FROM EDEN TO EROS:
Origins of the Put Down of Women

Books by Richard Roberts

ON BEING ACCUSED OF TREASON, AND OTHER POEMS (1967)

TAROT AND YOU (1971, 1984)

TAROT REVELATIONS (1981)
  with Joseph Campbell

TALES FOR JUNG FOLK (1984)

From Eden to Eros:

Origins of the Put Down of Women

by

Richard Roberts

VERNAL EQUINOX PRESS
BOX 581
SAN ANSELMO, CA 94960

©1985 by Richard Roberts.

All rights reserved under International Copyright Conventions. Printed in the United States of America. No part of this book may be reproduced or translated in any form (including photocopying or microfilming) without written permission from the author, except in the case of brief quotations (350 words or less) embodied in critical articles and reviews. For information write Vernal Equinox Press, P.O. Box 581, San Anselmo, CA 94960.

First Edition, 1985

Library of Congress Cataloging in Publication Data
ROBERTS, RICHARD
   From Eden to Eros: Origins of the Put Down of Women
   1. Women — Psychology. 2. Women — Religion
   3. Discrimination against women 4. Identity — Psychology I. Title
85-051722
ISBN 0-942380-05-3

©1985 by Richard Roberts
All rights reserved

CONTENTS

Acknowledgments

Introduction

I.	EDEN	1
II.	PATRIARCHY	27
III.	MATRIARCHY	41
IV.	WITCHES	63
V.	NATURE, BODY, AND SEX	87
VI.	EROS	113
VII.	SOCIAL HARMONY	151
	Appendix of Footnotes	162

Grateful acknowledgment is made to the following publishers for excerpts from:

Princeton University Press: *The Great Mother, An Analysis of the Archetype,* by Erich Neumann, translated by Ralph Manheim, Bollingen Series XLVII, copyright 1955, ©1983, renewed by Princeton University Press. *Two Essays on Analytical Psychology,* by C.G. Jung, copyright ©1966, *Papers From The Eranos Yearbooks,* vol. 2, *The Mysteries,* edited by Joseph Campbell, Bollingen Series XXX, copyright ©1955, 1983 renewed by Princeton University Press. *The Hero With a Thousand Faces,* by Joseph Campbell, Bollingen Foundation XVII, Meridian Edition, copyright ©1956.

Harper and Row: *The Nag Hammadi Library,* edited by James Robinson, copyright ©1977 by E. J. Brill, Leiden, The Netherlands. Harper and Row paperback edition copyright ©1977. *The Laughing Savior,* by John Dart, copyright ©1976. *The Way of the Animal Powers,* by Joseph Campbell, Alfred van der Marck Editions, copyright ©1983. *The Secret Life of Plants,* by Peter Tompkins and Christopher Bird, copyright ©1973. *Womens Mysteries,* by Esther M. Harding, copyright ©1971. *Knowing Woman: A Feminine Psychology,* by Irene Claremont de Castillejo, copyright ©1974.

Avon Books: *The Tree of Life,* copyright © 1974. *Tantra,* by John Rawson, copyright ©1973.

Dover Publications, Inc.: *The Mallens Maleficarum,* translated by Rev. Montague Summers, copyright ©John Rodker, London, 1928, copyright ©1971 Dover edition. *Star Names: Their Lore and Meaning,* by Richard Allen, copyright ©1963.

Vintage Books, Random House, Inc.: *The Gnostic Gospels,* by Elaine Pagels, copyright ©1979 by Elaine Pagels. *The White Goddess,* by Robert Graves, copyright ©1958, by arrangement with Farrar, Straus, Giroux copyright ©1948 Robert Graves. *The Occult,* by Colin Wilson, copyright ©1971.

Viking Press, Inc.: *The Masks of God: Occidental Mythology* and *Creative Mythology,* by Joseph Campbell, copyright ©1964 and 1968.

E.P. Dutton: *Greek Astronomy,* by Sir Thomas Heath, copyright date unknown. University of California Press, *The Gods and Goddesses of Old Europe, 7000 to 3500 B.C.,* copyright ©1974.

Prometheus Press: *Larousse Encyclopedia of Mythology,* copyright ©1960.

The Free Press: *Ancient Judaism,* by Max Weber, copyright ©1952.

Inner City Books: *Descent to the Goddess,* by Sylvia Brinton Perera, copyright ©1981.

Oxford University Press: *Gaia, A New Look at Life on Earth,* by J.E. Lovelock, copyright ©1979.

Bantam Books: *Psychic Discoveries Behind the Iron Curtain,* by Sheila Ostrander and Lynn Schroeder, copyright ©1970.

Ballantine Books: *The View Over Atlantis,* by John Michell, *copyright* ©1972.

Westminster Press: *Receiving Women,* by Ann Belford Ulanov, copyright ©1981.

Harcourt Brace & Co.: *Contributions to Analytical Psychology,* by C.G. Jung, copyright ©1928.

Prentice-Hall: *The Inner World of Choice,* by Frances Wickes, copyright ©1976.

Henry Holt: *The Inner World of Man,* by Frances Wickes, copyright ©1948.

G.P. Putnam's Sons: *Striving Twoards Wholeness,* by Barbara Hannah, copyright ©1971.

Doubleday: "The Process of Individuation" by M.L. von Franz, in *Man and His Symbols,* copyright ©1964.

Spring Publications: *Eros on Crutches: Reflections on Amorality and Psychopathology,* by Adolf Guggenbuhl-Craig, copyright ©1980.

Alfred Knopf: *The Serial,* by Cyra McFadden, copyright ©1977.

This book is dedicated to the women of the world, past present and future.

Special thanks to Joseph Campbell, Doctor Dean Edell, Peg and Jerry Kranz, Nancy Parsifal, Jane and Rob Butts, Colin Wilson, George Sayre, Ken Quigley, Lisa Spann, Gloria Taylor, Raymond Reed, Denny Zeitlin, Mel Bowman, Darryle Isaac, Nick Raggio, Nina and Mark Bredt.

INTRODUCTION

The majority of this book was written in 1973 for inclusion in *Tarot Revelations,* my collaboration with Joseph Campbell. While writing that book, a friend who had converted to Judaism was undergoing a psychological crisis that involved a search for authority in his otherwise rudderless life. His crisis manifested in part with extreme guilt feelings whenever he commenced a sexual experience with a woman. One night is particularly memorable. He had dined with a beautiful fellow law student from his college and had retired to his bedroom when from above I heard him cry, "Evil, evil! The Bible has branded fornication sinful!" Shortly thereafter the young lady came running down the stairs and out the door.

It was then that the full impact of the negativity of the Judeo-Christian tradition hit me, for here was an otherwise intelligent young man behaving like a candidate for a rubber room in a mental hospital. In the succeeding weeks, he would debate me during the dinner hour about the validity of the Bible as the Word of God. When I would return to my room to proceed with the writing of *Tarot Revelations,* my mind would be full of his arguments to the extent that I would be responding to the negativity that he had presented in his harrangue.

When Mr. Campbell came for one of his visits, reviewing what I had written he said, "Dick, none of this has anything to do with Tarot." In his creative wisdom he told me he thought the material might make *another* book, but that it did not belong in our collaboration. Therefore, most of what now appears in this book as chapters two, three and four, "Patriarchy", "Matriarchy" and "Witches", was created during this time.

During his visits Mr. Campbell did his best to enlighten our distressed friend, explaining to him that he was misreading myth as history, that mythology — the Bible's and all the world's — represented psychic "events", larger than life and mere history, for the patterns or archetypes of these events are eternally true, recurring as they do in the psyches of every member of the human race. But lacking any inner, psychic authority, our friend had to hold on to some external authoritarian power and could not be dissuaded.

My subsequent realization that the witchcraft craze was a male hysteria, explained by Jung's concept of the anima, the feminine archetype in the male unconscious, led to my personal recognition that the war between the sexes, from ancient history up to now, would be resolved only through recognition of the role of the archetypes in our individual lives. The marriage of the warring opposites, or the processes whereby they can be married, constitutes the material of chapter six, written for the most part in the late 1970s.

Chapter five, "Nature, Body, and Sex," was written somewhat earlier, and bears the insight that one's attitude towards personal nature, body and sex, is conditioned by one's attitude towards the goddess, or Great Mother, in the form of nature and planet (Gaia).

In the 1980s, when I discovered the astronomical basis for the tree, serpent, and woman of Eden, it became abundantly clear how patriarchy had fabricated the Eden tale in the very first book of the Bible in order to bring about the fall from heaven of the figures of devotion of the original religion of Goddess worship enshrined in the sky. That is to say, the heavenly Tree of Life, its guardian serpent, and the Goddess herself were disparaged in order to lay the dogmatic groundwork for patriarchy's rape of her religion. This has become patriarchy's basis for the put down of women which has followed us to this very day, with devastating effects on both women and men in all areas of society. The author hopes the reader may come away enlightened from the reading of this book.

CHAPTER I
EDEN

WHERE DID THE PUT DOWN BEGIN?

In the Garden of Eden, of course. To put the whole Genesis story into a nutshell (or an apple core), death came into the world with sex, Eve's specifically. Ever since then guilt has accompanied sex, and blame has followed woman down through the centuries. Beneath patriarchy's antipathy to Eve and the fertility goddesses that preceded her, lies a fear of sex and a fear of death. Unless one takes the Genesis account as the literal word of God, we are reading a highly prejudiced account designed specifically to denigrate women, to limit their religious and social roles in the community, and to keep them in domestic subservience. The result of this put down in the past two millenia has been a stunting of feminine growth in respect to social, psychological, creative, and spiritual development. I state emphatically that the Eden account is intentionally prejudiced because I have evidence, which we shall explore in this chapter, that serpent, tree, and woman were elements of an astronomical configuration revered by the pre-patriarchal cultures that worshipped a feminine deity, The Great Mother.

Let us examine the scenario of the Garden with particular regard for the serpent's role, since in Genesis he is the evil antagonist that devised man's Fall with woman's complicity, whereas in similar scenes in religions contemporary or precedent to Judeo-Christianity, the serpent's role was benign and evolutive rather than evil, and immortality results from following this ancient god's instruction. We have a hint of this in the Genesis story, because eating of the tree does *not* bring the death promised by God ("ye shall surely die"). God lied, and ironically the forked tongue of the serpent spoke the truth.

A fascinating but quite different account of the Garden drama is offered by the Gnostics, sometimes called early Christians. We have evidence of their presence in the Near East and Egypt from about the Second Century B.C. onward. Knowledge of the Gnostics was sparse indeed until 1945, when the fifty-two papyri texts were discovered at Nag Hammadi on the Nile in Egypt.

GOD IS A WOMAN—HALLELUJAH!

The Biblical Creation myth holds that it is the Breath or Word (Logos) of God that causes inanimate matter to take life. In the Gospel of John, we recall:

> In the beginning was the Word, and the Word was with God. He was in the beginning with God; all things were made through him, and without him was not anything made that was made. In him was life, and the life was the light of men.

In this respect, the Judeo-Christian tradition accords with earlier versions of Creation, but in Gnosticism the Diety is Pistis Sophia, *Pistis*, the feminine Greek for "faith," and *Sophia*, feminine Greek for "wisdom." When she breathes on the Abyss, a shadow comes into being beneath the Ogdoad, the starry realm where she reigns. The shadow becomes matter, and the form it takes—the text tells us—is like an abortion. Ultimately this shadow/abortion assumes the shape of a great beast, lion-like and androgynous, without knowledge of its creation by Sophia. The next step involves the creation of the world, which seems to have been the reason for Sophia's creation of this monster, variously named *Saklas* (Aramaic for fool), *Samael* ("blind god" in Aramaic), and *Ialdabaoth*, "child of chaos," since he was created from the watery Abyss.

It is at this point in the myth of creation that Judeo-Chrisian mythology commences with Genesis and the world's creation. After the world's creation, Saklas really does behave like a fool, falling victim to a bad case of chauvinism by declaring himself the supreme god. His traits match those of Yahweh, or Jehovah, the angry god of the Old Testament, wherein he is described as warlike, jealous, and malicious, characteristics which the Hebrews exalted in order to bring down their enemies. Originally two Adams are created, one a spiritual essence or Light/Adam (Sophia's creation), the other of dust— that is, of a merely physical body. The "dirty" Adam is Yahweh's creation. Eve now enters the Eden scene in the Gnostic text, *On The Origin of the World*:

> Sophia sent Zoe, her daughter, who is called "Eve (of Life)," as an instructor in order that she might raise up Adam, in whom there was no soul so that those whom he would beget might become vessels of the light. [When] Eve saw her co-likeness cast down she pitied him, and she said, "Adam, live! Rise up on the earth!"
>
> Immediately her word became a deed. For when Adam rose up, immediately he opened his eyes. When he saw her, he said, "You will be called 'the mother of the living' because you are the one who gave me life."[1]

From the above two versions of the creation of the world and the creation of man, it may be seen that our religious heritage took a turn for the worse in opting for patriarchy and Yahweh over the Goddess Sophia and matriarchy.

Adam displays gratitude and homage to Eve as the one who gave him life. If we examine Eve's epithet "mother of the living," her full import in the tradition of the Great Mother comes to the surface. This homage was in the historical mainstream of the B.C. Mother Goddess religions, whereas the Genesis version would be adjudicated slanderous were it to be written today. The Judeo-Christian mainstream has hung its case on a rib. Why? It seems to be man's attempt to gain the upper hand in society—perhaps as a reaction against earlier matriarchial dominance. Saklas and his flunkies, the Archons, rulers of the seven planets, conspire to give Adam a good ribbing; according to *On the Origin of the World*: ". . . let us teach him in his sleep as though she came into being from his rib so that the woman will serve and he will rule over her."[2] However, there are even more slanderous tales! A Hebrew tradition teaches that the devil entered the world from the hole in Adam's side from which came the rib to make Eve. Thus, by insinuation, evil and woman are linked. The Moslem religion has perpetuated the put down of women longer and more severely than any other culture, desert Bedouin attributing the origin of woman's creation to the tail of a monkey. I could go on recounting these creation tales, but they serve no purpose other than to expose the pathology of the patriarchy that created them.

Returning to the Gnostic version of Eden, wherein the serpent is called "the one who is wiser than all of them," since Sophia herself is a personification of wisdom, we may expect to find a link to the serpent. In one Gnostic text, *The Nature of the Archons*, Sophia's consciousness enters the serpent's body, thereby imparting her wisdom to it, whereupon it is referred to as the instructor. In *On the Origin of the World*, on the other hand, Sophia creates the serpent in order to instruct Adam and Eve regarding their origins. Sophia, then, is mother to both the serpent and Eve, the "mother of the living."

> Then the one who is wiser than all of them . . .when he saw the likeness of their mother, Eve, he said to her, "What is it that god said to you? 'Do not eat from the tree of knowledge'?"
> She said, "He not only said 'Do not eat from it' but 'Do not touch it lest you die.'"
> He said to her, "Don't be afraid. You certainly shall [not die]. . . . For [he knows] when you eat from it your mind will be sobered and you will become like god, knowing the distinctions which exist between evil and good men. For he said this to you, lest you eat from it, since he is jealous."
> Now Eve believed the words of the instructor.[3]

Adam and Eve eat of the Tree and their consciousness expands; they are no longer in the dark. But the archons, soon learning of their transgression, curse them and all the creation of the earth. One thing which Eve learns from the instructor is the secret of creation, sexual intercourse, in which she instructs Adam. This gives Adam and Eve a power like that of the archons to be creators themselves, and brings down the wrath of Saklas and the archons. Once again we see the link of Eve, sex, and evil. In Genesis, the primordial parents are naked, that is, aware of their sexual differences, and ashamed of the knowledge they have acquired. The Gnostic text from *Origin* ends on the same sour note as Genesis. Because of the archons' curses, "there is no blessing from them. It is impossible that good be produced from evil." Indeed, some of the Gnostics display the same revulsion to the sins of the flesh as the Judeo-Christians. But it has been suggested that our library of Gnostic texts is the result of prejudicial preservation by ascetic Christian monks, those desert dwellers having kept only those Gnostic texts that suited their point of view.

Be that as it may, the cast of characters in the Garden of Eden may be analyzed symbolically, resulting in some amazing revelations. For this drama has antecedents in other religions, most important of which is the serpent's link to the Great Mother of the matriarchies; hence, the reason in the context of patriarchy for the denigration of Eve, the serpent, and sexual knowledge.

Watching the serpent cast his skin, early man noticed the similarity to the moon's cycle, casting off its own death (the dark of the moon) with rebirth at the new moon. Of all animals, therefore, snakes were the most likely symbols of immortality. All religions hold out the possiblility of immortality, but in the matriarchies this is accomplished by cycles of regeneration which reflect natural process. Too, just as a serpent disappears into the earth, the moon vanishes in the earth's shadow at the dark of the moon, to be reborn again at the new moon. The female fertility cycle links woman, moon, and serpent, with the dropping of the egg (ovulation) in time with the burgeoning full moon on the fifteenth day of the cycle. In truth it may be said that Eve, Serpent, and Tree, in the Garden of Eden are all aspects of one principle—fertility. Going a step further, they are all forms of the Great Mother Goddess.

Let us examine the mythic roots of the tree of the knowledge of good and evil, of which Adam and Eve did partake. But more importantly, what is the ultimate source of the tree of life, which God defends with "Cherubims and a flaming sword *which turned every way*, to keep the way of the tree" (Genesis 3:24) "lest he (Adam) put forth his hand, and take also of the tree of life, and eat, and live for ever:"(Genesis 3.22)

This Tree of Life, or Tree of Heaven, appears in the mythology of practically every B.C. culture. In a sense, Eve bears the same relation to Sophia her Creator/Sustainer that the Eden tree does to Mother Earth. Indeed, in Genesis 3:6, when we read "that the tree was to be desired to make one wise" if we recall that Sophia meant wisdom, then the affinity of Sophia and Eve is closer still.

The tree in Eden is at the middle of the Garden, a dead giveaway that it is the World Axis/Tree common to earlier mythologies.

. . .it is into the hidden and mysterious depths of this Great Earth Mother that the roots of the tree descend. Through these penetrating roots the tree participates in the regenerative life of the waters and the soil. From germination to death the tree remains bound to its mother the earth, the permanent source of its renewal. In the autumn, seed and leaf return to the earth out of which, from the mysterious rising of the sap in the spring, they emerged. This sap, drawn from out of the depths, is the milk of the Great Goddess herself, the heavenly ambrosia, elixir of the gods, by means of which the dead attain immortality. Standing at the 'centre of all that surrounds it' the Tree of Life, like the Fountain of Life, is an image of the endless renewal of the cosmos from a single centre or source.[4]

The "endless renewal of the cosmos from a single centre or source" indicates that the World Axis/Tree also has a cosmic dimension. The stars were thought to hang upon a dome vaulting the earth like a vast temple. In turn, the dome of heaven rested upon the distant four quarters of the earth, to which no one in the ancient world had ventured. The four quarters are indicated in Genesis 2:10-15 with reference to four rivers. The Eden tree, standing at the center, therefore, has an implied vertical axis which extends to a cosmic source whereby the world is renewed. This heavenly point is the pole star around which earth and sky rotate daily and annually (the seasonal round), the Unmoved Mover of all creation. This pole or World Axis was prevalent in the mythologies of 4,000 B.C. where it was most commonly symbolized as a sacred tree. A secondary manifestation of the center is in mythologies of the sacred mountain. This concept rendered in architecture is the essence of the meaning of the ziggurat and pyramid, containing four sides and a central pinnacle. The Great Pyramid at Ghizeh, for example, is positioned so that its eastern side faces precisely the rising of the sun at the vernal equinox.

By use of the modern computer, we can reconstruct the skies of earlier millennia in order to divine the star that was the "orientation point of the great Karnak temples of Rameses and Khons at Thebes, the passage in the former, through which the star was observed, being 1500 feet in length; and that at least seven different temples were oriented toward it."[5] This star was Eltanin, Gamma Draconis, or the serpent's eye in our constellation Draco. It "was known there as *Isis*, or *Taurt Isis*. . . . Also, *Apet, Bast, Mut, Sekhet*, and *Taurt* were all titles of one goddess in the Nile worship, symbolized by Gamma Draconis."

"It was nearer the pole than any other bright star about 4,000 years ago."[6]

The pole star 6,000 years ago was Thuban, Alpha Draconis. If we consider that the cosmos is renewed from this center, then the spiritual significance of the pole star far exceeds its utilitarian value as a navigational guide.

"The star [Thuban] could be seen, both by day and night, from the bottom of the central passage [380 feet long, directed northward to this star, doubtless by design of the builder, from a point deep below the present base, at an inclination of 26°17′ to the horizon of the Great Pyramid of Cheops (knum Khufu) at Gizeh, in 30° of north latitude, as also from the similar points in five other like structures; and the same fact is asserted by Sir John Herschel as to the two other pyramids at Abousseir.

"Herschel considered that there is distinct evidence of Thuban formerly being brighter than now, as its title from its constellation, and its lettering, [alpha] would indicate; for with Bayer it was a 2nd-magnitude,—in fact the only one of that brillancy in his list of Draco,—and is generally so in star catalogues previous to two centuries ago."[7]

Whether as Isis in Egypt, or as Inanna in Babylonia, the Great Mother and the Tree of Life are one and the same, as the following illustration indicates: "From the centre of an Egyptian celestial tree, planted in the 'waters of the depths,' a goddess, epiphany of the Great Earth Mother, distributes the food and drink of immortality."[8]

As we have seen, the sap of the Tree of Life, or the Heavenly Tree, "is the milk of the Great Goddess herself, the heavenly ambrosia, elixir of the gods, by means of which the dead attain immortality."[9] The parallel tree in Eden is the oft forgotten other tree.

". . . and now, lest he [Adam = Man] put forth his hand, and take also of the tree of life, and eat, and live for ever;" (Genesis 3:22)

Thereupon, the Lord God drove out Adam and Eve and placed Cherubims and a flaming sword to guard the tree, presumably so that Man could not attain immortality, the fruit of the tree of life.

Not only does Eve correspond to the Great Mother Goddess, and the Tree of Life to the Heavenly Tree, but also in the earlier and contemporary mythologies the fruits which bestow immortality are guarded, not by a flaming sword, but by dragons and serpents. Furthermore, these trees, dragons, and serpents had corresponding astronomical configurations. The Genesis account, therefore, appears to be a deliberate denigration of serpent and Eve, the celestial objects of worship of the other religions.

Figure 1

In addition, we must not overlook the fact that the Tree of Life, or Heavenly Tree, bore fruit bestowing immortality because it was the "tree" of the pole star, the point from which cosmos was generated, The Unmoved Mover.

I am grateful to Miss Gloria Taylor for the suggestion that since dragons are thought to breathe fire, the fiery tongue or breath of the dragon may have been transformed into a flaming sword in the Genesis account. Indeed, some language expert may be able to find a root word for sword which has a variant of fire, tongue, or breath.

At all events, we need to investigate briefly the accounts of dragons and serpents guarding treasures of immortality. In Greek mythology, Night, visible as the starry sky, gave birth to the Hesperides, whose golden apples at the end of the world are guarded by a serpent. Atlas had been condemned to stand before the Hesperides and to bear upon his shoulders the vault of heaven so in this myth we certainly have a celestial reference.

As far as I have been able to determine, every culture contains a mythology of a serpent or dragon which represents the ancient and formidable Goddess of nature. Being feminine, according to the descriptions we have of the monster, we may associate dragon and serpent with the Great Mother of the earlier matriarchies. Anyhow, the monster stands for the previous order, and as such is symbolic of chaos, which is conquered by a solar hero who stands for the new, patriarchal order. Furthermore, along with serpent and dragon, the animal most commonly fought— and put to death—by solar heroes is the bull, which is equated with the moon, and the Great Mother of the matriarchies. In the mythologies of Scandanavia, India, China, Egypt, Sumer and Greece we find the central motif of a vanquished serpent/dragon. In Sumer, the monster is the adversary, a concept which is transformed in 2,000 years to our devil, the evil antagonist of God, and responsible for Adam's Fall through Eve's complicity. It is the ramifications of this for women throughout history—and especially for today—which will be my major concern in this book, but first let us discover what happened to all those vanquished serpent/dragons of the old natural order.

In Babylonia, Marduk cut Tiamat in half, forming the earth with one part, and then flinging the other into the sky, where it now shines down on us as Draco, the Dragon. Presently Joseph Campbell will tell us of Indra's victory over Vritra, a cosmic serpent, Zeus' over Typhon, whose head knocked against the stars, and Yahweh's over Leviathan, serpent of the cosmic sea. In Norse myth, Odin flung the serpent Midgart into the darkness of the heavens. And in Greece, Minerva took on a dragon in the war between the Olympian gods and the Titans and their heirs. When she hurled the dragon skyward, it became entangled in the World Axis/Tree before it could unwind its coils.

Interestingly enough, in each culture these dragon/serpents are visible in the constellation Draco, the Dragon. Even in Central America, the Plumed Serpent of the ancient Aztecs has very probable correlations with Draco. But our most telling version comes from the Greek myth of Heracles (Hercules). Describing Draco's head, Aratus tells us:

> On his head blazes not one star alone but two on his temples and two in his eyes, while one underneath marks the end of his under-jaw. His head lies obliquely, and seems just as if it were nodding towards the end of Helice's tail; his mouth and right temple are quite straight opposite the tip of the tail; the said head moves where the limits of rising and setting are confounded.
>
> Just there dwells a Phantom like to a man toiling painfully. No one knows his story nor to what task he is bound, but all alike call him On his knees. The Phantom that toils on his knees is like one sitting with knees bent; from both shoulders his hands are raised and stretched out, one this way, one that, to a fathom's length. He has the tip of his right foot over the middle of the head of the crooked Dragon.[10]

The "Phantom" in the sky, kneeling near Draco is identified, however, by Eratosthenes.

> . . .this, they say, is Heracles, whose foot is on the Serpent (Dragon). He stands clearly visible with his club uplifted, and with the lion's skin wrapped round him. The story is that, when he went in search of the golden apples, he killed the dragon, their appointed guardian, who had been placed there for this very purpose, that he might do battle with Heracles. Hence it was that, when the labour was accomplished at great risk, Zeus, who thought the struggle worthy of a memorial, placed the figure among the stars. The dragon is seen with

his head aloft, and Heracles stands over him, having one knee bent but standing with the other foot on the dragon's head, stretching out his right hand with the club in it as if about to strike, and with his left hand holding the lion's skin wrapped about him.[11]

Now on any clear night that we look up at the sky we are presented with a most interesting picture, an encapsulation, as it were, of at least the last 6,000 years of our religious history. Hercules' lion's skin identifies him with the sign of Leo, ruled by the sun; hence he is a solar hero of the new patriarchal order. His right hand holds a club, his new-won power, while the foot holding down the dragon's head symbolizes his ultimate victory. But the vanquished dragon in turn symbolizes the old order of the matriarchies, and the Great Mother herself. Relevant to our topic, this celestial scene represents an epiphany of the put down of women. Transplanted to Eden, the sordid seeds would grow into the raison d'etre for the projection of evil onto the women suffering under patriarchy.

Now although we know how the serpent/dragon came to be a constellation according to patriarchy (flung into the sky when vanquished), we do not know the myths of matriarchy whereby the serpent occupied the place of greatest honor in the heavens, for it was said that the constellation which possessed the pole, truly reigned supreme. The reason for this is obvious. The cosmos is ever reborn from the point of the pole star, the Unmoved Mover. Interestingly enough, Thuban's relative position in Draco corresponds to the place of the birth canal of an actual serpent. As Joseph Campbell has often told us, the ancients associated the serpent with immortality because the evidence of the sloughed skin suggested that it survived its own physical death.

Under patriarchy, Christ would come to occupy the place of honor, the pole. That is to say, the Tree of Life or Heavenly Tree would become The Cross, and Christ would be the Fruit of immortality to be gained by men. Again a dragon/serpent would guard the treasure of immortality; the fallen serpent of Eden would prevent Adam's attaining immortality, and be the cause—with woman—of his expulsion from Paradise.

However, the evidence indicates that some of the patriarchal writers of the Bible knew of the exalted serpent mythology, and were less than honest in transforming this divine source into the adversary of their new religion. For example, the references in Revelations 12:1-9 are clearly to celestial figures:

> And there appeared a great wonder in heaven; a woman clothed with the sun, and the moon under her feet, and upon her head a crown of twelve stars. . . .
>
> And there appeared another wonder in heaven; and behold a great red dragon having seven heads and ten horns, and seven crowns upon his heads. . . .
>
> And there was war in heaven: Michael and his angels fought against the dragon, and the dragon fought and his angels,
>
> And prevailed not; neither was their place found any more in heaven.
>
> And the great dragon was cast out, that old serpent, called the Devil, and Satan, which deceiveth the whole world: he was cast out into the earth. . . .

Michael, then, is another solar hero who does Yahweh's work in conquering the dragon, and the casting out from heaven is a fanciful rendering of the reduction of a cosmic deity to devil.

Before we pass on to a discussion of the Goddess as the serpent's bride, I should like to present a sketch of the ceiling of the Mithraeum at Ponza, an island off Italy. Mithras was a solar god, but the cult's roots extend back into the era of the Great Mother and integrate symbology that is not wholly patriarchal in spirit. I noted in *Tarot Revelations* that the origins of alchemy's secrets are to be found in Mithraism.

In *Occidental Mythology*, Joseph Campbell presents a profound analysis of Mithraism which we recommend to the reader.

There is also an astronomical reference to be recognized in the symbols of the bull and scorpion; for in the centuries during which the foundations of all astrological iconography were laid (c.4300-2150 B.C.), the zodiacal sign of Taurus, the Bull, stood at the vernal equinox, and Scorpio, the Scorpion, at the autumnal. Leo, the Lion, was then the sign of the midsummer sun, when its decline toward winter began, and Aquarius, the Water Carrier, was in the house of the winter solstice, where the sun god, *Sol invictus*, was annually reborn, on December 25![12]

Now if we analyze Mithras' slaying "of the Primeval Bull— which was the role assigned in the orthodox Zoroastrian system to the wicked Angra Mainyu, the Antagonist,"[13] we note that the sword of the sun (Mithras) pierces the bull's flesh. Referring once more to Joseph Campbell's astronomical correlation, we realize that the sun's rays first pierce the bull (Taurus) in 4300 B.C., when Taurus stands at the vernal equinox and Scorpio is the opposite sign at the autumnal equinox. The scorpion holds the bull's testicles in the scene of the tauroctony. The Mithraic tableau depicts, therefore, a specific moment in time when these two signs, Taurus and Scorpio, were the year's poles, c.4300 B.C.

Figure 2

Examining the zodiac at Ponza, we see that the only accurate lines of demarcation between signs are those of the same era, for only the line between Taurus and Gemini is completed by the opposite line between Scorpio and Sagittarius. Also of interest is the fact that if the line is completed it passes through the Draco serpent at the point of the pole star Thuban. Thus, when Thuban was the pole star, Scorpio and Taurus stood at the poles! The creator of the serpent was not accurate in his depiction of Draco, as the shape is all wrong, but its presence suggests its creator rendered it so in order to depict the most highly significant moment in time according to the Mithraic calendar.

One last word on astronomical serpents and mythology. Since Eltanin in Draco (Gamma Draconis) is the Great Mother as Inanna, according to most early sources, and since Dumuzi, her consort was transformed into a serpent, my intuition is that it may not be too long before new fragments are discovered which present evidence that he and the constellation Draco are one and the same. Significantly, he makes an annual descent to earth and return to heaven, which journey may be read in Draco's circumpolar motion.

THE SERPENT'S BRIDE

The history of mythology—primitive, occidental, oriental, and creative—is told wonderfully in Joseph Campbell's four volume series *The Masks of God*. In Chapter One of *Occidental Mythology*, "The Serpent's Bride," he tells the history of that damning event in the Garden:

No one familiar with the mythologies of the goddess of the primitive, ancient, and Oriental worlds can turn to the Bible without recognizing counterparts on every page, transformed, however, to render an argument contrary to the older faiths. In Eve's scene at the tree, for example, nothing is said to indicate that the serpent who appeared and spoke to her was a deity in his own right, who had been revered in the Levant for at least seven thousand years before the composition of the Book of Genesis. . . .

In *Primitive Mythology* and *Oriental Mythology* I have discussed a number of such deities who are at once the consorts and sons of the Great Goddess of the Universe. Returning to her bosom in death (or, according to another image, in marriage), the god is reborn—as the moon sloughing its shadow or the serpent sloughing its skin. Accordingly, in those rites of initiation with which such symbols were associated (as in the mysteries of Eleusis), the initiate, returning in contemplation to the goddess mother of the mysteries, became detached reflectively from the fate of his mortal frame (symbolically, the son, who dies), and identified with the principle that is ever reborn, the Being of all beings (the serpent father): whereupon, in the world where only sorrow and death had been seen, the rapture was recognized of an everlasting becoming![4]

GODDESS OF THE TREE

We shall analyze some drawings of early archeological seals which present scenes which at first suggest our own Biblical mythology of the Garden of Eden, but with important differences. As Joseph Campbell notes:

> Nor is there any sign of divine wrath or danger to be found in these seals. There is no theme of guilt connected with the garden. The boon of the knowledge of life is there, in the sanctuary of the world, to be culled. And it is yielded willingly to any mortal, male or female, who reaches for it with the proper will and readiness to receive.
>
> Hence, the early Sumerian seal . . .cannot possibly be, as some scholars have supposed, the representation of a lost Sumerian version of the Fall of Adam and Eve. Its spirit is that of the idyll in the much earlier, Bronze Age view of the garden of innocence, where the two desirable fruits of the mythic date palm are to be culled; the fruit of enlightenment and the fruit of immortal life. The female figure at the left, before the serpent, is almost certainly the goddess Gula-Bau (a counterpart, as we have said, of Demeter and Persephone), while the male on the right, who is not mortal but a god, as we know from his horned lunar crown, is no less surely her beloved son-husband Dumuzi 'Son of the Abyss: Lord of the Tree of Life,' the ever-dying, ever-resurrected Sumerian god who is the archetype of incarnate being.[15]

Since the ancients did not know the meaning of the nocturnal lights in the sky and were unaware of the earth's motion on its axis, they interpreted the stars and planets as gods and goddesses, and most—if not all—of their mythology had an astronomical basis for the nightly procession of gods and goddesses.

The Tree of Life or Cosmic Tree was a vertical axis, passing through three separate zones, sky, earth, and underworld. At its upper or heavenly end, the Tree was fixed to the pole star, around which the stars rotated. Figure 3, the picture of the Sumerian seal is of especial interest to us in our attempt to understand the true origins of the myth of the Garden because at opposite ends of the picture we have the symbol for Taurus, the horned crown worn by the goddess at right, and the symbol for Scorpio, the serpent at left. Taurus and Scorpio, of course, are polar opposites in the zodiac, but what is most compelling here is that at the time of the height of the religion of the Mother Goddess (4-2,000 B.C.), the pole star was Alpha Draconis. Our dragon (Draconis) was their serpent, atop the World Axis/Tree when Taurus and Scorpio were the spring and fall poles of the year. The serpent's body wound around the tree and moved nightly as the earth rotated on its axis. The modern mind cannot begin to comprehend the supernatural effect which the stars' nightly procession had on early humankind. To them, the objects of light were alive and divine, since their realm was the heavenly sphere.

Figure 3

11

Further evidence of my thesis may be found in the Tree of the Hesperides vase painting of Figure 4. Noting the uniform representation and star-shape of the tree's leaves, the only conclusion possible is that a celestial tree is intended. Furthermore, how can it be that the goddess feeding the serpent floats in mid-air? In his interpretation in Occidental Mythology the Tree of the Hesperides, Joseph Campbell tells us that according to Hesiod's Theogony, the Hesperides were daughters of the cosmic goddess Night; thus this Greek myth may incorporate elements of an earlier mythology, specifically the World Tree with the constellation Draco coiled about it circa 4,000 B.C. The Larousse Encyclopedia of Mythology designates the Hesperides' abode as "beyond the river-Ocean [the Milky Way], at the extreme western limits of the world, where they personified the clouds gilded by the setting sun. They lived in a wondrous garden and guarded the golden apples which grew there. Since, however, the Greeks had two identical words for 'apple' and for 'flock of sheep', it has been wondered if the Hesperides were not rather guardians of the celestial flocks which in Indo-European mythology symbolised clouds."[16]

Figure 4

The latter interpretation of celestial clouds would be more in keeping with a celestial tree. Furthermore, there is a most interesting detail in the vase painting which further suggests an astronomical configuration. Note the posture of the goddess floating in mid-air. She appears to be seated as if on a throne. The left eye of the serpent in the constellation Draco is named Rastaban, or Alwaid. The right eye, not visible in this vase depiction of the serpent, was named Eltanin, which as we noted earlier was identified with a number of titles of the goddess in Nile worship. A line of stars (?) extends horizontally from the posterior of the floating sister to the center of the Tree/serpent in the approximate area of Thuban, the pole star "throne of Inanna." Or, we may infer that the floating sister is the constellation Lyra, in proximate celestial vicinity of the head of the serpent; thus the bright star Vega may have had associations with a goddess figure in ancient star lore.

At all events, the key figures of the Eden scene are all present; yet the spirit of Figures 3 and 4 is considerably different from the way they are cast in the biblical version. The reasons for the biblical put down of the goddesses are quite clearly presented in the following words of Joseph Campbell's interpretation of the spirit of the vase painting of the Tree of the Hesperides:

> And all is precisely as things would have remained in Eden, too, if the recently installed patriarch of the estate (who was developing his colorable claim to priority not only of ownership but even of being) had not taken umbrage when he learned what things were going on....
>
> In the older mother myths and rites the light and darker aspects of the mixed thing that is life had been honored equally and together, whereas in the later, male-oriented, patriarchal myths, all that is good and noble was attributed to the new, heroic gods, leaving to the native nature powers the character only of darkness - to which, also, a negative moral judgment was now added![7]

THE DRAGON FIGHT

Coining a term from anthropology and archeology, Erich Neumann says, "We have to make do with psychological sequence-dating in dealing with the archetypal stages. The uroboros comes 'before' the stage of the Great Mother, and the Great Mother 'before' the dragon fight. . . ." In terms of the psyche, the uroboros stage is undifferentiated consciousness, and, therefore, unconsciousness, the womb life. The Great Mother stage is the stage in which the personal mother is thought to be an extension of the individual ego. The dragon fight, therefore, is the stage of separation of ego from the mother. In the ego's fight to emerge (like the baby's effort to draw the first breath), the mother may be repressive, so that she may be viewed with hostility. But the projection of evil onto the serpent signifies that the psyche senses a threat to its development and continuing emergence. At the same time, the separation from the mother is the cause of the separation into opposites, on the part of the ego, of all the contents of consciousness it encounters.

The uroboros is represented symbolically by a snake with tail in mouth, signifying the bound (yet limitless!) dimension of the psyche. In alchemy, the symbol is represented often by a winged dragon with tail in mouth. When the ego has differentiated from the unconscious and the mother, it projects into the outer world the earlier limited, bound, undifferentiated stage, and goes to do battle with whatever force might again restrict it. This is known as the attempt to slay the dragon. The hero never recognizes the dragon as being at home, that is, within his unconscious, and, therefore, must ride out to find the dragon, maiden, and the treasure, which the dragon guards, limits, and restricts. The maiden is the Great Mother in yet another form, but unless the hero has truly slain the dragon, he will get mother again when he rescues from bondage the maiden and marries her. When she conceives by him and a new potential hero appears in her womb, the whole cycle begins again, the struggle for new consciousness ever present in every life.

Now from the point of view of patriarchal mythology, and masculine ego consciousness, Eve, the Great Mother, and the personal mother, are identified with the serpent in our "psychological sequence-dating," for Eve heeds the serpent and does his bidding and, therefore, is identified with him, while the individual ego remembers the stage of the uroboros (serpent with tail-in-mouth), and associates the blissful undifferentiation with the personal mother.

In the last stage, the ego seeks to slay the dragon, that is, all the elements of childhood and adolescence associated with home and the mother. And in terms of mythology and religious history, the fight with the dragon has its counterpart in what I call the Quarrel with the Serpent. The Quarrel is basically what we have discussed earlier, the denigration of the serpent, "a deity," as Joseph Campbell has told us, "revered in the Levant for at least seven thousand years before the composition of the Book of Genesis." Yet the Biblical thrust directed at the serpent is that which sets it in opposition to the divine, and judges it evil, the reason being, as we have seen, that the new patriarchal god opposes what divinites have gone before it, and it suffers no new rival. At the same time that the serpent is denigrated, Eve "falls" also, a clue once again that both stand for the one natural and divine principle that was encompassed in the Great Mother, the deity Yahweh sought to unthrone. However, the eventual victory of Yahweh will have repercussions down to our present day in an area as seemingly unrelated to the Garden of Eden as ecology. For as Joseph Campbell tells us:

> Wherever nature is revered as self-moving, and so inherently divine, the serpent is revered as symbolic of its divine life. And accordingly, in the Book of Genesis, where the serpent is cursed, all nature is devaluated and its power of life regarded as nothing in itself: nature is here self-moving indeed, self-willed, but only by virtue of the life given it by a superior being, its creator.

In Christian mythology, supplementing the Old Testament, the serpent is normally identified with Satan, and the words addressed by Yahweh to the serpent in the Garden ("I will put enmity between you and woman, and between your seed and her seed; he shall bruise your head, and you shall bruise his heel") are taken to refer to the crucified son of Mary, by whose wounds Satan's force was to be broken. As pointed out in *Occidental Mythology*, the resemblance of the Christian legend of the killed and resurrected redeemer to the old myths of the killed and resurrected gods, Tammuz, Adonis, Dionysus, and Osiris, presented a certain advantage to the preachers of the new gospel, but on the other hand, also a danger. For whereas on one hand the resemblances made it possible for them to claim that in the historical reality of Christ's crucifixion the merely mythic promises of the earlier religions had been surpassed, on the other hand the obvious resemblances also made it possible for converted pagans to regard the new revelation as simply one more transformation of Hellenistic mystery lore; and in fact, many sects of the first five or six centuries can best be understood in just that way.

Saint Hippolytus (d.c. 230)...opens a vista into the hidden sense, or "higher wisdom"...of serpent veneration through his account of the cosmology of an Ophitic Christian sect of his day called the Perates:

Their cosmos consists of Father, Son, and Matter, each of which three principles contains infinitely many forces. Midway between the Father and Matter, the Son, the Logos, has his place, the Serpent that moves eternally toward the unmoved Father and moved Matter; now it turns to the Father and gathers up forces in its countenance; and now, after receiving the forces, it turns toward Matter, and upon Matter, which is without attribute and form, the Son imprints the ideas that had previously been imprinted upon the Son by the Father.

Moreover, no one can be saved and rise up again without the Son, who is the serpent![18]

The Son, Logos, Serpent of the Ophites is dramatically apparent in the night sky as the constellation Draco, and Draco's counter-clockwise motion about the pole is precisely what is described in St. Hippolytus text: "the Serpent that moves eternally toward the unmoved Father and moved Matter; now it turns to the Father...and now...it turns toward Matter...For it was he who brought the paternal models down from aloft, and it is he who carries back up again...."

As the earth rotates on its axis, the head of Draco's serpent appears to dip towards earth, its coils following after, and then the appearance of an ascent occurs; the unmoved pivot for the serpent's circumpolar swing is of course Thuban, the pole star, back towards the snake's tail.

Campbell then notes that in this cosmos, Christ appears to be an incarnation of the serpent. The Gnostic system finds the origin of evil in the creation of the world by the Demiurge, the god of the Old Testament, himself created for the purpose of creating the world. Entrapped in matter there is light, the divine essence of Sophia, wisdom. In order to free light from bondage to matter, the Serpent/Son makes a second descent to the world, "and the Bible story of the serpent in the garden is an account of this appearance. For the serpent there caused the male and female, Adam and Eve to violate the commandment of the Demiurge, and so commenced the work of redemption."[19]

Now in *Occidental Mythology*, Joseph Campbell presents a line drawing reproduced here from an Elamite painted bowl of the late Sassonian period (226-641 A.D.) which shows the serpent coiled around the world tree.

I believe this picture is yet another representation of a map of the sky, specifically in relation to the world of the Taurean Age circa 3240 B.C. The interpretation of this picture is dependent upon the attribution we give to the curious symbol in the upper lefthand corner. To me it is unquestionably a star, and since we have the World Axis/Tree and serpent it is logical to suppose that the star is the pole star. Furthermore, the star is shown at the center of a cross, indicating the four directions. The celestial center of four directions would be the pole star.

Figure 5

To continue our unravelling of the mystery of the serpent around the tree in Eden, and the beginning of the origins of the put down of women, let us examine—with Joseph Campbell's help— one more ancient cylinder seal. Here we see "the Mesopotamian hero Gilgamesh in dual manifestation, serving as the guardian of a sanctuary, in the way of the lion-birds of Gudea's cup. But what we find within this sanctuary is of neither human, animal, nor vegetal form; it is a column made of serpent-circles, bearing on its top a symbol of the sun. Such a pole or perch is symbolic of the pivotal point around which all things turn (the *axis* mundi), and so is a counterpart of the Buddhist Tree of Enlightenment in the 'Immovable Spot' at the center of the world. Around the symbol of the sun atop the column, four little circles are to be seen. These, we are told, symbolize the four rivers that flow to the quarters of the world. (Compare the Book of Genesis 2:10-14) Approaching from the left is the owner of the seal, conducted by a lion-bird (or cherub, as such apparitions are termed in the Bible) bearing in its left hand a pail and in its right an elevated branch. A goddess follows in the role of the mystic mother of rebirth, and below is a guilloche—a labyrinthine device that in this art corresponds to the caduceus. So that, again, we recognize the usual symbols of the mythic garden of life, where the serpent, the tree, the world axis, sun eternal, and ever-living waters radiate grace to all quarters— and toward which the mortal indvidual is guided, by one divine manifestation or another, to the knowledge of his own immortality."[20]

Figure 6

Now I would agree with Joseph Campbell in all elements of his eloquent interpretation of this seal save one. Once again, the symbol atop the serpent circles of the *axis mundi* has four points, the same as the other cylinder seal which we have analyzed. To the naked eye the sun appears as a circle, whereas a star appears to shine from points because of the earth's atmosphere; therefore, the star atop a column of entwined serpents may be interpreted as Alpha Draconis. And, lastly, the four circles surrounding the star may signify the four compass points, or the four directions of the world, north, east, south, and west, which surround and begin at the center of the world, the axis mundi, marked by the pole star, Alpha Draconis.

Since Mesopotamia is one of the lands over which the Great Mother ruled as Inanna, it is of great interest to note here that the scholar Archibald Sayce had researched the celestial compilations of the Akkadian king Sargon. Sargon called Alpha Draconis Tir-An-na, the Life of Heaven. Another possible translation is Throne of Inanna; thus it may be her throne that is depicted in the intricacies atop the axis mundi in the picture which Joseph Campbell has just discussed.

When I mentioned to Joseph Campbell my theory regarding the cosmic interpretation of the serpent, he very kindly referred me to another book which was to supply further evidence, Marija Gimbutas' *The Gods and Goddesses of Old Europe* (7000 to 3500 B.C.)

Let us begin with excerpts from Gimbutas' chapter "Cosmogonical and Cosmological Images." In the symbology of snakes, horns, crescents, and the cross, we have most compelling evidence that the Judeo-Christian tradition took for its own imagery that by virtue of its ritual utilization over many millenia had acquired archetypal status in the psyches of the worshippers of Old Europe. These numinously endowed symbols could not be unceremoniously cast out, for they would linger on beneath the surface of conscious worship. It became necessary, therefore, to transform the meaning of each symbol to suit the new religion.

A striking development in art at the inception of the agricultural era was its persistent representation of a number of conventionalized graphic designs symbolizingabstract ideas. These ideograms, recurring on figurines, stamp seals, dishes, cult vessels, and as part of pictorial decoration of vases and house walls, were used for thousands of years throughout Old European civilization, and help to expand our understanding of its cosmogony and cosmology, and of the functions of the deities it sustained.

The symbols fall into two basic categories: those related to water or rain, the snake and the bird; and those associated with the moon, the vegetal life-cycle, the rotation of seasons, the birth and growth essential to the perpetuation of life. ...

The snake and its abstracted derivative, the spiral, are the dominant motifs of the art of Old Europe, and their imaginative use in spiral form design throughout the Neolithic and Chalcolithic periods remained unsurpassed by any subsequent decorative style until the Minoan civilization, the sole inheritor of Old European lavishness. The Chalcolithic Butmir, Cucuteni, and East Balkan peoples created large bulbous vessels, adopting the snake-spiral as the basis of the entire ornamental composition. This art reached its peak of unified symbolic and aesthetic expression c.5000 B.C. ...

The mysterious dynamism of the snake, its extra-ordinary vitality and periodic rejuvenation, must have provoked a powerful emotional response in the Neolithic agriculturalists, and the snake was consequently mythologized, attributed with a power that can move the entire cosmos. ... The organization of the motifs demonstrates that the imagery is genuinely cosmogonic: the disc and snake compositions appear in bands occupying the middle of the vases associated with belts of the upper skies. ... " The Cucuteni civilization is clearly affiliated with its southern neighbors of the East Balkan tradition, and forms the northerly outpost of Old European culture [reaching in an oval from what is today Bucharest to Kiev] extending as far as the middle Dnieper in the northeast. Ethnically, it appears to have comprised a medley of the indigenous inhabitants, and infiltrating Mediterraneans. Southwestern and East Balkan influences played an important part in transforming local ceramic styles, both at the inception and during the evolution of the Cucuteni culture, which in its classical period, around 4500-4000 B.C., achieved a remarkable artistic maturity in its ceramic products.[21]

This period, 4500-4000 B.C., we recall, is the time when Scorpio and Taurus are at the poles. Gimbutas does not disappoint us when it comes to the serpent in interpreting the designs of ceramic painting of the period. "The involved ornamentation of Cucuteni and East Balkan ceramic painting is a glorification of nature's dynamism. Its graphic expression is organized around the symbol of the snake, whose presence was a guarantee that nature's enigmatic cycle would be maintained and its life-giving powers not diminish. The snake was the vehicle of immortality. Some vases flaunt a gigantic snake *winding or stretching over the whole universe*, over the sun or moon, stars and rain torrents." [Italics mine]

The central figures in the Eden scene, tree, serpent, and Eve, are now in the perspective of what they had been to the worshippers of the Great Mother in the era 7,000 B.C. down to her "demise" at the beginning of the Iron Age. The following quotes from Joseph Campbell culminate my argument that a cosmic meaning, the constellation Draco must be attributed to the mythological serpent, and his denigrated descendant, Eden's snake.

By the early Iron Age (c. 1200 B.C.) the period when the influence of the Great Mother has waned considerably, Joseph Campbell observes as follows:

...the literatures of both Aryan Greece and Rome and of the neighboring Semitic Levant are alive with variants of the conquest by a shining hero of the dark and—for one reason or another—disparaged monster of the earlier order of godhead. . . . [The following italics are mine, not Campbell's] "The chief biblical example was Yahweh's victory over *the serpent of the cosmic sea*, Leviathan. ..."

The counterpart for the Greeks was the victory of Zeus over Typhon, the youngest child of Gaea, the goddess Earth—by which deed the reign of the patriarchal gods of Mount Olympus was secured over the earlier Titan broods of the great goddess mother. The Titan's form, half man, half snake, we are told, was enormous. He was so large that *his head often knocked against the stars and his arms could extend from sunrise to sunset.* . . .

The resemblance of this victory to that of Indra, king of the Vedic pantheon, over the cosmic serpent Vritra is beyond question. The two myths are variants of a single archetype. Furthermore, in each the role of the anti-god has been assigned to a figure from an earlier mythology—in Greece, of the Pelasgians, in India, of the Dravidians—daemons that formerly had symbolized the force of the cosmic order itself, the dark mystery of time, which licks up hero deeds like dust: the force of the never-dying serpent, sloughing lives like skins, which pressing on, *ever turning in its circle of eternal return*, is to continue in this manner forever, as it has already cycled from all eternity, getting absolutely nowhere. . . .

. . .in India the old mythology of the serpent power presently recovered strength, until, by the middle of the first millenium B.C., it had absorbed the entire pantheon and spirit of the Vedic gods—Indra, Mitra, Vayu, and the rest—transforming all into mere agents of the processes of its own, *still circling round of eternal return*.

So, to recapitulate, we have two references to cosmic serpents while the third was so large that it knocked its head against the stars. The cosmos signifies the starry night sky, therefore, I feel quite confident in attributing the serpents vanquished by the new heroes of patriarchy to the constellation Draco. Now if we look again at Campbell's last two paragraphs, specifically the italicized material regarding a *turning, circling, eternal return*, we must realize that to one watching the night sky, the coils of the descending serpent appear to entwine about the pole, returning eventually to the same place (the eternal return). And so the serpent of Eden stands revealed.

The scriptures we have believed for two thousand years, pertaining to original sin and the inherent evil of women, that have given patriarchy its authoritarian validation for treating women as witches and economic slaves, proves to be a misreading—probably deliberate—of an astronomical myth that accurately and yet poetically explained the nature of the cosmos thousands of years before Genesis.

As the Life Principle, it is clear that the Tree is Eve and Eve the Tree. Also, the serpent's spiral coils suggest the lunar goddess because of the cyclical nature of the world of phenomena; birth and death, fertility and decay, etc. But the Genesis version adds a second tree, so that we have the Tree of Life, the tradition of the lunar goddess, and the Tree of the knowledge of good and evil.

In effect patriarchy introduces duality, the pairs of opposites of which good and evil are primary examples, along with life and death, conscious and unconscious, and left and right brain function. In the tradition of the Great Goddess, the one Tree of Life encompassed all pairs of opposites. Now in Genesis, Eve is cut off from her Tree and she is identified with the evil principle of the Tree of good and evil. Further, her other lunar aspect, the serpent, is denigrated as the evil antagonist to life. Whereas in reality, she and serpent are aspects of the life principle itself! A curious business, indeed. But can we find a motivation in this patriarchal axe-grinding? I think so.

Through all the Eden drama, Adam is completely passive, a befuddled interloper into a woman's Mystery. The serpent and Eve converse, and Eve makes a decision, and then initiates the soul-less Adam. It is significant that yet another Tree, Christ's Cross of death and resurrection, accomplishes mankind's salvation in the Christian tradition. But patriarchy and matriarchy embrace vastly different ideas of what the end of mankind shall be. *The former discards time, the end of time being the desired goal.* The Judeo-Christian Heaven, from what one hears of it, is totally static, so dull in fact that in his play *Don Juan in Hell,* Bernard Shaw was moved to make Hell the more attractive.

In the Mysteries of the Great Goddess, death is not an end in itself, but a portal to new birth, the natural round never ending, fallen seeds rooting again. Christianity postulates a resurrection of the physical body, hence, the prohibition against cremation. But the spouse of the Great Goddess is reborn as her son, who will again become her lover, and father himself once more from out of his death, as the moon is reborn with each cycle; therefore, the religions of the Great Mother instruct us to live in harmony with nature. I shall discuss the importance of this theme in regard to modern ecology in a subsequent chapter, but we should note that Yahweh is a god of natural catastrophes.

There is no doubt in my mind that the Gnostics were writing on Jehovah (Yahweh), the Old Testament God, when they spoke of Saklas, Samael, Ialdabaoth. His anger has fueled our guilt, even over two millenia. Beneath the surface of patriarchy's antipathy to fertility goddesses and the eternal round of natural process lies a fear of nature, sex, and death. To die and not be resurrected in the body is the Christian's great fear. "The wages of sin is death," we have heard all our lives. To the patriarchist, life is like an infection that can be caught if one is not always on guard.

Also beneath the surface of the concomitant trappings of Christianity—celibacy and monasticism—lies the fear of life itself. And even deeper in the unconscious of the collective psyche of the Judeo-Christian tradition lurks an overwhelming fear of sexual intercourse with women. Since this process regenerates life itself, manifest antipathy to life characterizes the monastic strain so prevalent in religious history. This fear of sexual knowledge of women returns us full circle to the Garden and the Tree of the knowledge of Good and Evil, death and damnation being its legacy to us, even unto this modern day.

Recently I met a man who had been the Catholic chaplain for a university, until he married and was forced to relinquish his position. To him I put this question. "How does the sexual knowledge of woman impair you and render you unfit to perform your pastoral duties?" Of course, he could not answer this, since by marriage he did not deem himself unfit, nor can the Church answer. But behind the dogma that demands celibacy of priests lies the patriarchal notion that contamination—in the spiritual sense—results from sexual knowledge of woman. Eve the temptress, Eve the consort of the serpent!

When we get into our chapter on nature and the body, we shall see how our attitudes towards sex and nature are integrally linked, since our bodies are our immediate nature. Then we shall see how our individual attitudes towards ecology are mirrored by our sexual attitudes, since—once again— our bodies are our nature. Most fascinating of all, however, is that there are always parallels in left and right brain functioning; therefore, patriarchal antipathy to nature, the body, and sex has remarkable similarity in the macho desire to rape women and rape nature!

Indeed, the hunters out to shoot deer, or to cut down forests, (to tame nature), are psychologically the types most likely to rape women. They are total left-brain types, completely shut off from any emotional relation to their victims, be they deer, forest, or women. As we progress in our attempt to understand the sexes, we shall have some answers as to why women are most at ease—and men most often ill at ease—while relating; yet the solutions to the war of the sexes are not beyond attainment once we realize the psychological resons for the differences.

But before that happens, the old devils have to be laid to rest, and the reasons for men's uneasiness with sexual relations brought into the light. Patriarchal thinking takes place in left-brain functions, as we noted in introduction. Emotional relating, women's forte, is a right-brain function. A man cannot perform sexually if his mind is on left-brain matters. Since worries are often focused in this area, business, money problems, etc, being in the wrong area of the brain at the wrong time is the most frequent cause of psychic impotence.

At the same time, if the person is capable of easily moving his focus between left and right brain functions, the left-brain becomes an antidote against early ejaculation, as in the amusing story of a boy I once knew who was having his first sexual experience, to the envy of the rest of us who had not yet been initiated by the goddess. When he got close to orgasm, and if he wished to prolong the act further, he began to recite in his mind batting averages of major league ballplayers. This switch from right-brain ecstasy to left-brain figuring saved the day until he wanted to switch back again!

But, if the man sees the woman as evil or dangerous in some way, then she is to him a true daughter of Eve, and the old serpent again rears his ugly head. The Fall in the Garden, therefore, meant contamination by sexual contact, according to the Judeo-Christian tradition.

THE SECRET OF SEXUAL INTERCOURSE

Earlier I spoke of the serpent as the Instructor of Eve, whereupon she became the initiator of Adam in the secret of creation, sexual intercourse. I also noted that in the Genesis drama of the Garden, Adam appears to be an interloper into a woman's mystery. If for a moment we can think back in time to that period when we ourselves were innocent of the "facts" of life, we may recall our own myths of creation. In effect, how did we answer the question, "Where do babies come from?" This innocence is akin to that experienced by primitive man, for sexual intercourse contained a secret, or mystery, in that primitive man had not made the connection between the sexual act and the result—the child. When a mere man, Adam, is initiated into the mystery by Eve, she having been initiated by the serpent-god, we can see the reason for the archon's wrath, for in possession of this knowledge man has become godlike. In another sense, the immortality of the species is assured, since with his new knowledge man can perpetuate his species. Thus, the necessity in the eyes of the archons and Saklas/Yakweh to place a joker in the deck, the Tree that confers death, the catch 22 negating the knowledge of the secret of creation.

Once again we must remember that according to Genesis and our Judeo-Christian heritage, death enters the world (Eden) through sexual initiation. And, once again, we must remember the effect that this teaching has had on us through guilt and the expectation of punishment because of sexual experience. In Church dogma this experience need not be with another, for masturbation—the sexual experience of one's self!—is also deemed sinful and worthy of divine retribution at death. I cannot help thinking that this ecclesiastical reaction is a reflection of the archons' reactions to Eve's revelation and initiation of Adam. The archons' reactions are mirrored by Yahweh; he is jealous that the secret is out; he is angry that his law has been transgressed; and he is damning in his condemnation of mankind (Adam and Eve).

Now although today few take the Bible to be the Word of God, and, therefore, their conscious minds are seemingly uncontaminated with sexual guilt, the unconscious minds of men and women harbor the gnawing shame of Adam and Eve. Sex is somehow "dirty," and very few are at ease during sexual intercourse. A compulsion to get to the end of the act goads them on. We shall deal with the psychology of sex in our modern world in a subsequent chapter, but for now let us turn back the clock to the time of our innocence.

In the pre-Judeo-Christian era, the reproductive function of the female was not recognized as inherently her own. After all, in the human cycle, birth follows intercourse by nine months; consequently, the fertile power of the female was thought to reside with the moon goddess. In other worlds, at this stage in humankind's evolution, the secret was not out. Genesis is the myth of the loss of innocence (expulsion from the idyllic Garden) because the secret is given to man by the Initiator against the wishes of God. In a sense, therefore, our Judeo-Christian myth is a new development in the evolution of man, and for that reason a myth of great import and validity. What has diminished its import, however, and its significance for the evolution of human consciousness, is that it has been misread and misinterpreted. The god reigning 6,000 years before Yahweh's appearance in mythology, the hero serpent, has found his role reversed, and he has become antagonistic to man, equated with the dark, demonic principle that seeks to thwart man's spiritual evolution. At the same time Yahweh is equated with the Good, though in reality his edict would have thwarted man's evolution *had it not been violated by Eve.*

Eve is the moon goddess of 6,000 B.C. in modern dress, or modern undress, and Yahweh's antipathy to her is recognition of her and her serpent/lover's precedence as preservers of the matriarchal link to mankind's prehistory. Sophia, mother of Saklas/Yahweh, possessed a heavenly light which the archons sought to derive from her. This Light, or Holy Spirit, was imparted to mankind. In the form of the moon goddess, this same heavenly light was the fertilizing force for all life on the planet. Indeed, without it, or during its dying phase, life could not flourish, for seeds could not germinate, plants could not grow, nor could animals or humans bear young. The moon, therefore, is the actual power of growth, and not a poetic metaphor for the goddess. Without her presence earth is a wasteland.

The Mother Goddess religion, therefore, is a spiritual principle of nurturing and fertility, in which Mother Earth—not the next life—is the sacred plane of endeavor. The rites of the Great Mother are *ecstatic* dance, song, and fertility rites, versus the *monastic* tendency of patriarchy; consequently we may say very generally that the Mother Goddess religion is a "Be here now" religion, whereas Biblical patriarchy is "Not of this world." Christ constantly stressed that he was the prophet of a new order, one that had not yet come, but which would be realized in Heaven, his Father's kingdom. Being in the world was but a preparation for this other life, compared to which life in the world was a living death. This carries philosophical weight only if one is willing to reject life, which the Church Fathers did, as we have seen from their writings.

But let us examine the implications. First of all, in Goddess worship the outer world (nature) is sought out and cultivated. By this I do not mean "tamed" or conquered agriculturally. Instead one places oneself in the position of the initiate to the initiator (nature) with homage, expectation, and gratitude. Contrastingly, monasticism slams the door on the outer world, often with the condescending attitude that it is corrupting.

In chapter five we shall see how one's personal nature is represented by by one's body. Here we can see pronounced and disturbing discrepancies between the two religions, for in the monastic orders the body—like outer nature—is tamed and disciplined, a devil's house of lust that must be brought to task. Again, the role of Adam as an interloper into a woman's mystery comes to mind, for he was initiated into the mystery of sexual intercourse.

In the same way, personal procreation stands in relation to the universal mystery of fertility and regeneration. Hence, the individual participates in the Greater Mystery and effects a relation.

Besides one's body, there is an inner nature of which we may speak now in this era of the unveiling of the psychological mysteries, and which we shall discuss further in chapter five. Adam was made aware by Eve of his body and its function. In this respect, she fulfilled the role of what the psychologist C.G.Jung has termed the *anima*, the soul of man, and the feminine principle in the unconscious. Jung postulated the theory of the archetypes of the collective unconscious. The archetypes may be thought of as psychological components in the psyche similar to an entire psychic family. The ego and the conscious mind act as if they constitute the entire family; however dream analysis reveals the nature of the unconscious members of the psyche. Just as a man's conscious orientation is masculine, his unconscious contains a compensating component, the anima, or feminine archetype. This woman within directs him, whether or not he is aware of it, in all his relations per se, for the relation of his conscious mind to his own anima dictates what his personal relations shall be. This fact is manifest to those who have studied Jungian psychology in order to gain emotional autonomy in the act of Eros, since the Eros initiation is not only a new relationship to the body, but also an instruction into the correspondence between the outer relation in one's life and the inner relation to the woman in one's psyche. Thus, Eve functions as Adam's anima, and the Eros initiation of Adam instructs him regarding sexual intercourse's synchronous magic in relation to universal fertility and procreation (outer nature). Also, she awakens him to a new world of inner relation, his own feminine component. Whereas he had been alone in Eden, he is now in an I-Thou relation. So too, the lonely ego, realizing it is no longer autonomous, enters into relation with the unconscious feminine component.

Finally, I must mention my visit to a planetarium, where by the miracle of a star projector, and the courtesy of the director, I was transported back in time some 6,000 years to the era of the Great Mother and saw the serpent rightfully restored to the pole. It was a moment of awe, for I was seeing the same divinities as did those who gazed above in 4,000 B.C. Proceeding up from the earth and out the top of my skull was the Tree of Life itself, culminating in Thuban, the pole, the very center of cosmic generation. And I was centered again myself, and saw the serpent descend and ascend about the pole, reminding me of the spirit of life he brought to earth, and the descent of my own spirit to earth, and its eventual return. And there, shining as Eltanin, his brightest eye, was the star known in Egypt as Isis, and Inanna in Babylonia, the Great Mother once more. All homage to Her.

TABLE ONE *

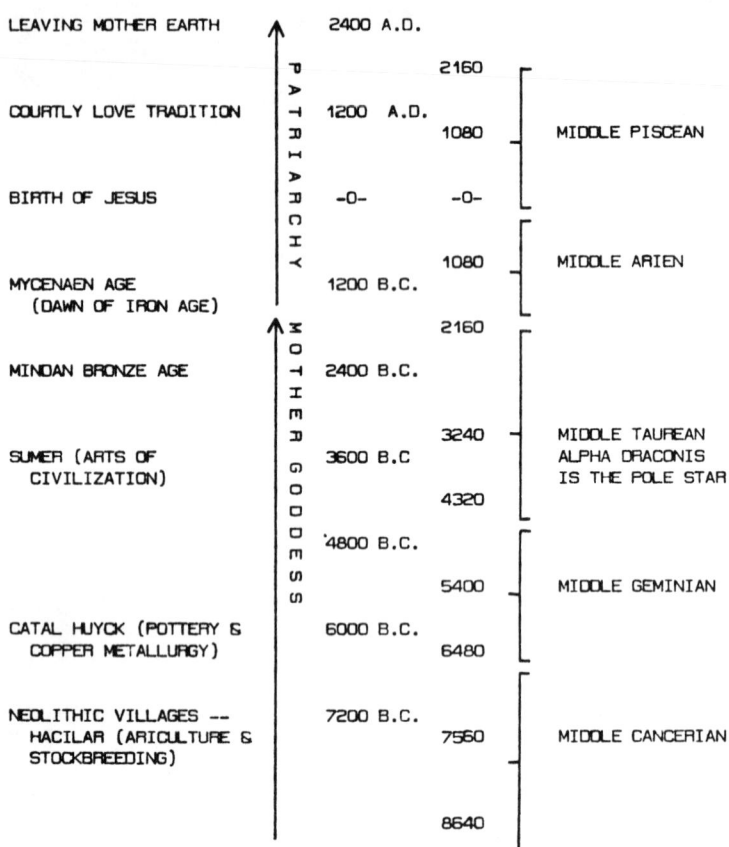

* In terms of the perspective of this book, the history of the Mother Goddess, important historical changes occur every 1200 years, as shown at the left. Calculated by the precession of the equinoxes, the comparative astrological ages are of a duration of 2,160 years, as shown at the right.

CHAPTER II
PATRIARCHY

I have found that the most important changes in the historical perspective with which we are concerned—that of the Mother Goddess—occur every 1200 years. The table of correspondences shows these changes at left, while at right the equivalent astrological age is listed. For example, the Taurean Age runs from 4320 B.C., the dawn of the Iron Age. With the advent of the development of armor, sword, and spear, militant patriarchy began its march across the face of Mother Earth. The very last date of significance which I have noted is 2400 A.D., "Leaving Mother Earth." Predictably, if the technology which commenced in 1200 B.C. is on schedule, we may begin to bid farewell to Gaia (see Chapter 5), rocketing off into space to colonize distant planets of other star systems, the technology which had its onset in 1200 B.C. in the form of the iron war chariot now transformed into chariots of fire.

The earliest depiction of the Great Mother is carved on a limestone block in a rock shelter at Laussel, France, c. 20,000 B.C. Joseph Campbell's book *The Way of the Animal Powers* notes fourteen sites of Great Mother images westward from the Don River across Europe!

Our table of correspondences commences with 7200 B.C. We are speaking in terms of approximate dates, of course, but about this time there is evidence of profound changes in human life, which heretofore had depended rather precariously upon hunting and food gathering. Now the soil is cultivated and the herds controlled (penned) and bred. Nomadic wandering is no longer necessary, but upon the fertility of the crops and herds depend the lives of the villagers. Invoking the powers of the Mother Goddess through rituals of sympathetic magic becomes a way of insuring fertility. James Mellaart found evidence of a continuous Mother Goddess culture at Catal Huyck in Anatolia (Turkey) from about 7200 B.C. down to 5400 B.C., excavations of entire villages revealing that each home had a shrine to the Goddess. Ceramic ware and naturalistic statues of the Goddess appear in archeological stratum dating from 5700-5400 B.C., so the progressively civilizing influence of the Goddess continues during the 3600 years from 7200 B.C. up to 3600 B.C., the general date given for the appearance in Mesopotamia of the arts of advanced civilizations: writing, mathematics, architecture, astronomy, and government. Sumer was the most advanced city-state of 3600 B.C., possessing all of the above arts necessary for high civilization, and best known for the building of ziggaruts, tiered temples for both worship and observation of the gods and goddesses in the sky, the planets.

The Great Mother's role was two-fold. Not only did she bring forth life and nourish it, but she received the dead back into her body, the earth, in order that they might be reborn again. Attis, Adonis, and Tammuz were the son/consorts of the Goddess, representing the dying and reborn gods of corn and grain. Venus was the planet in the sky associated with Ishtar, a goddess of fertility, and Eltanin in Draco was Isis and Ianana.

Dominant as the center of civilization until 2400 B.C., Sumer rules the period from 3600-2400 B.C., its power waning as civilization shifts south to Egypt and east to Crete, where snake goddess statues appear from the Minoan era down to Mycenaen times in 1200 B.C. From 1200 B.C. onwards the influence of the Great Mother wanes considerably, going underground for the most part with the end of the Bronze Age and the beginning of the Iron Age. Iron was used for forging stronger swords and the wheels for war chariots. The Mycenaen invaders of Crete were taller than the people of Minoan Crete, and possessed the warlike qualities typical of the Aryan invaders.

Regarding this crucial period in history, Joseph Campbell tells us, "For it is now perfectly clear that before the violent entry of the late Bronze and early Iron Age nomadic Aryan cattle-herders from the north and Semitic sheep-and-goat herders from the south into the old cult sites of the ancient world, there had prevailed in that world an essentially organic, vegetal, non-heroic view of the nature and necessities of life that was completely repugnant to those lion hearts for whom not the patient toil of earth but the battle spear and its plunder were the source of both wealth and joy."[2]

In one intellectually concise, and at the same time poetic, sentence, Joseph Campbell has delineated the primary differences between matriarchy and patriarchy. Further on, in *Occidental Mythology*, he speculates as to why the partriarchal impulse in Greece produced poetry, the *Illiad* and *Odyssey*, whereas in the Levant the product was religion. Campbell's words have great value for us in trying to comprehend the profound psychic and cultural changes humankind faced as the transfer from matriarchy to patriarchy took place at the crucial date in our table, 1200 B.C. or thereabouts:

> And so we arrive at the epic date of the deeds of Homer's heroes: The date as well, of those of the Book of Judges. The two heroic ages were simultaneous. In both dominions there had been a long period of interplay and adjustment between settled agricultural and intrusive pastoral-warrior peoples, after which, very suddenly, overwhelming onslaughts of fresh pastoral-warrior folk (in Palestine the Hebrews, in Greece, the Dorians) precipitated a veritable *Gotterdammerung* and the end of the world age of the people of bronze. The exploits of Homer's "divine race of heroes" fall in the period c.1250-1150, and following a lapse of about three centuries their epics took form, their dates coinciding approximately with the biblical, as follows:
>
> c. 850 B.C.: Illiad - Yahwist (J) Text c. 750 B.C.: Odyssey - Elohim (E) Text
>
> It is all too neat for mere coincidence, and, as Freud has remarked, there is the further problem of why in the case of the Greece what appeared was poetry, and of the Jews, religion.[3]

One answer, perhaps, as to why the Levant produced a religion which strongly emphasized laws and covenants (e.g. the Book of Judges mentioned by Campbell), whereas Greece produced a pantheon of gods, all of whom displayed very human traits, is evident in the fact that poetry is the language of the White Goddess, the Great Mother in the role of muse, and the Greeks, despite being outwardly patriarchal, incorporated the feminine principle in their mythology. " . . .the Olympians never were confused by the Greeks with the ultimate Being of being. Like men, they had been born of the Great Mother. Though stronger and of longer life than men, they were their brothers. Moreover, they were but temporary governors of the universe, which they had wrestled from an earlier generation of divine children of the goddess, and they would lose it—as Prometheus knew—to a later. Properly they were the archetypes of the ideals of the Greek city state, and with its passing they passed too."[4]

And earlier, in *Occidental Mythology*, Joseph Campbell tells us:
> Jane Ellen Harrison demonstrated over half a century ago [in *Prolegomena to a Study of the Greek Religion*, 1903] that in the field festivals and mystery cults of Greece numerous vestiges survived of a pre-Homeric mythology in which the place of honor was held, not by the male gods of the sunny Olympic pantheon, but by a goddess, darkly ominous, who might appear as one, two, three, or many, and was the mother of both the living and the dead. Her consort was typically in serpent form; and her rites were not characterized by the blithe spirit of manly athletic games, humanistic art, social enjoyment, feasting and theatre that the modern mind associates with Classical Greece, but were in spirit dark and full of dread. The offerings were not of cattle, gracefully garlanded, but of pigs and human beings, directed downward, not upward to the light, and rendered not in polished marble temples, radiant in the hour of rosy-fingered dawn, but in twilight groves and fields, over trenches through which the fresh blood poured into the bottomless abyss.[5]

The "darkly ominous" goddess of "the bottomless abyss" suggests dominance by the unconscious, traditional antagonist to light/consciousness, and secondly, the evolving ego's fear of being pulled back into darkness/unconsciousness. We shall have more to say of this shortly in analyzing the various reasons for patriarchy's supplanting matriarchy. However, if the reader will refer once again to our table of 1200 year increments, with the next date zero, the birth of Jesus, when patriarchy gained further impetus, it would seem that between 1200 B.C. and 1200 A.D., the goddess/feminine principle had gone underground, into the collective unconscious, not to emerge again until the era of courtly love, as the collective *anima* or feminine projection of Western culture.

This erotic flowering, in the poetry of courtly love and in the radical concept of marriage, awakened sleeping monsters in the psyches of monks and nuns, and was followed by a collective repression of the anima and the erotic impulses thereof. This repression bred new monsters in the psyches of monks and inquisitors, whereupon witches rode the nightskies of the Renaissance, projected onto the face of the moon, the Mother Goddess herself, and projected also onto the innocent persons of the women of Europe, England and America. If the 1200-year intervals of our table prove viable, we may expect another collective rise of the anima from the psyche about the year 2400 A.D. Or, 2400 A.D. may signify the century when we depart Mother Earth for other planets and other galaxies.

THE FEMININE GODDESS IN GNOSTICISM

The Gnostics venerated the serpent and seemingly were aware at least of the older religion of the Great Mother. In their Mother Goddess, Sophia (wisdom) there is a sure parallel to the Great Mother, for as the serpent is wise and descends the World Axis/Tree, and Inanna descends from light to the underworld, so too Sophia in descending moves from the Ogdoad, or starry realm, to earth, which by comparison to the great Above, seems to be just as much "the pits" as Ereshkigal's kingdom of the dead was to Inanna. So light, divinity, descends from Above to Below, comprising the essence of all three myths. Matter without light is inanimate, but given the sacrifice of the descending serpent, or the Light of Wisdom (Sophia), *all* life may be infused with beauty. My theory here is that one's attitude towards matter determines the attitude towards cell, body, sex, women, and nature. Then shall the flesh be exalted or mortified? The two attitudes depend upon whether or not one sees matter as imbued with spirit, or "fallen," devoid of spirit. When the latter is the case, then the body is to be mortified, sexual rapture is thought to be the devil's work, and nature is to be tamed. Women, then, personify the danger of damnation, that is, to the traditionalist of the Judeo-Christian religion. But, are there not more enlightened views of the feminine in Christianity? For some startling new perspectives on Jesus and women we must return to the recently discovered Nag Hammadi texts mentioned previously. Here, some of Jesus' sayings present a quite different picture of his attitude towards women than is traditionally presented. And, most astounding of all, an eye-witness account in one book states that Simon of Cyrene is crucified in Jesus' stead, who laughs and mocks his persecutors from afar.

" I did not succumb to them as they had planned. But I was not afflicted at all. Those who were there punished me. And I did not die in reality but in appearance . . .it was not I. They struck me with the reed; it was another, Simon, who bore the cross on his shoulder. It was another on whom they placed the crown of thorns. But I was rejoicing in the height over all the wealth of the archons and the offspring of their error and empty glory. And I was laughing at their ignorance."[6]

The story of the laughing Savior is one of the most startling element of the Nag Hammadi texts, and I share it with my readers here because it presents Jesus in a different light, unlike the Biblical tale in which he is a hapless victim of the forces seeking his death. My own personal opinion, for what it is worth, is that if Jesus were of the Christ consciousness, he would be above submission to the tortures of crucifixion. The Biblical rebuttal is that he did this for humankind in becoming flesh; however the Gnostic version has greater appeal for me.

For women, the Gnostic texts present material on Jesus that suggests that Christianity was not misogynist originally, but that some of the early Church fathers may have deliberately suppressed certain sayings of Jesus that did not suit their philosophies. Indeed, the Nag Hammadi texts may have been hidden and buried to prevent their destruction by zealous priests of a more traditional persuasion.

One amazing treatise, *The Gospel of Philip*, has Jesus kissing Mary Magdalene. "According to this treatise," says Wesley W. Isenberg in the introduction, "the existential malady of humanity results from the differentation of the sexes. When Eve separated from Adam, the original androgynous unity was broken. The purpose of Christ's coming is to reunite 'Adam'and 'Eve'."[7]

Indeed, in a later chapter when we put Adam and Eve back together again in the hierosgamos, a psychic marriage resolving all pairs of opposites, our concluding realization will be very much like the words of Jesus in *The Gospel of Philip*:

> Light and darkness, life and death, right and left, are brothers of one another. They are inseparable. Because of this neither are the good good, nor the evil evil, nor is life life, nor death death. For this reason each one will dissolve into its original nature. But those who are exalted above the world are indissoluble, eternal.
>
> Names given to world things are very deceptive, for they divert our thoughts from what is correct to what is incorrect. Thus one who hears the word 'God' does not perceive what is correct, but perceives what is incorrect.[8]

Thus also to the traditional labels of masculine and feminine. In uniting masculine and feminine in the sacred marriage, Jesus hints of a sacred marriage-to-be between himself and a "Mary," who appears in *The Gospel of Philip* as a manifestation of Sophia (wisdom), the feminine deity that descended from Light/Spirit to earth, only to become entrapped in matter. According to *The Gospel of Philip*:

> Some said, "Mary conceived by the Holy Spirit." They are in error. They do not know what they are saying. When did a woman ever conceive by a woman?. . . .
>
> For it is by a kiss that the perfect conceive and give birth. For this reason we also kiss one another. We receive conception from the grace which is in each other.
>
> There were three who always walked with the Lord: Mary his mother and her sister and Magdalene, the one who was called his companion. His sister and his mother and his companion were each a Mary.[9]

This presents an entirely different picture of Jesus than that in the Bible, for there he eschews the company of women, *or so the apostles say*, perhaps in jealousy. Here Jesus walks about conversing with his mother, sister, and "companion," his bride-to-be in spirit.

Further elaboration on the concept of Sophia is provided by John Dart accordingly:

The figure of Wisdom ("Sophia") in Proverbs has been cited by Bultmann as a key to the Gnostic redeemer concept. Once residing with God on high, Wisdom comes down to earth and attempts to spread her knowledge. She warns those who scorn her that she will laugh and mock them when calamity comes.

The mocking idea is carried over in *The Nature of the Archons* and *On the Origin of the World*. In those Gnostic writings, Sophia and Eve, her daughter, both patterned after Wisdom in the Jewish literature, mock the Archons.

Eve is pursued by the lustful archons in both texts, but she laughs at their senselessness and blindness. She fools them by providing a substitute image of herself for them to rape. Just so the living Jesus in later stories provides a substitute for the archons to crucify!

Sophia Zoe also laughs at the archons' desire to create a man in *On the Origin of the World*. She laughs because she knows they are blind. And when it was evident to the chief Archon's minions that there was a higher realm, they laughed at the Archon for saying he was God and that no one existed before him.[10]

In The *Gospel of Philip*, Sophia is described as barren, without child, a trace of salt. Then we read, "But where *they* will be in their own way, the Holy Spirit will also be, and her children are many." To whom do *they* refer? Evidently the reference is not to the apostles, they would say, "But where *we* will be."

The conclusion of the alchemical process is a marriage whereby the darkness of salt is transformed to gold (light), obstensibly the same sacred marriage mentioned in *The Gospel of Philip*:

Those who are separated will be united [and] will be filled. Every one who will [enter] the bridle chamber will kindle the [light], for [it burns] just as in the marriages which are [observed,though they] happen at night. That fire [burns] only at night and is put out. But the mysteries of this marriage are perfacted rather in the day and the light. Neither that day nor its light ever sets. If anyone becomes a son of the bridal chamber, he will receive the light.[11]

And this ceremony, the *hierosgamos*, unites in alchemy Mercurius, an androgyne, frequently equated with the Holy Spirit (particularly in Jung), with Sun and Moon, or active sulphur and passive salt, masculine and feminine elements. John Dart notes that "Certain female biblical personages may come by an honored status partly because of the prominence of the Sophia myth in Gnosticism. Eve,for instance, was more than mere mortal in the Gnostic view,she was the divinely empowered daughter of Sophia."[12]

The last matriarchal religion before patriarchy took precedence, the Eleusinian Mystery, consisted of two dieties, the Mother goddess Demeter and her daughter Kore, or Persephone. Thus the suggestion that Eve is Sophia's daughter presents the possibility that certain Gnostics were aware of and *preserving* this tradition in a most esoteric way. Furthermore, Kore and Demeter are moon goddesses, and Kore, like Sophia, is barren, that is virgin, until raped by Hades (darkness) below. She is dragged off to the underworld, and the parallel to Sophia is present since she falls from Light above to become entrapped in matter below.

Therefore, if we can equate Sophia with the lunar goddesses, Christ may be compared to the Solar Logos. Adding the third principle mentioned, the androgynous Holy Spirit, the line from Philip's gospel now seems clearly to describe the "ceremony," or mystic marriage, the hierosgamos of Sophia, Christ, and the Holy Spirit. And if not, why the reference to children? Again the line reads: "But where *they* will be in their own way, the Holy Spirit will also be, and her children are many."

But let us move on a few pages to where the evidence is even more compelling. Here, neither salt, nor Sophia are used as names for her, but she is called Wisdom, the literal translation in Greek of the name *Sophia*. Recall again that Sophia created the universe.

> As for the Wisdom who is called 'the barren,' she is the mother [of the] angels. And the companion of the [Savior is] Mary Magdalene. [But Christ loved] her more than [all] the disciples [and used to] kiss her [often] on her [mouth]. The rest of [the disciples were offended] by it [and expressed disapproval]. They said to him, "Why do you love her more than all of us?" The Savior answered and said to them, "Why do I not love you like her?" When a blind man and one who sees are both together in darkness, they are not different from one another. When the light comes, then he who sees will see the light, and he who is blind will remain in darkness."
>
> The Lord said, "Blessed is he who is before he came into being. For he who is, has been and shall be."[13]

Here Jesus seems to be laughing again, albeit up his sleeve, for if Mary Magdalene is Wisdom, and so he has told the disciples, then she is also Light, the divinity which fell into the darkness of matter; but the disciples, unable to see her divinity, are like blind men who remain in darkness.

One question then remains. Is Mary Magdalene a supra-personal being, as Jesus is also Christ, or is she but one woman, embodying the divinity in *all* women, whom Jesus has selected as his companion? In the same sense, therefore, all men embody Christ's divinity.

Elaine Pagels' book *The Gnostic Gospels* is clearly the most concise and readable of the commentaries on the Nag Hammadi texts, particularly in regard to the role of women in the early Christian Church:

> ...the heretic Marcion, had, in fact, scandalized his orthodox contemporaries by appointing women on an equal basis with men as priests and bishops. The gnostic teacher Marcellina traveled to Rome to represent the Carpocratian group which claimed to have received secret teachings from Mary, Salome, and Martha. The Montanists, a radical prophetic circle, honored two women, Prisca and Maximilla, as founders of the movement.
>
> Our evidence, then, clearly indicates a correlation between religious theory and social practice. Among such gnostic groups as the Valentinians, women were considered equal to men; some were revered as prophets; others acted as teachers, traveling evangelists,

healers, priests, perhaps even bishops. This general observation is not, however, universally applicable. At least three heretical circles that retained a masculine image of God included women who took positions of leadership—the Marcionites, the Montanists, and the Carpocratians. But from the year 200, we have no evidence for women taking prophetic, priestly, and episcopal roles among orthodox churches.

This is an extraordinary development, considering that in its earliest years the Christian movement showed a remarkable openness toward women. Jesus himself violated Jewish convention by talking openly with women, and he included them among his companions. . . .

While Paul acknowledged women as equals "in Christ," and allowed for them a wider range of activity than did traditional Jewish congregations, he could not bring himself to advocate their equality in social and political terms. Such ambivalence opened the way for the statements found in I Corinthians 14,34f., whether written by Paul or inserted by someone else: " . . .The women should keep silence in the churches. For they are not permitted to speak, but they should be subordinate . . .*it is shameful for a woman to speak in church.*"

Such contradictory attitudes toward women reflect a time of social transition, as well as the diversity of cultural influence on churches scattered throughout the known world. In Greece and Asia Minor, women participated with men in religious cults, especially the cults of the Great Mother and of the Egyptian goddess Isis. While the leading roles were reserved for men, women took part in the services and professions. So women took up education, the arts and professions such as medicine. In Egypt, women had attained, by the first century A.D., a relatively advanced state of emancipation, socially, politically, and legally. . . . .

Women of the Jewish communities, on the other hand, were excluded from actively participating in public worship, in education, and in social and political life outside the family.

Yet despite all of this, and despite the previous public activity of Christian women, the majority of Christian churches in the second century went with the majority of the middle class in opposing the move toward equality, which found its support primarily in rich or what we would call bohemian circles. By the year 200, the majority of Christian communities endorsed as canonical the pseudo-Pauline letter of Timothy, which stresses (and exaggerates) the anti-feminist element in Paul's views: "Let a woman learn in silence with all submissiveness. I permit no woman to teach or to have authority over men; she is to keep silent." Orthodox Christians also accepted as Pauline the letters to the Collossians and to the Ephesians, which order that women "be subject in everything to their husbands."

Clement, Bishop of Rome, writes in his letter to the unruly church in Corinth that women are to "remain in the rule of subjection" to their husbands. While in earlier times Christian men and women sat together for worship, in the middle of the second century—precisely at the time of struggle with gnostic Christians— orthodox communities began to adopt the synagogue custom, segragating women from men. By the end of the second century, women's participation in worship was explicitly condemned: groups in which women continued on to leadership were branded as heretical.

What was the reason for these changes? The scholar Johannes Liepoldt suggests that the influx of many Hellenized Jews into the movement may have influenced the church in the direction of Jewish traditions, but, as he admits, "this is only an attempt to explain the situation: the reality itself is the only certain thing." Professor Morton Smith suggests that the change may have resulted from Christianity's move up in social scale from lower to middle class. He observes that in the lower class, where all labor was needed, women had been allowed to perform any services they could (so today, in the Near East, only middle-class women are veiled).[4]

And so we see that the situation of women, both socially and spiritually, gradually became more oppressive, so that from 200 A.D. to 1200 A.D., the advent of courtly love, a kind of psychological Dark Ages set in. After Jesus' death, and without his protective influence, the mysogynist tendencies in Christianity surfaced with a vengeance, and all women were made to bear the brunt of Eve's guilt. It seems to me that the attitude towards women is a good indication of the level of civilization of a particular culture. When rape, murder, and treating half the society like chattel prevail, then we are looking at Dark Ages indeed.

THE CHURCH FATHERS ON WOMEN

Let us examine some of the writings of the early Church fathers in order to further define patriarchy's put down of women. In the year 1100, at the Council of Constance, the Church established celibacy as a ground for acceptance into the clergy. Before then, there was a certain *naturalness* in the idea of a married priest, for, indeed, the Judeo-Christian tradition only gradually supplanted the naturalness, or man-nature relatedness of the earlier Mother Goddess religions. Significantly the above date tells us that eleven centuries of the Church calendar were required before such a chauvinistic edict could be passed. But what of the antipathy to woman before 1100?
Although married himself, Tertullian (A.D.c.160-c.230) demonstrates a real abhorrence for feminine contact—as if it were with the devil himself! After reading the following, we may wonder whether his marriage was consumnated, or whether he married for social conveniency.

In Book 1, *On the Apparel of Women*, he states, "CHAPTER 1 INTRODUCTION. Modesty in Apparel Becoming to Women, in Memory of the Introduction of Sin into the World Through a Woman." In the following first paragraph, Tertullian advises women to dress in humble garb, we may suppose so as not to appear "uppity," "walking about as Eve mourning and repentant, in order that by every garb of pentinence she might the more fully expiate that which she derives from Eve,—the ignoring, I mean, of the first sin, and the odium (attaching to her as the cause) of human perdition. 'In pains and in anxieties dost thou bear (children) woman; and toward thine husband (is) thy inclination, and he lords it over thee.' And do you not know that you are (each) an Eve? The sentence of God on this sex of yours must of necessity live too.'

Tertullian continues: "*You* (women) are the devil's gateway: *you* are the unsealer of that forbidden tree: *you* are the first deserter of the divine law: *you* are she who persuaded him (Adam) whom the devil was not valiant enough to attack. *You* destroyed so easily God's image, man. On account of *your* desert—that is, death—even the son of God had to die."

Accordingly, he concludes that ornaments of beauty "are the baggage of woman in her condemned and dead state, instituted as if to swell the pomp of her funeral."

According to Tertullian, the angels fell "from God and heaven on the account of concupiscence after females." Having been "enticed into connubial connection with them," the gift they bestowed upon women was the art of makeup and ornamentation that they (women) "might become offensive to God."

In his tract *On Exhortation to Chastity*, he reiterates that "dress is the genius of carnal concupiscence, which again is the cause of fornication." He notes marriage is lawful but not polygamy: "one woman, one rib, for Adam was the one husband of Eve, and Eve his one wife." In Chapter IX he impugns marriage itself as akin to adultery:

"It is laws which seem to make the difference between marriage and fornication; through diversity of illicitness, not through the nature of the thing itself. Besides, what is the thing which takes place in all men and women to produce marriage and fornication? Conmixture of the flesh, of course; the concupiscence whereof the Lord put on the same footing with fornication. Accordingly, the best thing for a man is not to touch a woman . . .for from marriage results wombs, and breasts, and infants. And when an end of marrying? I believe after the end of living!"

Indeed!

The anti-life stance is so heavy-handed no one need miss it. Behind the nurturing imagery of the human mother (womb, breasts, and child), stands the Great Mother, the fertility goddess supplanted by Judeo-Christianity, and it was towards her that the Church Fathers' tirades were directed—however unconsciously— though they fell about the heads of the living women of their day.

Even though we would be hard-pressed to find such extreme denigrations coming from a representative of the Church today; nevertheless, it must be remembered that the negative effects of this heritage still reside in the psyches of many men. *Hence, the put down of women has been equally devastating in its effect on men.*

THOU SHALT NOT!
VERSUS
'GET IT ON!'

The putdown of women which began in ancient Judaism, winds like a serpent's shape through both Old and New Testaments, and is reiterated and enforced in the Koran of Islam. Probing to the heart of the matter, it is possible to discern two very different types of religions. The rites and celebrations of the Mysteries of the Goddess placed the individual celebrant in a special relation to natural and cosmic process. In a sense, *every* woman herself was the incarnation of the Goddess. The individual's conduct was thought to influence natural and cosmic rhythms; therefore, each individual *played a larger part* in the order of things than that demonstrated by his or her mundane existence.

By contrast, from the Ten *Commandments* (italics mine), through all of the Bible and the Koran, patriarchal religions present a series of laws, prohibitions, social contracts, and canons of conduct to be followed to ensure status within the body of the Church/State and before the final *judgment* of God. God and worshipper are separate, and one may pray to God in supplication, but the prayers are like the suits of primitive tribesman to their local chieftains, requests that wrongs be righted, lives rewarded, and greivances redressed, whereas the chanting, singing, and celebrations for the Mother Goddess involved her presence in the very heart and body of the celebrant. One dare not "approach" God on his Judgment Throne anymore than approach a judge's bench without permission. This God is remote, inaccessible, and man corrupt.

Basically the differences between Mother Goddess religion and patriarchy are as simple—and as complicated—as the differences between women and men, and right and left brain functions. Patriarchy accents the law, commandments, judgements, rules of conduct to be followed, or, in summary, knowledge and intellectuality. Goddess worship accents dance, poetry, music, and in these rhythms finds harmony with rhythms in body, nature, and the *cosmic* patterns of the stars. There is a desire to immerse oneself in nature, in life, rather than to tame, conquer, or subdue nature out of suspicion and fear. Women may be called moody by men, but their bodies reflect the cyclical processes in nature, the Mother Goddess, whose moods are the seasons themselves. This intrinsic harmony with nature inspires nurturing tendencies in women, nurturing of crops, livestock, and children, stressing *relation* rather than knowledge.

In a sense, the two *kinds* of religion are so vastly different that one may wonder just where *is* the religion in patriarchy. A Buddhist, given the Bible to read by a Western friend, eventually returned it with the remark, "I can't find any religion in it!"

To the adherents of patriarchy, it seems a good thing that man has moved in this direction. "In place of magical ritual man has developed rational bureaucracies of vocationally specialized men in ecclesiastic, political, and economic organizations . . . .Specific historical and social reasons led early Jewry to Yahwe. Yahwe [Jehovah, the God of the Old Testament] is a war god. He is a jealous god, a god of anger and . . .natural catastrophies (locust plagues, pestilence, earthquakes, floods) . . .opposed to fertility deities (Baalim and Astarte) and orgiastic cults. As an invisible god he is opposed to all symbolic representations. The Jews are his chosen people on the basis of a contract with mutual rights and obligations. He is the god of the collectivity rather than the individual which is jointly responsible to him. Granted the fulfillment of special conditions, Yahwe has pledged to lift up the down-trodden and deliver them, not in the beyond, but in this world, His chosen people must show themselves worthy of Yahwe by obeying his commandments. The relation between Yahwe and his chosen people unfolds in historical time from the creation through the vicissitudes of the Exodus, from the conquest of Palestine, kingly glory to the Exile, diaspora and the fulfillment of the promise."[15].

RELIGION AS SOCIOLOGY

It is my position, however, that we do not have a religion described above, but a sociology, a relation between a social collective of mutually elect (by birth) people and a King/Judge/Commander, whose godly figure integrates royalty, the law, and the military.

"Besides Yahwe's personal traits, also, his position as guardian of the sociolegal order brought him into opposition to the divine mythologies circulating in Canaan as throughout the Middle East. This distinguished him also from the great universal deities of the surrounding culture areas. The primary field of activity, including Ikhnaton's sun god, was the realm of nature. The political destinies usually were guaranteed by the local god of the residence, the social orders by one or several functional deities and only secondarily by the great god of heaven. Yahwe, too, was originally a god of nature, He was a god of certain natural catastrophies, which the Levitical exhortation considered expressive of his wrath against disobedience. The more important the Torah became in Israel, the more firmly was his behavior related to the individual's greater or lesser obedience and good will toward Yahwe.

"Thus all nature mythologies were subordinated to a sober, rational orientation of divine action. The reception of universalistic, cosmological myths into the Yahwe conception was unavoidable for the cultured stratum of Israel. This had far reaching ramifications for the form assumed by the myths. They were turned in ethical direction."[16]

In other words, they were reduced from Mysteries to models for conduct!

It seems manifest, therefore, that men's "religions" were originally nothing more than early tribal customs that became sociological systems, validated by priestcraft and sacred texts, with the purported stamp of divine approval. A woman, or women, in the practice of the art of sympathetic magic first "discovered" religion, that is, the connection between inner psychic reality and outer events. This involved "intuiting" a different order of reality from the evidence of the senses. Indeed, ecstasy and altered states of consciousness induced by wine and narcotic plants facilitated perception of this other reality.

In Judaism "the whole attitude toward life was molded by the conception of a God-ordained social and political revolution to come (since Jewry had become a parish people), and ritualistic correctness, circumcision, dietary prescriptions and the Sabbath rules combined with ethical universalism, hostility toward all magic and irrational salvation striving."[17]

Hostility toward all magic may in part explain Judaism's antipathy to the Mother Goddess, but one is left with the feeling that Judaism is nothing more than the creation of lawyer/priests feathering their own nests by laying down rules for the community to follow. Unless one believes that God handed Moses ten tablets, then we must face the fact that the "religion" being written by the lawyer/priests was making themselves indispensable to the community, through "ritualistic correctness, circumcision, dietary prescriptions and Sabbath rules." Furthermore, in the area of diet and circumcision, these priests gave themselves new professional roles in the province of medicine, so that they acted as doctors, lawyers, and judges, while wearing obstensibly only the priest's hat.

I am somewhat uncertain as to the priests' role in the business community, but by driving the money lenders from the temple, Jesus' action indicates that the nest-feathering extended beyond the boundaries of the medical and legal professions. Christianity as we know it in the bible seemed to succumb to the sociological influence of Judaism, and in so doing to lose the mystery and wonder which is the essence of the religious impulse. The Nag Hammadi texts cannot be explained away by the sociological overview, which may explain in part why they "disappeared." As we have seen in our analysis of some excerpts from the texts, they do indeed restore the mystery dimension to Christianity, offering a goldmine of material which shall be scrutinized for decades to come. It is the undiscovered mystery dimension of Jesus which offers not only the salvation of the church members, but also the collective salvation of Christianity, for the sectarian squabbles over dogma only serve to alienate further those persons—whether men or women—seeking a bonafide religious experience. But for now, let us turn back the clock to examine the characteristics of matriarchal culture with specific reference to the deity of Old Europe, the Great Mother.

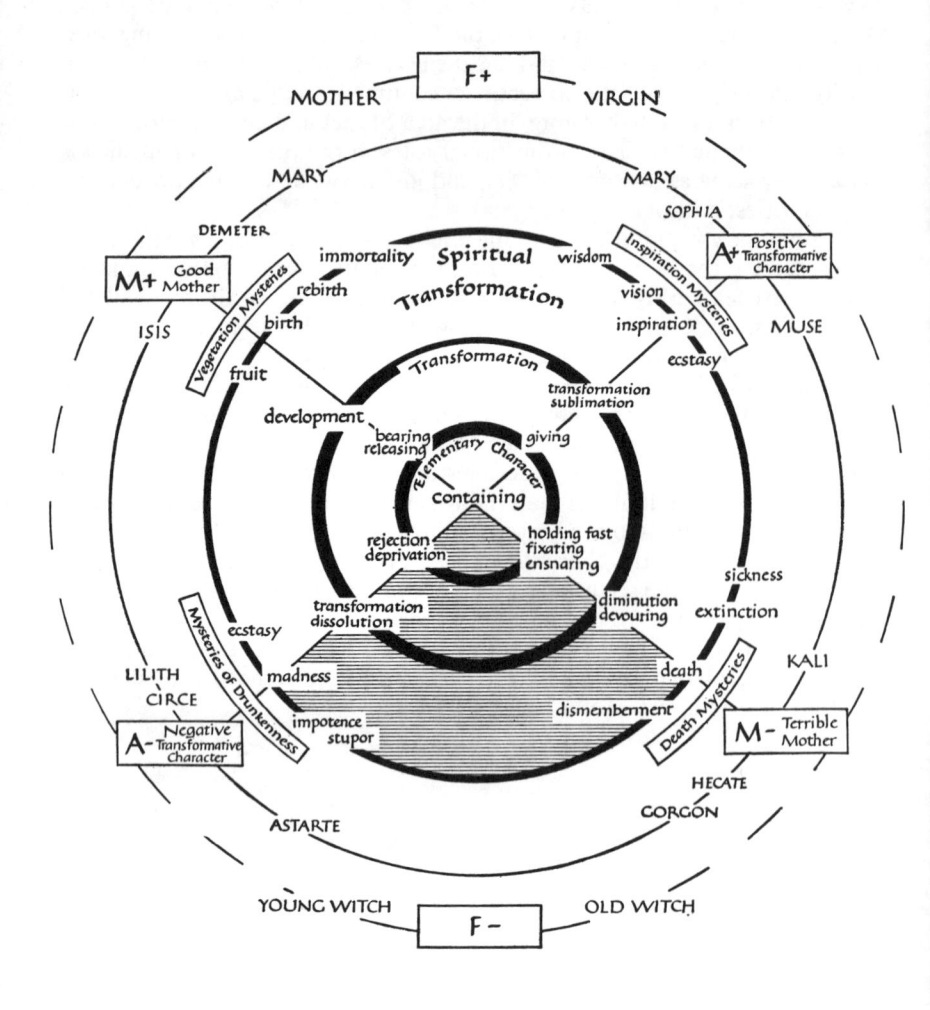

Figure 7

CHAPTER III
MATRIARCHY

THE GREAT MOTHER

The diagram above is from Erich Neumann's *The Great Mother* which is an all-encompassing study of the feminine from both mythological and psychological perspectives. Since my focus is on the origins of the put down of women in the Judeo-Christian tradition, we can only concern ourselves with areas of Neumann's chart which are germane to our discussion; however, for the reader who wishes to investigate other aspects of The Great Mother, the diagram shall be a helpful jumping-off point for further study. It should be remarked as well that *The Great Mother* contains 185 full-page plates illustrating the archetype of the Great Mother as she is depicted in artistic creations from Paleolithic sculpture down to contemporary paintings.

In sharp contrast to the psychic sickness of patriarchy stands the Eleusinian mysteries (V.Century B.C.). Here we begin with humankind's *harmony* with nature, which—because of patriarchy's antagonism to the Mother Goddess—became in the Judeo-Christian tradition antipathy to nature. Because I believe that one's attitude towards nature is a projection of one's attitude towards his or her own body, I am devoting an entire subsequent chapter to this topic in order that we all may see the reasons for our sexual attitudes in a clearer light.

According to Catholicism, God is not immanent in nature,or at least that is the intellectual import of the following newspaper excerpt: "In Rome, the Rev. Gino Conetti, a Vatican theologian who warned against astrology and horoscopes last month on the ground that destiny is linked to God rather *than nature*, has issued a warning against magic and magicians." In essence, God versus nature, or Yahwe versus The Great Mother.

Neumann's diagram encompasses in circular form what is known as the Great Round, the cycle from birth to death, shown at opposite poles M+ and M- for positive and negative Mother. At the same time, the diagram is round and symbolically womb-like, "bearing" and "releasing" at the positive pole, and "holding fast, fixating, ensnaring" at the negative pole. Any religion of the Great Mother stands in superior relation to any creation of patriarchy, it seems to me, because by encompassing the pairs of opposites, birth and death, matriarchy enables the worshipper to integrate psychically the many pairs of opposites confounding the human condition both *within and without*,e.g. good and evil, male and female. Therefore, from the psychological perspective, that religion is a form of therapy, stimulating health and well-being. Indeed, the psychiatrists of today have become the high priests of a new religion, usurping the role vacated by default by the priests of the Judeo-Christian religion.

As we gaze at the Great Round encompassed by the archetype of the Great Mother, we note that nowhere does the so-called Devil appear, and the concomitant concept of evil, from whence cometh guilt. Of course, there are negative elements in the archetype of the Great Mother, but these are trials for the initiate, preparing him or her all the more for dealing with life, and not psychic problems created by the very nature of the religion itself, such as guilt, in patriarchy's case.

Therefore, the greatest challenge to the psychic well-being of the initiates to the religions of the Mother Goddess involves the innate fear of annihilation of consciousness with death, at pole M− of the diagram. These are the Mysteries of Death, which have at the opposite pole what Neumann calls "Vegetation Mysteries," which we may paraphrase as "Mysteries of Fruition," that is, of seed and growth. Again, just as early humankind had not yet learned the secret of sexual intercourse, the secret of plant cultivation was also unknown. Interestingly enough, the Judeo-Christian tradition sought to leap over the philosophical challenge of life and death by *transcendence* to heavenly realms, with rewards and judgments meted out after life. This dissociation from life's vitality bred the monastic psychic condition, in which life is not to be experienced to the fullest, but eschewed, and woman, the bearer of life and the carrier of the sexual impulse to generation, is to be avoided like the plague, lest damnation follow *knowledge* of her. Now given today that the monastic life is neither available nor desirable for most of us, the concomitant condition is anxiety and guilt from experiencing life's forbidden fruits.

THE ELEUSINIAN MYSTERIES

These rites involve Demeter, the goddess at the "M + Good Mother" pole. Sadly, although we have statuary and sanctuaries attesting to the worship of the Great Mother at Catal Huyck (7,000 B.C.), there is no literature relevent to her worship earlier than Astarte (13th century B.C.) and the Eleusinian mysteries (5th century B.C.). But the literature relating to the Eleusinian mysteries is vastly compelling, for the mysteries of life and death, poles of the one great riddle of meaning are revealed to the initiate, thereby facilitating one's ability to *function* in life as a productive member of the community, rather than precipitating flight from life to cloister away from imagined perils to the soul. The vegetation mysteries, as Neumann tells us, "are all closely connected with the fertility rituals of the Great Mother, which have to do with growth and the increase of life."[1]

It was perhaps antipathy to these same fertility rituals which further prompted patriarchy's dis-ease with nature, body, and sex, beyond that already instilled by its misreading of Eve's "fall" and the serpent on the World Tree.

"The Great Earth Mother who brings forth all life from herself is eminently the mother of all vegetation. The fertility rituals and myths of the whole world are based upon this archetypal context. The center of this vegetative symbolism is the tree. As fruit-bearing tree of life it is female: it bears, transforms, nourishes; its leaves, branches, twigs are 'contained' in it and dependent on it. The protective character is evident in the treetop that shelters nests and birds. But in addition the tree trunk is a container 'in' which dwells its spirit, as the soul dwells in the body. The female nature of the tree is demonstrated in the fact that treetops and trunk can give birth, as in the case of Adonis and many others."[2]

Adonis, we recall is one of the fertility gods of the Great Mother, her son/spouse/consort. Born of the Great Mother, he in effect, *dies* of her. Many a Ph. D. thesis has been written on Christ's agony on the wooden tree of death, the cross, and the relation of his death to the earlier dying and resurrected gods. Furthermore, we have long forgotten the reason for the Christmas tree, and its symbolic association with the sun god's victory over darkness, the moon, and the mother goddess. For Christ is born at the winter solstice, the darkest time of the year when the sun's strength is weakest. The illuminated *ever*green tree, which does not lose its foliage even in winter, thereby—like Christ—symbolizes immortality. In Giotto and other religious painters, the heads of Christ and the saints are surrounded by aureoles of light, signifying the new birth of light and also the transfigured spiritual enlightenment.

But now let us proceed to an examination of the Eleusinian mysteries, which although no longer flourishing were still within memory at the time of the life of Jesus. Reconciling the mysteries of both life and death, the Eleusinian mysteries, according to the Homeric *Hymn to Demeter*, were:

... established by the goddess herself and those who took part in them could look forward to a far better lot in the afterworld. . . . But this was not men's only reason for giving thanks to the Eleusinian goddess. Her unique favors included the promise of agricultural fertility, the ennoblement of human life, the cultural gifts which overcame the bestial in man. The goddess, said Isocrates at the beginning of the fourth century B.C., gave us two things when she came to Eleusis: first the fruit of the field, to which we owe our transition from an animal to a human life; and second the rites, participation in which makes us look with joyful hope upon the end of life and upon existence as a whole . . .

Let us first consider the principal goddesses of the Eleusinian cult. They are, as everyone knows, Demeter and her daughter, Kore, 'the maiden,' or Persephone. Here we can disregard the other Eleusinian deities, except for Pluto, king of the underworld, who abducted Persephone and made her his wife. Searching for her vanished daughter, Demeter came to Eleusis; there she found her, there she made her peace with the gods and gave to men the holy mysteries and agriculture. This is the narrative of the Homeric Hymn. Despite her Greek name, Demeter is indubitably descended from a preHellenic culture. . . . [3]

Here we might add that Demeter is "indubitably descended" from the goddess of Catal Huyck, circa 7,000 B.C., for her function is to preside over both life and death. "She was worshipped as the giver of grain, but other fruits and blossoms were considered among her gifts and she was associated also with the growth of man, to whom after death she was a mother, receiving him in her womb, the womb of the earth."[4]

But the heritage of the goddess of the Eleusinian mysteries goes back even further in time. As Neumann tells us in discussing "The Primordial Goddess," chapter nine of *The Great Mother*, "With the Stone Age sculptures of the Great Mother as a goddess, the Archetypal Feminine suddenly bursts upon the world of men in overwhelming wholeness and perfection. Aside from the cave paintings, these figures of the Great Goddess are the earliest cult works and works of art known to us." And here Neumann adds in a footnote that these figures of the goddess are the earliest known works of art "whether we take them to be twenty thousand or only twelve thousand years old." [5] Neumann continues:

> Of the Stone Age Sculptures known to us, there are fifty-five female figures and only five male figures. The male figures, of youths, are atypical and poorly executed, hence it is certain that they had no significance for the cult. This fits in with the secondary character of the male godhead, who appeared only later in the history of religions and derived his divine rank from his mother, the Goddess. . . .
>
> With their emphasis on the impersonal and transpersonal, these figures of the Great Mother Goddess are primordial types of the feminine elementary character. In all of them the symbolism of the rounded vessel predominates. The belly and breasts, the latter often gigantic, are like the central regions of this feminine vessel, the 'sole reality'. . . .
>
> The unshapely figures of the Great Mother are representations of the pregnant goddess of fertility, who was looked upon throughout the world as the goddess of pregnancy and childbearing and who, as a cult object not only of women but also of men, represents the archetypal symbol of fertility and of the sheltering, protection, and nourishing elementary character. [6]

Here, therefore, is most of what we know of the Stone Age Great Mother. Fortunately, however, much more is known of the Great Mother through the Eleusinian mysteries, encompassing the pairs of opposites of death and fertility at two of the poles of Neumann's diagram. In these mysteries, as Walter Otto tells us,

> . . .we find a powerful intuition that seems extremely strange to modern thinking, while to early peoples it was as natural as of existence itself had spoken to them. And among many so-called primitive peoples, it still forms the basis of important usuages and myths. The substance of this intuition is that generation and fertility, and particularly the growth of grain, are indissolubly bound up with death. Without death, there would be no procreation. The inevitability of death is not a destiny decreed by some hostile power. In birth itself, in the very act of procreation, death is at work. It is the base of all new life. In the Bible, procreation, birth, and agriculture as well occur outside of paradise and appear only after death has been decreed for man. Certain primitive peoples of today still preserve a tradition—which is symbolically enacted at regular festivals—that a mythical woman had to die in order that the grain might spring from her dead limbs; and that only by initiation into her death can man become potent and life be renewed.

This then is the core of the myth of Persephone, to which the Eleusinian mysteries attach. Man receives the fertility which is indispensable to him from the hand of death. He must appeal to the Queen of the Dead. And this he can do; for here in Eleusis her divine mother mourned for her, here she returned to her mother, and here the goddess created agriculture.[7]

Now this is indeed an important insight, one which will serve to help us discriminate between the religions of matriarchy and patriarchy, for if death is part of natural process, then life may be embraced, enjoyed to the fullest, whereas in patriarchy (death having been decreed by the deity) there is an unnatural repugnancy towards life, nature, fertility, and woman herself *since she is the vehicle of procreation*.

Let us take our investigation of the differences between patriarchy and matriarchy a step further. The separation of the angry Yahweh from his creation, man, is highly significant in the Judeo-Christian tradition. Man may worship from afar, while the deity sits enthroned in heaven, perhaps hearing the supplicant's prayers; yet the worshipper never partakes of the divine. "But here in Eleusis" Otto tells us, "there was more. The privileged initiates stood in an essential *relation* to the event they were to witness. They had been brought closer to the goddess by the preceding ritual, the fasting, the drinking of the potion, and so on, a *bond had been forged between her and them*. They had been taken into the myth, as it were, and in this stupendous moment the myth became reality. . . . The cult is its present form the reenactment of an archetypal event, situated in the past but in essence eternal. And the moment when this myth is realized is the festival of the gods, the holy day, recurring at a fixed interval. On this day the whole memory of the great ancestral experience is again true and *present*. The gods are *at hand*, as they were at the beginning of time, not only as majestic figures demanding reverence, but as what they are: supreme realities of the *here and now*, primal phenomena of the movement of being, creating and suffering powers of *the living moment* which also encompasses death."[8]

Now in the foregoing quotation all the italics are mine, and if the reader will review them again he or she will see that they accent the temporal relation between the celebrant/worshipper and the goddess. In particular, the accent on the here and now contrasts sharply to patriarchy's Last Judgment after life, *post mortem*, the future "event" for which the good Jew, Christian or Mohammedan should live; yet living for that possible event, none can deny that the here and now of day-to-day life is neither embraced nor enjoyed, lest damnation be the result.

But what about the goddess' role in the matriarchal afterlife? In the Eleusinian mysteries it was said that the final revelation was of an ear of corn at the season when none could grow, signifying the return of the goddess from the underworld.

The stupendous moment has returned, the moment when the young goddess was ravished by darkness, when the divine mother sought her, mourning and lamenting her, until she learned that she was Queen of the Dead, and would remain so; but she rises up again and with her the grain, to which men owe their civilization. And the mystai are witnesses of this event, which in essence is not a play, but divine presence, realized myth. Persephone is present, for mankind, for the congregation, in the great moment that time has brought to pass. And she will be present again for every single man when the moment of death has come, that terrible festival of the death night, with which, the Eleusinian Mysteries have so often been compared.[9]

What about the Christian dependency upon salvation from a redeemer or savior? Was the Mother Goddess not such a savior for the celebrant in the Eleusinian mysteries? In a sense, yes, but the salvation she offered was that of nature itself, the resurrected grain, available to all humankind, and not merely to a Chosen Few who by good deeds and life-negation had earned a place in the afterlife. Unlike the remote Yahweh, the Great Mother is immanent in life and death, eternal for the celebrant.

The Eleusinian mystes lived the miracle of intimacy with the goddesses, he experienced their presence. He was received into the sphere of their acts and sufferings, into the immediate reality of their sublime being. His famous vision was no mere looking on. It was sublimation to a higher existence, a transformation of his being. What wonder then that the beholder of this vision should have been confident of a higher destiny in life, and in death, where Perephone was queen!

. . . In the cult, the human community meets the godhead. They were taken into its sphere, just like those primeval ancestors who were known to have enjoyed the most beautiful intimacy with the gods in the Golden Age when men still lived in Paradise. Now, with the beginning of the festival, with the coming of the gods themselves,that wonderful age was back again, the myth was present and fully real. . . . we shall find its meaning very great and its truth all the more profound in that *it does not make man dependent on the favor of any single power*, but links him through a higher presence with the great movements and moments of a divine cosmos.[10] [Italics mine]

THE CALENDAR

Of what significance was the calendar in relation to the rituals of Demeter and Kore? As we shall see, the Christian religion utilized the winter solstice and spring equinox in its two most important holy days, Christmas and Easter. And we shall see the significance of these times in the Eleusinian rites.

Nocturnal cults, and particularly those of a primordial mother, almost always bear a demonstrable relation to the moon. . . . the Athenians celebrated their great mysteries in the month of Boedromion (roughly our September). . . hence in the period of the autumn equinox, and the lesser mysteries in the month of Anthesterion (approximately our April) "when the sun is in the sign of Aries," hence in the period of the vernal equinox. "The Attic months followed the course of the moon. . . . [But] the Athenians celebrated their festivals according to the numbered calendar days. . . . The festival was celebrated on the day of the month bearing the determined number, even if the calendar was a little wrong. How else could Selene have complained of neglect?" From this complaint attributed to the moon (Selene) it can be seen that at one time at least the cult was related to the moon; and it is well known that difficulties arise in any attempt to make a lunar accord with a solar calendar. The Emperor Julian's precise dating presupposes Julius Caesar's solar reform of the calendar and perhaps even a distinct "reform" of the Eleusinian mysteries themselves in line with the imperial cult of sun worship, for beginning in the fourth century a priest of Mithras filled the office of hierophant at Eleusis. Thus the imperial Helios had vanquished the Earth Mother of the Greeks in the calendar as well as the Mysteries.[11]

And finally, what of the so-called fertility rites of the Mother Goddess which scandalized the early Church Fathers? We shall see that they were nothing more or less than a celebration of life itself.

And here let us recall the agrarian women's festival of the Haloa.
. . . celebrated in the month of Pyanepsion (in our October, or perhaps early November.) This festival was devoted to the mysteries of Demeter and Kore . . . "the officials [archons] must set up tables and serve all good things of land and sea. . . . Wine was served in abundance, and with it pastries in phallic and ctenic (animal) shapes. After the officials had set the tables, they withdrew and turned the room over to the women. . . . Men were not admitted. The women behaved with great freedom, manipulated phalluses and toy animals, made lewd speeches, or listened to the priestess who whispered about secret love. . . ."

The famous procession along the "sacred road," leading from Athens to Eleusis, on the nineteenth of Boedromion, must have been a popular festival....from time to time a halt was made and, according to Plutarch (*Alcibiades* 34,) "sacrifices and dances were held and other customary usages carried out."

On the twentieth of Boedromion, "the high festival began in the dark night; on this day the moon does not appear until several hours after sunset. We know from the *Frogs* of Aristophanes that the procession following the image of Iacchus [the divine child] became a *lampadephoria*, a torchlight dance. . . . In the *Ion*, Euripides speaks of the festive *lampas* of this sleepless night, in which the dance revolves around the Eleusinian Kallichoron, 'the well of the beautiful dance,' even the stars of heaven and the daughters of Nereus in the waves accompany the dance."[12]

Well, what a beautiful spectacle, and what a beautiful religion! We can picture the celebrant at the center of this beautiful procession, intoxicated with the majestic rhythms of the cosmos overhead, while underfoot stamping the earth in delight of the moment, drum and flute reverberating in head and heart, the Great Mother's presence everywhere, above and below. Life is celebrated! Life, though linked to death, life!

Now, although we have experienced rites and rituals of the Great Mother, let us now attempt to recreate the psychology of the Eleusinian mysteries. That is to say, what effects did the rites have upon the celebrants, and what individual feminine psychology can we ascertain?

The woman experiences herself first and foremost as the source of life. Fashioned in the likeness of the Great Goddess, she is bound up with all-generating life principle, which is creative nature and a culture-creating principle in one. The close connection between mother and daughter, who form the nucleus of the female group, is reflected in the preservation of the "primordial relationship" between them. In the eyes of this female group, the male is an alien, who comes from without and by violence takes the daughter from the mother. This is true even if he remains in the place of the female group but much more so if he carries the woman off to his own group.

Abduction, rape, marriage or death, and separation are the great motifs underlying the Eleusinian mysteries....The one essential motif in the Eleusinian mysteries and hence in all the matriarchal mysteries is the *heuresis* of the daughter by the mother, the 'finding again' of Kore by Demeter, the reunion of mother and daughter.[13]

The *heuresis* is the meaning of the torchlight parade of initiates, and Demeter is often depicted bearing a torch.

Psychologically, this "finding again" signifies the annulment of the male rape and incursion, the restoration after marriage of the matriarchal unity of mother and daughter. In other words, the nuclear situation of the matriarchal group, the primordial relation of daughter to mother, which has been endangered by the incursion of the male into the female world, is renewed and secured in the mystery. And here Kore's sojourn in Hades signifies not only rape by the male—for originally Kore-Persephone was herself the Queen of the Underworld —but fascination by the male earth aspect, that is to say, by sexuality.

In the myth this is reflected by two symbols, the pomegranate and narcissus. The redness of the pomegranate symbolizes the woman's womb, the abundance of seeds its fertility. Outwitted by Hades, persuaded to taste of the "sweet morsel," the pomegranate seeds, she consummates her marriage with him and belongs to him for at least part of the year. With regard to the other symbol, the seductive narcissus, "which beguiled the maiden," we read in the Homeric "Hymn to Demeter":

> It was a thing of awe whether for deathless gods or mortal men to see; from its root grew a hundred blooms and it smelled most sweetly, so that all wide heaven above and the whole earth and the sea's salt swell laughed for joy. And the girl was amazed and reached out with both hands to take the lovely toy; but the wide-pathed earth yawned. . . .

Through this embodiment of the seduction that fills the whole world, through desire to seize the phallus, she "succumbs" to Hades and is carried off by the male from "Mycone," the moon country of virginal dreams.

Kore's resurrection from the earth—the archetypal spring motif—signifies her finding by Demeter, for whom Kore had "died," and her reunion with her. But the true mystery, through which the primordial situation is restored on a new plane, is this: the daughter becomes identical with the mother; she becomes a mother and is so transformed into Demeter. Precisely because Demeter and Kore are archetypal poles of the Eternal Womanly, the mature woman and the virgin, the mystery of the Feminine is susceptible of endless renewal. Within the female group, the old are always Demeter, the Mother; the young are always Kore, the Maiden.

The second element of the mystery is the birth of the son. Here the woman experiences an authentic miracle that is essential to the orientation of the matriarchate: not only is the female, her image, born of woman, but the male as well. The miracle of the male's containment in the female is expressed at the primitive level by the self-evident subordination of the male to the female: even as lover and husband, he remains her son. But he is also the fecundating phallus, which on the most spiritual plane is experienced as the instrument of a transpersonal and suprapersonal male principle. Thus, at the lowest level of the matriarchate, the male offspring remains merely that which is necessary for fertility.

But at the mystery level, where the Kore who reappears is not only she who was raped and vanished but also a Kore transformed in every respect, her childbearing too is transfigured, and the son is a very special son, namely, the luminous son, "the divine child."[14]

And now we begin to see the debt which Christianity owes to the matriarchal Eleusinian mystery, for the birth of the divine child, known in Egypt as Horus, and in Greece as Dionysus, was celebrated in a temple dedicated to Kore, at the time of the winter solstice, to which Christmas corresponds.

The winter solstice, when the Great Mother gives birth to the sun, stands at the center of the matriarchal mysteries. At the winter solstice, the moon is full and occupies the highest point in its cycle, the sun is at its nadir, and the constellation of Virgo rises in the east. "From this position the first month in the oldest known Semitic-Babylonian calendar, which begins with the winter solstice, takes its name: *muhurile*, the confrontation of the gods. From this basic position it follows that in astral mythology the moon has an upper-world character, and the sun an under-world character. The moon signifies life; the sun signifies death."[15]

The birth of the solar-child seems to be a much later mythological accretion then the original matriarchal unity of mother and daughter. Growing in the womb of the Great Mother like a still, small point of light, the solar-child may be likened to the initial influence of patriarchy, growing greater each day. Indeed, the solar-child's birth also indicates the beginning of the trend towards the solar calendar.

In the earlier phase of the myth (pre-4,000 B.C.) the moon was the son of the goddess, whose twenty-eight phases represented his sacrificial body, rendered into twenty-eight pieces. At a later date, the dark of the moon was identified with the goddess' rape and abduction to the dark regions of Hades. Seen rising from the earth each day, and descending at night, it was thought that the early sun-god resided in the underworld.

The belief that "a mythical woman had to die, in order that the fruits of the field might spring from her dead limbs," was it seems to us, the foundation of the original matriarchal form of the "queen's ritual," in which woman had to sacrifice herself for the fertility of the world. From all we know of it this queen's ritual was a symbolic marriage of death, in which the royal pair of the year were killed together.

In Eleusis "The community expected its salvation from what took place in the subterranean hall." It is believed that this central event was a forced marriage, ritually enacted by the hierophant, the priestess of Demeter, and those who were to be initiated. This *hieros gamos* was also experienced as a death situation, for the Eleusinian mysteries were compared to a "gruesome celebration of the death night."[16]

From the point of view of a feminine psychology, the Eleusinian mysteries represent the various stages of psychic development of woman. Obviously there is a great discrepancy between the religion we have just discussed, which facilitates feminine growth, and the subsequent dogma of patriarchy designed to denigrate and stifle feminine growth.

In connection with the *heuresis*, finding again of Kore by Demeter, or rather their reunion, the mystery of the marriage of death expresses the transformative character of the feminine as manifested in the experience of growing from girlhood to womanhood. Rape, victimization, downfall as a girl, death, and sacrifice stand at the center of these events, whether they are experienced through the impersonal god, the paternal uroboros, or, as later, personalized and placed in relation to a male who is in every sense 'alien'.

But Kore is not merely overcome by the male; her adventure is in the profoundest sense a self-sacrifice, a being-given-to-womanhood, to the Great Goddess as the female self. Only when this has been perceived, or emotionally suffered and experienced in the mystery, has the *heuresis*, the reunion of the young Kore turned woman, with Demeter, the Great Mother, been fulfilled. Only then has the Feminine undergone a central transformation, not so much by becoming a woman and a mother, and thus guaranteeing earthly fertility and survival of life, as by achieving union on a higher plane with the spiritual aspect of the Feminine, the Sophia aspect of the Great Mother, and thus becoming a moon goddess.[17]

Examining matriarchy, we find the divinity immanent in nature and humankind; no separation, no duality, no distance between Creator and creation, celebrant and Goddess in a unique RELATION. Patriarchy, however, begins with separation (of worshipper and Deity), and by the 20th Century humankind is in isolation from the Deity or forsaken by Him (Existentialism). Indeed, the very best minds of our own century seem to be either outright atheists or, at least, agnostics. What reason can there possibly be for this? Patriarchy, and the masculine mind in general, seeks to KNOW. Knowledge involves seeking evidence: weighing, measuring, and classifying the evidence at hand. This works very well in the area of most scientific endeavours, but God and the universe are ultimately a Mystery that recede before science, eluding the human mind, escaping compartmentalizing. Thus a truly patriarchal religion can never be anything more than canons of conduct, laws, and ethical systems, since the divine defies rendering as a mathematical formula. God or Goddess may be intuited, and thereby surely known, but the scientific method does not provide a way of knowing the divine.

Women's Mysteries, as Esther Harding has so aptly named matriarchal religion, involve a relation to the divine through an EXPERIENCE of it, involving the unconscious mind also and the five senses, as well as the feeling and intuition functions of the psyche. Music, song, dance, poetry, *visual* art,and sexual ecstasy are all utilized to experience the RELATION between the Goddess, the Infinite Mystery of the Universe, Nature, and the celebrant—standing always at the center of the cosmos. The seasonal *round* is charged with mana in matriarchy, one's own life harmonized with that of Nature, death retaining a beauty poignant as the fall of an autumn leaf. Particularly with the advent of Deism in the 18th century, in which the world is viewed as a mechanical construct, patriarchy observes the seasonal process with the dispassionate eye of a clockmaker, uninvolved and uncaring. The difference between the desire to relate and the desire to know is also the primary difference between women and men.

Now that we have observed some of the rites and rituals of the Great Mother, and the psychological effects and implications for feminine consciousness, let us now observe specific differences between matriarchy and patriarchy with regards to time, music, dance, and poetry.

In terms of the evolution of consciousness, psychic stress commences appropriately enough with the biblical Fall, not an historic time at all but a mythic time, and therefore, true in terms of the psyche, a time when the ego begins to emerge from the matrix (womb) of the unconscious, when conscious and unconscious divide into good and evil, light and dark, and masculine and feminine. In this Eden we can imagine a society, a culture, indeed a world, in which the Feminine principle pervades through the focus on *experience* and on *relation*. The masculine stress on *knowing*,knowledge, as a way to dominate— and thereby dismiss—Nature, has not yet come to the fore. For by classifying the mana, or supernatural mystery of nature, the power of Mother Goddess herself could be rendered innocuous, or so it was thought. Night was the realm of the lunar goddess, but Neumann tells us, "For it is still as true as ever that the revelations of the moon-spirit are more easily received when night animates the unconscious and brings introversion, than in the bright light of day." The light of day was for commerce, tallying the profit and the loss in the market place of those towns and cities that were proliferating in the nuclear Near East. And appropriately enough, the fragments of the Semitic languages preserved from those days compute business transactions, tallies of those mundane endeavours that today would land in the garbage can or shredder. The masculine aptitude for business begins in those times of the demise of the Mother Goddess; yet today, as more and more women ride off to mercantile wars, we sense the presence of the animus spurring on their chargers. But with this difference. To merely work is not meaningful to woman. It is not her natural inclination.

To work, thereby establishing meaningful relations, and to give herself *experience* she cannot come by otherwise—as in the home—is meaningful to woman. Commerce is ruled by time, but patriarchal time is not matriarchal time, as we shall see.

TIME

Let us begin by examining concepts of time other than those we know today. A modern watch is a marvel. It can tell not only time to the second—or swifter, but also the day, month, and year (calendar), and the calculation of the calendar was no mean feat in matriarchal times. We know, for example, that Stonehenge (circa 2,000 B.C.) was an accurate computer of sun/moon positions, particularly their conjunctions, and of the key times of the year connected with planting and harvesting. This suggests a blend of patriarchal (scientific) consciousness for matriarchal purposes (fertility).

Modern woman, though she may wear a wristwatch that measures quantitative time, bears within her body a clock of qualitative time, defined individually by her monthly periodicity. This "clock" defines her psychological *experience* of each day by mood, determining the very essence of her emotional life. Further, the relation of her inner cycle to the outer moon, ruler of sexual relations in the form of the goddess, defines and conditions her own sexual relations. What modern woman has not tried to plan a weekend or occasion around the restrictions of her period—real or imagined. Indeed, in some women cramping and excessive bleeding can be positively debilitating. By contrast, modern man goes along *knowing* about woman's other time, but totally unable to relate to that "time." Blissfully shooting glances at the calculator/computer/machine on their wrists, monuments to patriarchal efficiency, men feel secure in the *knowledge* that their time is measured by the turning of the earth on its axis in its twenty-four hour solar time. The sun—as patriarchal science sees it—is unchanging, and, therefore, like men, undefined by mood (!), whereas the moon's periods (*like the woman's*) define inner and outer qualities of life. Waxing moon and waning moon are polar opposites, as are full moon and dark of the moon, and symbolically and psychologically have quite different qualitative effects.

Let us hear from Erich Neumann:

> We can most clearly represent to ourselves the archetypal character of the moon's periods by the changing force of their radiations. For they are centers of the waves through the world and permeate psycho-biological life. Moon-time conditions human living, too. New moon and full moon were the earliest sacred times; the dark of the moon, as the victory of the dark night dragon, was the first typical time of darkness and evil. . . .
>
> The periodicity of the moon, with its nocturnal background, is the symbol of a spirit that waxes and wanes, conforming to the dark processes of the unconscious. . . . At this stage of matriarchal consciousness, the ego's task is to wait and watch for the favorable or unfavorable time, to put itself in harmony with the changing moon, to bring about a consonance, a unison with the rhythm of its emanations. . . . Its response to the rhythm, the times and tides of waxing and wan-

ing, of crescendo and decrescendo, give it something of the quality of music. Therefore, music and dance, because of their accent on rhythm, play in important role in creating and activating matriarchal consciousness, and in establishing a consonance between the ego and feminity and its ruler, the moon spirit![18]

A woman's time, therefore, is "seasonal" within the monthly cycle, being both barren and fertile, a microcosm of the annual season of twelve months. Hence, each day is qualified by the bodily hormonal processes that influence psychic processes, thus, matriarchal time is qualitative not quantitative.

THE CALENDAR

When the Romans adopted the solar calendar of 365 days, five days fell outside of the traditional lunar year of twelve months of 30 days each. Being outside the calendar, they did not count with the church and state, and sins, revels and excesses committed on those days were forgiven and came to be the licentious time we now call carnival.

We know that swearing originated in prohibitions pertaining to taking Gods' name in vain, that is, invoking Him by naming Him. It can be imagined that the Goddess was also invoked, praised, prayed to, and named for luck in love and fertility. Again, such naming set up and reasserted the original *relation* between celebrant and Mother Goddess. Indeed, since she had borne all the earth's children, how could she subsequently deny them? Yahweh, however, had no relation with individuals, only with his Chosen People by covenant, so it was thought that his wrath could be invoked by naming him and thereby forcing his attention on the blasphemer.

The patriarchal solar calendar artificially separated humankind from nature and the year, since "months" were no longer defined by the monthly cycle of the moon. Given these changes in time and the calendar, it is of little wonder that the celebrant ceased to feel that he or she was the center of the universe, which one could not help feeling under matriarchy. The separation of humankind from nature was a corallary manifestation of the gradual separation of the ego from the unconscious. In primitive humankind, what is "outside" in the natural world is seen as an extension of consciousness; hence the psyche is projected into the world and inanimate objects are endowed with life, nature spirits have to be appeased, and magical rites are utilized to influence the natural world favorably towards the celebrant. If the world is fertile, man flourishes; if not, he perishes.

MUSIC

As an expression of the rhythmic relation of the celebrant to the rhythms of nature, music was usurped by patriarchy to praise the glory of the Judeo-Christian King of kings; yet even in this seemingly innocuous area patriarchal fear of the goddess and the unconscious manifests. Recounting the history of music for the PBS television network, Yehudi Menuhin documents certain musical forms that could not be sung by choirs, banned in effect, because they were thought to be diabolic. In matriarchy the celebrant is at the center of the universe, in *relation* to the goddess, whereas in patriarchy there is no relation of the individual to the deity other than that granted collectively by covenant. Dance in matriarchy contains phases like those associated with planting at the new moon, for example. There are also "birthing" dances to place the fetus in harmony with celestial patterns. Also known was orgiastic dancing to inspire sexual arousal and release, thereby promoting fruition of crops, without which the culture might die like an infertile seed.

Music, particularly that which utilized the singing voice, flute, and drum, was probably almost always used in conjunction with dance to facilitate the centering of the celebrant in relation to the cosmos and the Mother Goddess. Certainly no one could have come away from *experiencing* the rites of such a festival with the feeling that nature, Goddess, and spirit were separate or without *relation.* to the celebrant. Perhaps, then, we need not new myths today, but old rituals to properly realign ourselves to the mystery dimension.

In dance there was a direct manifestation of the Goddess, and an immediate *relation* or connection between the celebrant and the Goddess, for more than any other art form, dance reflects the rhythmic processes of nature, the Great Mother. As we have seen, the first concept of time was cyclic, nature a reflection of the Eternal Round in which everything born in nature died, but was reborn again, as the Moon goddess herself appeared anew from the dark of the moon. The year itself was a direct manifestation of the Great Mother, proceeding from birth in the spring to death in the fall, reborn anew in the spring of the next year. Dance in matriarchy, therefore, took its patterns directly from those observed in nature, and was at first imitative of the Eternal Round of cyclic change. Spiral patterns when danced effected the convergence of the cosmic cycles of the Great Mother with the spiral movements of the dancer, celestial motion being circular. The dancer, as the *pivot* of worship, thereby established once again the unique relation of the celebrant and the center of the cosmos,the World Axis/Tree around which the serpent wound; the Eternal then manifested in the immediate here and now of the dance,endowing the worshipper with sanctity, identification, and rapture.

The natural ecstasy of the dance would become anathema to patriarchy for a number of reason, as we shall see, not the least of which was that the "instrument" used in dance is the human body, and the body was severely denigrated in patriarchy. However, in matriarchal dance rituals the body was the vehicle of the *experience* of the Great Mother, the cosmic rhythms *above* mirrored below, in the dancer's spiralling movements, so that ultimately all separation was transcended as celebrant and deity became one. Such a concept is heresy in patriarchy since the creation can never approach his Creator.

Very probably dance began in our most primitive ancestors not as imitations of celestial movements but as mimicry of animals. Since early humans were hunters (before becoming planters) sympathetic magic was initiated in order to assure the hunt's success. Humans learned to dance from observing and imitating the animals. The first "gods" worshipped were totem ancestors, animals embodying the collective spirits of the dead animals, upon which the tribe depended for food, and from whose bodies were fashioned clothes, tools, and new weapons to slay more animals. Earliest dance, therefore, depicted a dance/drama, as it were, in which a dancer, clad in the skin of the animal sought, mimicked its movements, whilst other dancers in the garb of warriors relentlessly stalked the animal/dancer until a spear thrust brought down the prey. It may have been deemed necessary in those rites to actually kill the animal/dancer, or at least to shed his blood, in order to effect a successful end to the hunt. In the rituals of the hunt/dance, we may have the origins of human sacrifice.

As humans evolved to planting cultures dependent upon vegetation, the life-principle was no longer the totem-animal god, but the god who embodied the life of the grain; thus he became personified as a man, the son/consort of the Great Mother, whose sacrifice as the dying corn and grain ensured the culture's survival. At the same time, dance patterns evolved from the erratic movements of symbolic prey bent on eluding pursuers, to spiral movements depicting the god's cyclical descent and resurrection, and the even grander circle above of the spiralling cosmos, wherein the Great Mother reigned supreme. It is at this time in history, we may assume, that dancing becomes origastic and linked to fertility rites. Since the times of sowing and harvesting were crucial to the life of the culture, generally associated with the spring and fall equinoxes, dances were joined to promulgate growth. After the seeds had been tamped down, the dancers entered the rows and commenced a rhythmic stamping of the feet, accompanied by songs entreating the seed to rise from the soil, as the corn spirit had risen from his earthen grave. Couples copulated in the fields in order to confer fertility by sympathetic magic. Possibly human seed (sperm) was ejaculated upon the soil above the buried seed to simulate not only rain but also the life-giving dew thought to fall from the Moon Goddess at night.

Later in the year, possibly at the summer solstice, when the plants had emerged from the soil, new dances were initiated to instill greater growth, the dancers leaping ever higher around the shoots—the higher the dance, the higher the plant might grow. At the autumn equinox, when the plants were but barren stalks, the dancers again entered the rows, but this time they trod upon the dead plants, thrusting them down into the earth again, thereby burying the seeds from whence would reappear the young shoots in spring.

Besides fertility dance also has an opposite or funerary function. Both functions, however, aim to release life. The fertility function of dance we have just recounted. The funerary function endeavors to effect the release of the deceased, whether vegetation god embodied in corn or grain, or merely the human counterpart, the soul wandering the labyrinth of the underworld, where demons of darkness seek to hold him back from his eventual resurrection.* The Mystery of Birth and Creation has as its antithesis the Mystery of Death, but rather than signifying the end of life, as in patriarchy, death is seen in matriarchy as an adjunct of life, the dark half of the moon's face, which comprises a totality (with the light).

In matriarchy, the celebrant identifies with the sacrifice to the extent that it is not a divine *other* being (as in Christianity) but the divine immanent in the celebrant who is willingly sacrificed. Life, feeding on life, breeds death, which in turn breeds new life in the Eternal Round. Corpses were well provided with objects dear to them in life, and their bodies were painted with magic symbols

---

*In *Tarot Revelations* I wrote about the function of the twenty-two cards of the Major Arcana as a Western Book of the Dead, comparable to the Gnostic archons which seek to hold back the soul during its ascent to light.

and talismans designed to appease demons of the underworld and to vouchesafe the passage of the soul. The fear of death was abated by a noisy accompaniment from the dancers and musicians. In the absence of instruments, beating on the bark of trees (the origin of "drumming") invoked the nature spirits within, scaring off the demons of darkness. Whistling whilst passing a graveyard is a modern parallel.

Dancing in funerary rituals of the Great Mother took the form of winding circles about the body or bier. Within was a protected area or *temenos*, similar to that which the human child experiences within the encircling arms of its mother. Usually torches were carried, such as Demeter used in her descent to the underworld in quest of Persphone. Outside the circle was darkness and the unknown forces that sought to claim the corpse for their own, probably to feed upon it, since from earliest times humankind has buried its dead to prevent animals from feeding on them. As the circle of dancers moved ever more rapidly about the tomb of the deceased, tightening the circle, a funnel or cone of energy was created from which it was thought that the departed soul would draw new vitality and life; thus the purpose of the dance was to aid the dead in gaining new life. Since according to patriarchy the resurrection of the dead could only be effected by Yahweh at the Second Coming of Christ, the whole religious purpose of the dance was cast in an heretical light and seen as a demonstration of the Devil's work. Not only was funerary dancing suspect, but also fertility dances, since the body was damned out of hand as the Devil's playground.

But what if people still danced in spite of all these prohibitions? Under matriarchy dance had been a form of possession by the divine Great Mother, a way in which her power could manifest in the body of the celebrant. Under patriarchy, the dancer was seen to be possessed by diabolic powers; hence all dances—like all women!—were manifestations of an evil presence. Too, whether or not patriarchy identified it as such, spinning in circles recalled the cyclical nature of the religion of the Great Round, rebirth a *natural* corollary of death, not requiring Yahweh's intervention. Line dancing, signifying linear time and eschatology, the end of time with the coming of Christ at Judgement Day, would eventually be sanctioned by the Church, but only with the segregation of the sexes into opposite lines. The dynamism of the sexes joined in dance was recognized in the religion of the Mother Goddess, yet fearing this sexual energy, the Church replaced dance with prayer and meditation in cloisters isolated from the opposite sex. By Puritan times in America, merely dancing was evidence enough to send the miscreant to the gallows or stake.

One further observation in relation to dance and Christianity is worth our attention here. When the South began to import vast numbers of Africans captured by Arab slavetraders, after the passing of a generation the slave usually forgot the old religion and converted readily to Christianity. But in the Negro spirituals and in their dancing, relics of the old matriarchal religion remained. In a film called "Gospel" we see songs and gyrations whose origins are in the rituals of the Great Mother 4,000 years earlier, even though the words reflect a "gospel" vastly inappropriate to the euphoria of the singing dancers.

It should be noted in summary that dancing is peculiarly "matriarchal," in its predilection toward the unconscious. It may be apparent to the reader by now that dancing seems to short-circuit, so to speak, the rational processes of consciousness, enabling elements from the unconscious to "take over" consciousness, with possession or hysteria a possible result. It seems to me that persons with problems of sexual dysfunction due to psychic causes should begin not with surrogate lovers, but by beginning to dance, by themselves, and in whatever uninhibited manner they feel like expressing themselves. This would be a good process for initially opening the door to the unconscious

If we examine dance today, particularly in the courtship of the sexes, we find a revealing trend of sexual estrangement in the lack of physical contact while dancing, the *separation* of bodies indicating a lack of *relation*. Often one "partner" may be doing a dance that has no artistic connection to the movements of the other person. Further, frequently neither partner is looking at the other! And we are but 800 years removed from the tradition of courtly love.

> 'So, through the eyes love attains the heart:
> For the eyes are the scouts of the heart,
> And the eyes go reconnoitering
> For what it would please the heart to possess.'[19]

REASONS FOR SHIFT FROM MATRIARCHY TO PATRIARCHY

As we know, matriarchy, the worship of the Mother Goddess, was supplanted eventually by patriarchy. What were the reasons for the shift to patriarchy, which represents not only a change of outer religious orientation but also an *inner* change of consciousness?

On an individual and very personal level, duality commences with the separation of the child from the mother, who in the original unity is seen as an extension of the child. And synchronous with biological division, there is a psychic splitting of the ego from the matrix of the unconscious. Consciousness, the ability to reflect on one's self and one's relation to the outer world, rises like an island newborn from the floor of the unconscious. Collectively, therefore, humankind may have been experiencing an emergence of spirit, which rooted in nature and the body, was not yet spiritually imbalanced. As we have seen, however, simultaneous with the separation of consciousness from the unconscious, duality also emerges, the *real* serpent in the garden. The psychic at-one-ment with nature, which the matriarchal ego had experienced at first hand, now becomes fallen and lost.

> So he drove out the man, and he placed at the east of the garden of Eden Cherubims, and a flaming sword which turned every way, to keep the way of the tree of life.[20]

And nature becomes a waste land.

> ...cursed is the ground for thy sake; in sorrow shalt thou eat of it all the days of thy life; thorn also and thistles shall it bring forth to thee; and thou shalt eat the herb of the field....[21]

The emerging consciousness erects a dichotomy between itself and nature, setting the stage for the onset of one of the classic pairs of opposites, spirit versus matter, leading eventually to our 20th century waste land in which scientists, bringing to bear upon matter the most sophisticated instruments for weighing, measuring, and analyzing, determine that God is dead, there being no evidence of spirit in matter finite (physics) or matter infinite (astronomy). The necessity for there to be a link between spirit, nature, body and the unconscious, we shall investigate in subsequent chapters. The marriage, or restoration of unity to the pairs of opposites, shall then resolve all dichotomies, personal and collective.

Heeding the serpent's promise to acquire *knowledge*, therefore, humankind evolves, but the price paid is the pain of self-awareness.

And the Lord God said, Behold the man is become as one of us, to know good and evil.[22]

Therefore, since the emergence of ego consciousness from the unconscious was evolutive, we must acknowledge that the first reason for the shift from matriarchy to patriarchy may have been beneficial to humankind. As to the other reasons, which deal with external matters *outside* the psyche, it is possible to see them as resulting from the inner change in the collective psyche of humankind.

At first "strangers" begin to appear at the borders of matriarchy: warlike Indo-Aryan invaders. By 4,000 B.C., the numbers of invaders increase so dramatically that the civilizations of matriarchy fall to them. Nomadic, hunting for their food, they ride horses, then the ultimate weapon because of the greater mobility acquired.

"The Aryans' gods were gods of warfare and the hunt predating semitic Yahweh by hundreds and perhaps thousands of years. Like all conquerors they regarded their dieties as superior to those of the conquered peoples, for had not their god's power been greater, they could not have conquered, or so they reasoned. Yet for all their invincibility, their 'level of civilization was considerably below that of the contemporary high neolithic and hieratic city states of Mesopotamia.'"[23]

Because of the biological relation of child and mother, it is inconceivable that there could have been any kind of patriarchal worship in the original religions of our ancestors (50,000 - 10,000 B.C.). At the same time, since all mana (supernatural power) resided with the female, it is most likely that the social structure was dominated by the female sex. *Social* matriarchy involved descent and inheritance of property through the mother's line. All children borne by a mother were "legitimate" because they carried her familial name; hence, women had a sexual freedom to seek impregnation outside the marriage, if, indeed, marriage as we know it existed at all. This freedom must have made the men of that era extremely uneasy, and perhaps accounts for the rigid bounds men were to place women under with the advent of patriarchy.

Since the rituals of the Mother Goddess were mysteries which served to place the celebrant in proper *relation* to the mana of the Goddess for purposes of fertility (both in humans and in nature), it is my theory that loss of *religious* and *social* autonomy came about as a direct loss of sexual power. The female of all species gave birth; the male did not, so in this regard he had no power and could not rival the female. Again, the object of veneration and association with the Mother Goddess was the moon. Now according to mythology, the moon goddess instilled fertility by penetrating the womb with her dewy rays, the male function being merely to rupture the hymen. *The loss of feminine mana, therefore, would have occurred when it became common knowledge that the male organ was the source of fertility and not the moon.* In pre-literate cultures this information would have been passed on much in the same way it is today, through *graffiti* drawn on walls wherever humans paused to fulfill bodily functions.

By the time cultures with an established writing rise to the fore in the late neolithic, we begin to find the Goddess' power waning like the moon's. Of course, this new *knowledge* is akin to the emerging consciousness that came with the separation of the ego from unconsciousness, and it is the apple waiting to be plucked from the Tree of Knowledge. But the discovery of the secret of sexual intercourse has devastating ramifications for matriarchy. First of all, the moon loses mana, and its place in the sky and in the order of human worship is taken by solar power.

"In the days of moon worship, religion was concerned with the unseen powers of the spirit world, and even when the state religion was transferred to the sun, a god of war, of personal aggrandizement, and of the things of this world, the spiritual qualities remained with the moon deities. For the worship of the moon is the worship of the creative and fecund powers of nature and of the wisdom that lies inherent in instinct and in the at- one-ness with natural law. But the worship of the sun is the worship of that which overcomes nature, which orders her chaotic fullness and harnesses her powers to the fulfilling of man's ends. The masculine principle, or Logos, thus came to be revered in the person of the Sun God, and the godlike qualities inherent in man, his capacity to achieve and to order, to formulate, discriminate, and generalize, were venerated in a sun hero, who undertook his twelve labors and slew the dragons of ignorance and sloth, thus acquiring consciousness, a spiritual value of a different order."[24]

Concurrent with the shift from lunar to solar mana, we may assume that bartering *power* shifted from silver to gold coin, and that the standard for wealth and jewelry was set by the preciousness of gold. The silver rays of the moon which had been all powerful, now were secondary to the gold King-god in the sky.

Accompanying the moon's dethroning in the sky was an unseating of the female mother in the family, so that now inheritance, property, and wealth, would pass along patrilinear lines, until by the end of the first millenium after Christ, women would be mere baggage bought and sold, arranged for, until the novel idea of marriage emerged with the collective male anima during the era of courtly love. And so power passed from the moon, silver, and Mother Right to sun, gold, and kingship, resulting in total denigration of the female principle.

Finally, one last reason for the shift from matriarchy to patriarchy involves a synchronous shift within the human mind from right-brain to left-brain functioning. In his fascinating work, *The Bicameral Mind*, Julian Jaynes theorizes that up until about the First Millenium B.C. humankind functioned more in right-brain areas than in left. The right-brain governs creativity, music, poetry, dance, intuition, in short, endeavors that utilize a harmony with the unconscious, whereas left-brain functioning involves the more objective, logical, sequential kinds of thinking that we associate with the intellect—and with modern *thought*. Now the collective swing of mankind from right to left-brain predominance that Jaynes documents occurs *at the same time* that Robert Graves (in his epic work *The White Goddess*) notes a change in the language, away from "true poetry" and towards Apollonian objectivity and Socratic logic. I see the swing from right to left brain dominance as a psychic cause of the swing from matriarchy to patriarchy. Again, historians are wont to view the causes as coming from without, but my theory here is that collective psychic changes *cause* the collective historic events, which then becomes the manifest evidence. It is the classic question of the chicken and the egg, and which came first.

At all events, we do have a very nice series of parallel situations, whatever the origin of the causes, for in Jaynes' scheme the trend is away from mythic, poetic thinking (nature numinously endowed with mana). At the same time Robert Graves is describing similar tendencies in language. In Graves' case, he attributes the causes not to a change from matriarchal to patriarchal thinking, but to the influence of the patriarchal invaders.

My thesis is that the language of poetic myth anciently current in the Mediterrean and in Northern Europe was a magical language bound up with popular religious ceremonies in honor of the Moon-goddess, or Muse, some of them dating from the Old Stone Age,and that this remains the language of true poetry. . . .The language was tampered with in late Minoan times [1500 B.C.] when invaders from Central Asia began to substitute patrilinear for matrilinear institutions and remodel or falsify the myths to justify the social changes. Then came the early Greek philosophers who were strongly opposed to magical poetry as threatening their new religion of logic, and under their influence a rational poetic language (now called the Classical) was elaborated in honour of their patron Apollo and imposed on the world as the last word in spiritual illimination: a view that has prevailed practically ever since in European schools and universities, where myths are now studied only as quaint relics of the nursery age of mankind.

One of the most uncompromising rejections of early Greek mythology was made by Socrates. Myths frightened or offended him; he preferred to turn his back on them and discipline his mind to think scientifically: "to investigate the reason of the being of everything—of every thing as it is, not as it appears, and to reject all opinions of which no account can be given."[25]

This is an excellent thumbnail sketch of the trends that have led us to our so-called scientific stance of today, in which anything that cannot be weighed or measured is rejected out of hand, depriving us of the very spirit that animates life, creating a philosophical waste land.

CONCLUSION

For 20,000 years there is a pattern of worship of the Great Mother, who husbands the animals and bears mankind and plants alike from her body the earth. As if in vengeance for the patriarchal invasion, the rape of nature, and the social domination of the feminine principle, at the time of the culmination

of the shift of power from the Minoan goddess to the Mycenaen warrior (c.1200 B.C.), there is a cataclysmic eruption of the Mediterrean island of Santorini.
And with that explosion, the Great Mother goes underground, both literally and symbolically. When she next surfaces in the Middle Ages supernatural power now is deemed evil, devilish, and diabolical. Riding astride flying phalluses across the face of the moon, she goes to orgiastic rituals said to be contrived in darkness to bring down the solar Judeo-Christian god by means of her alliance with his dark antagonist, the angel Satan, who like Eve experienced a Fall, from his from divine grace. Thus goes the new party line. The Great Mother, Eve, in her incarnation as every woman, seeks through innate sexual evil, to sway men from the path of righteousness that leads to divine salvation, and by so doing to cause their damnation. This presents in summary the traditional Judeo-Christian, patriarchal view of women.

CHAPTER IV

WITCHES

The two dominant theories regarding witchcraft present the two disparate points of view which we have already discussed, those of patriarchy and matriarchy, Margaret Murray's books representing the latter, and Montague Summers' the former. Murray's book *The Witch Cult in Western Europe* appeared in 1921, followed in 1926 by Summers' *The History of Witchcraft and Demonology*. The very next year, Summers wrote an introduction to the 1928 edition of *The Malleus Maleficarum (The Hammer of Witches)*, originally published in 1486, a book directly responsible for the torture and murder of tens of thousands of women for a period of two and one half centuries. But according to Summers and the patriarchal point of view, "*The Malleus Maleficarum* is among the most important, wisest, and weightiest books of the world... One turns to it again and again with edification and interest: From the point of psychology, from the point of jurisprudence, from the point of history, it is supreme. It is hardly too much to say that later writers, great as they are, have done little more than draw from the seemingly inexhaustible wells of wisdom which the two Dominicans, Heinrich Kramer and James Sprenger, have given us in the *Malleus Maleficarum*."[1] A true patriarchist remains unchanged by time. Two thousand years of human evolution and scientific enlightenment have left Summers behind, alone with his Church and a firm conviction that the Devil is alive and well and still working his mischief.

Now since Murray's book had appeared five years before his own, and purported to explain the origin of the witch cult and its contemporary followers, Summers attacked Murray's explanation with all the zealousness of an inquisitor. He was, after all, a clergyman, and she only a Cambridge anthropologist—whatever that was—and merely a woman!

But what of Murray's theory? She says that originally she thought that witches were victims of their own personal delusions, crackpots who believed themselves to be in league with the Devil. But her studies showed that they were members of an ancient religion, and that the trial records and interrogations were highly prejudiced accounts made by the masculine members of the new patriarchal religion, which had supplanted the old religion, or so it was thought! Utilizing the methodology of the anthropologist, Murray set out comparisons between the Judeo-Christian Devil, and Pan of Greek mythology, and other horned gods of the Near East, particularly those painted on the walls of the Lascaux caves, circa 17-12,000 B.C. Highly influential in Murray's work was Sir James Frazer's 1890 compendium of folklore and myth,

The Golden Bough. The "golden" bough of the title was the mistletoe berry, which changes from white to yellow after being severed from the oak on which it thrives. A sacred grove of these oaks was found in Roman times at Nemi, Italy, and a man with a sword (known as the King of the Wood) once resided there as a priest in the service of Diana, the goddess of fertility and the moon.

After reading *The Golden Bough,* Murray made some inspired intuitions and concluded that the Devil of our tradition was a mystic hand-me-down from the earlier religions that Frazer described. Of course, others before her had noted the relation born out of the witches' Sabbath to earlier pagan fertility rituals. But her theory that witches were descendants of the moon goddess Diana, still practicing her ancient rites, became gospel in academic circles, indeed, so much so that the *Encyclopaedia Britannica* for years carried only her words of explanation as to the nature of witches.

The problem I have with this theory is that she placed her witch/priestesses in subservience to the Devil, as she had to do in order to make her theory fit the testimonies of the witch craze. In other words, the Sabbaths were not celebrations of the feminine fertility moon goddess Diana, but subservient rites to a male god. This is not in the spirit of matriarchy as we have examined it. Secondly, Murray did not have benefit of the most important archeological discovery of the last half of our century, the neolithic village of Catal Huyck, where the Great Mother clearly reigns alone. Murray's theory points to an earlier male diety from the archeological evidence available to her, but we now know that the horned figures of the Lascaux caves were not gods but shamams dressed in skins and antlers in order to effect sympathetic magic in the hunt.

Thirdly, there is absolutely no evidence whatsoever of an all-encompassing fertility cult of the Great Mother at the time when Christianity began to spread from the Near East to Europe, England, and Ireland. Patriarchal war gods dominated the Roman and Teutonic pantheon, so although being pagan, these religious cultures did not contain cults of women priestesses that could be associated in subsequent times with organized covens of witches. Indeed, as our historical tables show, we have to go back before 1200 B.C., to the reign of the Mother Goddess, in order to find priestesses performing rites in her service. Highly significant is the fact that none of the Renaissance witches confessed to being part of a cult of the Great Mother. Either they avowed their innocence of witchcraft, or they confessed to being in league with the Devil. Therefore, we can conclude that what was not in their own minds did not exist—that there was no cult of the Great Mother at that time.

As to Summers' theory that an entity of evil known as the Devil is still at work in the world trying to thwart human salvation, in order to consider it intellectually, we would have to throw out modern theories that state that men's "evil" is the product of society (the sociological theory), or their own doing, whether unconscious or conscious (the psychological theory). And along with these modern sciences we would have to reject also geology, if we include in our discussion an examination of the biblical creation of the earth in seven days, and ultimately discard all science in favor of the biblical interpretation of historical and, contemporary events. I refuse, however,to come down to Summers intellectual level. Has anyone else noticed that the religious Fundamentalists always point to the increased relaxation of morals in the world as evidence of the Devil's hand? Summers does not dissappoint us and uses that old chestnut again in his concluding words attesting to the validity and importance of *The Malleus Maleficarum* for us today when he says, "if we duly consider the world of confusion, of Bolshevism, of anarchy, and licentiousness all around today, it should be an easy task for us to picture the difficulties, the hideous dangers with which Henry Kramer and James Sprenger were called to combat and to cope; we must be prepared to discount certain plain faults, certain awkwardness, certain roughnesses and even severities; and then shall we be in a position dispassionately and calmly to pronounce opinion upon the value and the merit of this famous treatise."[2]

For the intellectual benefit of the biblical Fundamentalists, yes, the world is a lot more liberal than it used to be, but we believe it is that way not because the Devil made it that way, but because we made it that way, because we like it that way. We like other kinds of music then hymns; we liked jazz in the twenties and thirties, and now we like rock. We also like "suggestive" dancing, and movies, drinking, and some of us even take drugs. And, yes, we are trying to enjoy sex for recreational purposes rather than just procreational. Admittedly, some of us still feel a lot of guilt in this area, but after reading to the end of this book, a lot of our guilt hopefully may be laid to rest.

And now, for the spiritual benefit of the biblical Fundamentalists, let me say that none of the above "licentiousness" of today has anything whatsoever to do with our salvation. Some of us tried drinking to get to God, and others thought they could find him through drugs, and still others tried sex to find the Goddess, but whatever our separate paths, we reject utterly your contention that our salvation may be possible only through your squabbling churches, and only by following your Commandments and dogma. Precepts of conduct constitute a sociology, not a religion.

THE HISTORY OF WITCH HUNTS

The first millenium of the Christian era was free of witch hunts and persecutions of women. Official Church doctrine, manifest in the "canon Episcopi", took the stand that anyone believing in witches was either an infidel (Muslim) or a pagan, which classifications encompassed the other half of the "unsaved" world. Therefore, because of this curious "catch twenty-two" of Church doctrine, no Christian could accuse another Christian of witchcraft or launch a witch hunt.

Ironically it would be the Cathars, descendants of the Gnostics and practioners of sexual abstinence, who would trigger a witch craze that would have sex as its main focus and, indeed, obsession. Recalling Gnosticism, we remember that the Old Testament God had been created solely for the purpose of creating the world, but a bad case of chauvinism had led Ialdabaoth/Yaweh/Jehovah to forget his creator, and to attempt to usurp the role of the Ultimate Godhead, Sophia. Thus this "God" was equated with the Devil in the eyes of the Cathars. Gradually Catharism gained appeal, until by the end of the twelfth century there were no less than eleven bishops of the Cathar faith. Finally an exasperated Pope called for a crusade.

Colin Wilson has written on witchcraft in several noteworthy books: *Witches* (A & W , 1981) *The Mysteries* (Putnam, 1978) and *The Occult* (Random House, 1971). Having devoted so much research and thought to the subject, he is entitled to have more than one theory as to the cause of the witch craze phenomenon, which lasted roughly 400 years.

Let us hear from Colin Wilson in his chapter on witchcraft in *The Occult:*

> The infamous Inquisition was born in Toulouse in 1229, and its most determined agents were Dominicans, who traveled around and reported heresy wherever they found it... A cynic might take the view that cardinals dining on roast boar and good Italian wine felt threatened by the bleakly ascetic doctrine of the Cathars. At all events, the Cathars and Albigenses were bloodily stamped out; the few survivors withdrew to remote mountain villages, as did the Waldenses under similar persecution more than two centuries later. Domenic (later St. Domenic), founder of the Friar Preachers, who established his headquarters at Toulouse in 1215 vowed to dedicate himself to destroying Catharism... Two centuries later the Cathars no longer existed, but the Dominican inquisitors were fulminating against witches whom they called Waldenses, who met together at Sabbaths or 'valdesia'...
>
> The Dominicans kept asking the Church to give its official sanction to the crusade against witches, but the Church, remembering that the 'canon Episcopi' denied the existence of witches, held out for another century. Then, unfortunately, a superstitious paranoiac, John XXII, became pope. He was convinced that his enemies were plotting to kill him by magic; so it was he who finally gave way to the Dominican demand that 'sorcery' itself should become a crime, quite apart from the question of heresy. This was in 1326...

In 1275 a woman was tried at Toulouse on charges of heresy, intercourse with a demon, and giving birth to a monster. The woman, age 60, was burned. The first *secular* trial on charges of actual witchcraft took place in Paris in 1390. Wilson continues:

> Jehane de Brigue was accused of sorcery by a man she had cured when on the point of death! Jehane explained that she was not a witch, but that she had simply used charms, taught to her by another woman, which included 'In the name of the Father, the Son and the Holy Ghost'—from which it is clear that the fundamentals of 'charming' have not changed in six hundred years. Under threats of torture, confined in an icy and filthy dungeon over the winter months of 1390-91, Jehane finally 'confessed' to having a demon familiar named Haussibut.

For the next four hundred years, torture and execution of women accused of witchcraft continued. Ultimately the list of victims numbered in the millions. Colin Wilson continues:

> The witch craze was so horrible and so widespread that the human imagination cannot encompass it. We find it hard enough

to envision Hitler's murder of six million Jews over less than ten years, so it is quite impossible to imagine a campaign of torture and murder lasting for four centuries. It is true that witchcraft executions were on a smaller scale than the Nazi atrocities; but it must be remembered that each witch was tortured individually. Russell Hope Robbins seethes with moral indignation: 'The record of witchcraft is horrible and brutal, degradation stifled decency, the filthiest passions masqueraded under the cover of religion, and man's intellect was subverted to condone beastialities that even Swift's Yahoos would blush to commit. Never were so many so wrong, so long...' But after reading a dozen or so pages of his Encyclopedia of Witchcraft the student feels these words err on the side of mildness.

Colin Wilson goes on to discuss a number of possible causes for the witchcraft persecutions, one of which is political: "when the Church wanted to punish a Protestant populace, it sent Dominican inquisitors... But the psychological motivations are equally important. The beginning of the witchcraft craze corresponded with the Black Death and the Hundred Years' War. When people are oppressed and miserable, violence becomes a psychological necessity. And violence is always associated with sex, particularly in puritanical and repressive societies. Witches were made to confess to intercourse with demons, and minutely examined for the witch's mark (a spot on the body insensitive to pain)."

Colin Wilson then formulates his theories:

> But this is not to assert that all witchcraft from the thirteenth to the eighteenth centuries can be reduced to terms of imagination and sexual frustration. We know that a large percentage of people have occult power and always have had. These range from the ability to 'read character' to the ability to cause 'supernatural' happenings. Such powers are more common among simple country folk than people in towns. We also know that when the will and imagination are gripped with some strong idea, reality often seems to conform to it...

Colin Wilson continues: "After the publication of the *Malleus Maleficarum* in 1486, the new science of printing played its important part in the expansion of the witch craze." And further on he says, "What the inquisitors were doing was to create a body of myths and symbols that were supercharged with meaning and that consequently exercised an overwhelming gravitational pull on imaginative and bored women. The Devil literally finds work for idle hands and idle minds.

"I [Colin Wilson] would regard this as the most important element in the witch craze, more important than ecclesiastical politics, or even the persecution of 'natural mediums' and clairvoyants. And if this is so, then it must be recognized that the inquisitors and judges were not as blameworthy as we now believe. They knew little or nothing about the symptoms of sexual hysteria."

And with his discussion of Isobel Gowdie, the Auldearne witch who confessed in 1662, Wilson tells us, "They strip her and examine her minutely for devil's marks, and she finds it all deliciously voluptuous"[3] Well, perhaps, but we have no record of her thoughts. It seems rather more like a masculine projection that she found the experience voluptuous. Bored and idle women are the basis of Wilson's theory of sexual hysteria. To me it seems to be an extrapolation from the condition of women in the 20th century. From all we know of life then, women were anything but idle, times being so hard that one worked from sunrise to sunset. Further, Wilson's theory of female hysteria lays the groundwork for removing much of the blame from patriarchal society, and the individual judges and inquisitors in particular.

I would like to suggest yet another theory—male hysteria—to explain the majority of the cases in the witchcraft craze; yet this hysteria was unique largely to clerics because their own sexual nature, and their unconscious feminine element within the psyche, had been so repressed that an eruption of a distorted sexual nature could be predicted. Given the kind of negative programming to which the clergy had been subjected for 1400 years, specifically in regard to the evil and dangerous nature of women, it was inevitable that the projection of women as evil (witches) would arise from their individual unconscious, given the collective projection of evil which the Church had placed on women. Too, there was often sexual gratification for the inquisitors, for as we know, the most forbidden fruit is often the sweetest.

DUAL ASPECTS OF THE GODDESS

The antithesis of a witch is the Virgin Mary, who although she possessed a human body capable of sexual functioning, instead brought forth the Savior of Christianity without need of carnal process. Witches gathered in covens to each partake in orgiastic pleasure with the Devil, God's antagonist, whereas God's method of impregnating Mary remains a Mystery to this day.

The two poles of witch and virgin comprise the depths and heights of the masculine projection onto women, collectively, and the personal projection of the feminine component in the unconscious of men, *the anima*. In other words, women are either whores or mothers. The assumption of Mary into heaven, her elevation, indicates a spiritualizing trend, counterbalancing the Fall of Eve. Yet according to patriarchal logic, if all women can be equated with Eve as evil, then why not equate all women with the goodness of Mary?

On a deeper symbolic level, however, the two poles of the feminine principle suggest the light and dark, creative and destructive, heavenly and cthonic (underworld), aspects of the one goddess, the Great Mother. Indeed, the dual aspects, or the splitting of the goddess, give us a clue once again that we may be dealing with patriarchal thinking. However, if we examine the Babylonian myth of Inanna's descent to the underworld (circa 2,000 B.C.), we find there that Inanna, Queen of Heaven, has an underworld counterpart, Ereshkigal, Queen of the Great Below.

In the underworld, Inanna undergoes an actual death, her body hung on a peg three days turns into rotting green meat. As a result of her demise and absence from earth, the world experiences a Waste Land effect, necessitating the revival of the goddess. Enki, god of wisdom and the waters of life, is assigned the task and effects her resurrection, but not without leaving a scapegoat to take her place in the underworld. Sitting on the royal throne when she returns is her consort, Dumuzi (later called Tammuz), and she fixes him with the same deadly eye that Ereshkigal had cast on her.

Dumuzi, then, is the vegetation god that we have discussed earlier in the forms of Attis, Adonis, and Osiris, all, we may recall, slain by the boar, sacred animal of the Great Mother, implying that the goddess herself is the slayer of the vegetation god. In this myth, however, she needs no animal, releasing the demons to seize Dumuzi, thereby repeating the death-dealing role of her dark sister below. Although he is her beloved, only a sacrifice commensurate with her own insures the seasonal Great Round. But her murderous deed is not personally aggressive towards Dumuzi, it is her impersonal hand in nature that creates and nurtures, whithers and kills. Although the demons are agents of the goddess—like the boar—still he is her beloved consort.

You, beloved, man of my heart,
You I have brought about an evil fate....
Your right hand you have placed on my vulva,
Your left stroked my head,
You have touched your mouth to mine,
You have pressed my lips to your head,
That is why you have been decreed an evil fate...[4]

The goddess' duality (love/hate) are implicit in these lines; she gives birth, and destroys. As we progress through this chapter, we shall see how a profound ambivalence towards women pervades the conscious attitudes of men throughout history, an ambivalence conditioned by the archetypal feminine in the collective unconscious of men. Desire and death are pairs of opposites plaguing man, for although he may desire a woman, there is the disturbing half-realization that death may be the consequence.

You have pressed my lips to your head.
That is why you have been decreed an evil fate.

As goddess of night, the moon, and the unconscious, she is the White Goddess, as Robert Graves has so aptly named her. "The test of a poet's vision, one might say, is the accuracy of his portrayal of the White Goddess... The reason why the hairs stand on end, the eyes water, the throat is constricted, the skin crawls and a shiver runs down the spine when one writes or reads a true poem is that a true poem is necessarily an invocation of the White Goddess, or Muse, the Mother of All Living, the ancient power of fright and lust—the female spider or the queen-bee whose embrace is death."[5]

Thus it is intimacy with the female that the male fears, for her embrace may be fatal. In our last chapter, we shall examine in psychological depth differences between the sexes; what has kept them from achieving harmony in the past; and how this harmony, or sacred marriage, may be accomplished in the present. And there, in that investigation, we shall learn that man must learn the facility for intimacy, the relatedness that women seek from men and cannot find.

Perhaps the reason for male fear may be found in the ancient archetype of the love/death goddess, eternally present in the dark waters of the collective unconscious of modern men, and from these depths, the archetype still spins its black magic of contemporary fear. Modern man, therefore, must experience and relate to his archetypal feminine (the anima), and by so doing raise her from darkness into the light of consciousness, where the old Night Mare is deprived of her power to project her black magic into the man's relation, thereby poisoning it.

"The Night Mare", according to Robert Graves in *The White Goddess,* "is one of the cruellest aspects of the White Goddess. Her nests, when one comes across them in dreams, lodged in rock-clefts or the branches of enormous hollow yews, are built of carefully chosen twigs, lined with white horse-hair and the plumage of prophetic birds and littered with the jawbones and entrails of poets. The prophet Job said of her: 'She dwelleth and abideth upon the rock. Her young ones also suck up blood.'"[6]

The lowering of consciousness in the descent to the inspirational anima (the muse) in the unconscious, is one way of doing homage to the White Goddess. Commencing in the 11th century and continuing through the 13th century, we noted the collective emergence of the male anima in the traditions of chivalry and courtly love; yet in courtly love the female was denied only physically, for by this process of poetic inspiration and commensurate idealization of the woman, the flames of eroticism were fanned ever higher, so that a genuine sexual ecstasy was attained. The poems, therefore, expressed the exquisite longing for the anima, the idealized woman within. In courtly love the flesh and blood woman worshipped by the troubador received the projection of this longing, and since it was seldom consummated, disenchantment was not risked nor the love compromised. At the same time the psychic energy of the longing required a grail to contain it, and the poetic creation became that grail. Thus they served the White Goddess, or Great Mother, from within.

Ignoring her culminates in the patriarchal Waste Land, as we have seen. Repressing her has even more devastating effects, as we shall see. "Socrates" Graves tells us, "in turning his back on poetic myths, was really turning his back on the Moon-goddess who inspired them and who demanded that man should pay woman spiritual and sexual homage: what is called Platonic love, the philosopher's escape from the power of the Goddess into intellectual homosexuality, was really Socratic love... it was the male intellect trying to make itself spiritually self-sufficient. Her revenge on Socrates—if I may put it this way—for trying to know himself in the Apollonian style instead of leaving the task to a wife or mistress, was characteristic; she found him a shrew for a wife and... ended his life with a draught of the white flowered, mousey-smelling, hemlock, a plant sacred to herself as Hecate..."[7]

Hecate is the White Goddess in her witch aspect, and she appears this way to men whenever the sexual libido is repressed, thereby becoming quite nasty in the cauldron of the unconscious, and emerging from the depths as a woman covered in filth and slime and festooned with toads. It is my thesis that as the flames of eros were fanned by courtly love, the sexual energy of the Great Mother became more than men could handle, resulting in the flight from the goddess in the escape to the intellectual homosexuality of the monasteries. I call this a dis-ease, with the body, nature, and womankind.

But the titillated eros of the previous centuries of courtly love became the *tortured* eros of the subsequent centuries of the witch hunts. For no matter how rigidly the conscious mind seeks to shut her out, in dreams the anima will manifest, for the dream contents are compensatory to consciousness; that is, they present what is lacking in the conscious life. Therefore, we can predict the dreams of those monks who had sought to insure their places in Paradise by placing walls between themselves and the female sex. St. Jerome's hallucinations demonstrate the way in which the conscious mind may be possessed by unconscious components. Alone in the desert, he found himself in Rome, besieged by bevies of beautiful seductive girls.

We may assume that the way women appeared in dreams changed constantly from seductively enticing to hags, because although their frustrated biology would have presented erotic animas, the fear, repression, and ambivalence would have caused the animas to be transformed into figures of danger, ultimately lethal in intent to the dreamer.

Too, we must remember that the true function of dreams was not understood in the Middle Ages; indeed, only now in the 20th century are we beginning to fathom the mystery of dreams. Unfortunately, usually only those persons who have been exposed to psychoanalysis place any credence in the value of dream exploration in order to better understand the conscious mind and its dependency upon the unconscious for psychic equillibrium and health.

In the Middle Ages, dream figures were not recognized as aspects of the dreamer, rather they possessed supernatural attributions as real beings, almost always evil, that came from outside the psyche in order to do the bidding of the Devil. The more erotic the dreams, the more witches were thought to be afoot in the immediate neighborhood of the dreamer, so that on the morrow, causes had to be sought, witches identified, tried, and killed lest their nocturnal power utterly overwhelmed the dreamer. And what of a sickness, or nocturnal emission? The perpetrator must be found.

SUCCUBAE

One very important piece of evidence to support our theory that witches were projections of the male psyche is the succuba. Succubae were female demons that straddled men in their sleep, causing seminal discharge. We now refer to this phenomenon of nocturnal emissions innocuously enough as "wet dreams". But we must remember that the psyche, that is, the *psychological* nature of man was not "invented" until the late 19th century, and only gained mass acceptance in the second half of our century. Indeed, even today it has little or no credibility in the Fundamentalist religious communities, psychiatry seen as a hand-maiden of deviltry. Indeed, Freud's revelation that children possessed pre-puberty sexual desires has never been accepted or forgiven by the Fundamentalists.

However, we may ask, if carnal knowledge of demons was grounds for the condemnation, inquisition, and conflagration of women, why were men not condemned for the similar act of intercourse with a female demon?

Men visited at night by succubae were regarded as passive victims of the evil female demons. Why, then, no sympathy for the women who had been subjected to the agony of the Devil's ice-cold member? The answer exposes the transparency of the male hysteria. The projection of evil regarding feminine sexuality, in view of male inadequacy, made all the men victims of succuabae's unnatural lust, whereas the human women were regarded as having sought out the Devil for the purposes of unnatural sex. The projection of the put down said that one sex was always unnaturally lustful; thus women went to the fire for sex with demons, and men were commiserated with, given two aspirins, and sent home to recover their vital fluids. Obviously one hysteria feeds another, that is, it infected both sexes, but which came first?

The significant truth to bear in mind is that the religion of the Mother Goddess had no Devil, and sex had no sinful contamination; hence Christianity planted the first hysterical seeds, which were then fed by the repressions of the Middle Ages. The male hysteria focused relentlessly upon the sexual nature of witchcraft, and beneath this hysteria we see clearly *masculine inadequacy before the power of feminine sexuality*, the fertile and teeming womb of the Mother Goddess; and her incarnation in her every daughter on the planet. From patriarchy's point of view, Eve was the greatest witch and evil to come into the world. So given Eve's link to the Devil, it was no great matter to *project* evil onto womankind collectively, returning us once again to the origins of the put down of women.

Thus, men are the victims of female demons, just as Adam was seen as the victim of Eve's sexual transgression. We may suppose, therefore, to find the origins of the succubae in early Judeo-Christian literature. After the period of Babylonian captivity, the Hebrews returned bearing a rich mythology of names of various demons, Lilith being a kind of half-woman, half-serpent monster. Then in the Talmud she is said to have lived with Adam, begetting demons, after his expulsion from the Garden. Genesis, the first book of the Old Testament, contains two versions of the creation, the first includes Lilith, while the second is seen as the creation of a new race. Hebrew tradition notes a second marriage for Lilith with Satan (the progenitor of our Devil). Lilith then negotiates Adam's "Fall" through seduction while Satan works on Eve in his serpent form. As time goes by, the lore has Lilith reverting more and more to her sexually demonic, serpent form. What I see in the denigration of Lilith is the degeneration of the myth of the Great Mother. To the Hebrews in captivity, the Babylonian Great Harlot was none other than the fertility goddess, or Great Mother, with the male's negative projection attached.

THE HAMMER OF WITCHES

To substantiate my theory that the witch craze was a male hysteria involving sado-sexual persecutions, let us scrutinize the *Malleus Maleficarum*, in which most of the chapters deal explicitly with sex.

PART ONE: Question VI

Concerning Witches who copulate with Devils. Why is it that Women are chiefly addicted to Evil Superstitions?

As for the first question, why a greater number of witches is found in the fragile feminine sex than among men; it is indeed a fact that it were idle to contradict, since it is accredited by actual experience apart from the verbal testimony of credible witnesses. ...

Now the wickedness of women is spoken of in Ecclesiasticus XXV: There is no head above the head of a serpent: and there is no wrath above the wrath of a woman. I had rather dwell with a lion and dragon than to keep house with a wicked woman, he concludes: All wickedness is but little to the wickedness of a woman. ... Wherefore in many vituperations that we read against women, the word woman is used to mean the lust of the flesh. As it is said: I have found a woman more bitter than death, and a good woman subject to carnal lust. ... More bitter than death, that is, than the devil: *Apocalypse* VI 8, His name was Death. For though the devil tempted Eve to sin, yet Eve seduced Adam. And as the sin of Eve would not have brought death to our soul and body unless the sin had afterwards passed on to Adam, to which he was tempted by Eve, not by the devil, therefore she is more bitter than death. ...

To conclude. All witchcraft comes from carnal lust, which in women is insatiable. See *Proverbs* XXX: There are three things that are never satisfied, yea, a fourth thing which says not, It is enough, that is, the mouth of the womb. Wherefore for the sake of fulfilling their lusts they consort even with devils. More such reasons could be brought forward, but to the understanding it is sufficiently clear that it is no matter for wonder that there are more women than men found infected with the heresy of witchcraft. And in consequence of this, it is better called the heresy of witches than of wizards. ... And blessed be the Highest who has so far preserved the male sex from so great a crime: for since he was willing to be born and to suffer for us, therefore He has granted to men this privilege.

Now there are, as it is said in the Papal Bull, seven methods by which they infect with witchcraft the venereal act and the conception of the womb...

For... since the first corruption of sin by which man became the slave of the devil came to us through the act of generation, therefore greater power is allowed by God to the devil in this act than in all others. Also the power of witches is more apparent in serpents, as it is said, than in other animals, because through the means of a serpent the devil tempted woman.[8]

We have come full circle, therefore, to Eden, the serpent, and Eve, and learned from the "wisest and weightiest" book that "all witchcraft comes from carnal lust, which in women is insatiable". But with the new perspective which we acquired on Eden in chapter one, patriarchy's original denigration of the Mother Goddess, and her divine consort enshrined in the night sky, shines forth transparently. The enormity of this male hysteria is made manifest. More bitter than death, indeed! Behind the hysterical fear of women which fanned the flames that burned thousands of women lies the masculine fear of sex and death, as our continuing perusal of the Malleus Maelficarum demonstrates in chapters entitled "...the Way whereby Witches copulate with those Devils known as Incubi;" "How Witches Impede and Prevent the Power of Procreation;" "How, as it were, they Deprive Man of his Virile Member:"

As to the method in which witches copulate with Incubus devils.

... First, as to the devil and body which he assumes. ... It must be said that he assumes an aerial body, and that it is in some respects terrestrial in so far as it has an earthly property through condensation. ... Devils know how to ascertain the virtue in semen:

Therefore, to return to the question whether witches had their origin in these abominations. ... no one can affirm with certainty that they did not increase and multiply by means of these foul practices, although devils commit this deed for the sake not of pleasure but corruption. And this appears to be the order of the process. A Succubus devil draws the semem from a wicked man; and. ... passes that semen on to the devil deputed to a woman or witch; and this last, under some constellation that favours his purpose that the man or woman so born should be strong in the practice of witchcraft, becomes the Incubus to the witch. ...

But with regard to any bystanders, the witches themselves have often been seen lying on their backs in the fields or woods, naked up to the very navel, and it has been apparent from the disposition of those limbs and members which pertain to the venereal act and orgasm, as also from the agitation of their legs and thighs, that, all invisibly to the bystanders, they have been copulating with Incubus devils; yet sometimes, howbeit this is rare, at the end of the act a very black vapour, of about the stature of a man, rises up into the air from the witch. ...

It is certain also that the following has happened. Husbands have actually seen Incubus devils swiving their wives, although they have thought that they were not devils but men. And when they have taken up a weapon and tried to run them through, the devil has suddenly disappeared, making himself invisible.[9]

How Witches Impede and Prevent the Power of Procreation

Concerning the method by which they obstruct the procreant function in both men and animals. ...

But it must be noted that such obstruction is caused both intrinsically and extrinsically. Intrinsically they cause it in two ways. First, when they directly prevent the erection of the member which is accommodated to fructification. And this need not seem impossible, when it is considered that they are able to vitiate the natural use of any member. Secondly, when they prevent the flow of the vital essences to the members in which resides the motive force, closing up the seminal ducts so that is does not reach the generative vessels, or so that it cannot be ejaculated, or is fruitlessly spilled.

Extrinsically they cause it at times by means of images, or by the eating of herbs; sometimes by other external means, such as cocks' testicles. But it must not be thought that it is by the virtue of these things that a man is made impotent, but by the occult power of devils' illusions. Witches by this means procure such impotence, namely, that they cause a man to be unable to copulate, or a woman to conceive.

And the reason for this is that God allows them more power over this act, by which the first sin was disseminated, than over other human actions. Similarly they have more power over serpents, which are the most subject to the influence of incantations, than over other animals. Wherefore it has often been found by us and other Inquisitors that they have caused this obstruction by means of serpents or some such things.

For a certain wizard who had been arrested confessed that for many years he had by witchcraft brought sterility upon all the men and animals which inhabited a certain house. Moreover, Nider tells of a wizard named Stadlin who was taken in the diocese of Lausanne, and confessed that in a certain house where a man and his wife were living, he had by his witchcraft successively killed in the woman's womb seven children, so that for many years the woman always miscarried. And that, in the same way, he had caused that all the pregnant cattle and animals of the house were during those years unable to give birth to any live issue. And when he was questioned as to how he had done this, and what manner of charge should be preferred against him, he discovered his crime, saying: I put a serpent under the threshold of the outer door of the house; and if this is removed, fecundity will be restored to the inhabitants. And it was as he said; for though the serpent was not found, having been reduced to dust, the whole piece of ground was removed, and in the same year fecundity was restored to the wife and to all the animals.[10]

Here we have once more the denigration of the serpent, the pre-patriarcy consort of the Great Mother. As we noted in our Eden chapter, there is an insidious religious tendency which turns the gods or goddesses of the former faith into the evil antagonists of its own religion. But there is a further point to be made in this tale of the slandered serpent, for, as we recall, the serpent/consort, in union with the Great Mother, himself bore the powers of creation. Here, as in the reversal of good and evil in the night sky vision of the serpent wound about the pole, the serpent heritage of fertility is twisted, so that now his presence impedes fecundity. Further, we can recall the healing power of Asclepius' wand about which the two serpents entwined. This myth too has been slandered, for the serpent's presence under the house does not heal but harms.

How, as it were, they Deprive Man of his Virile Member

First, it must in no way be believed that such members are really torn right away from the body, but that they are hidden by the devil through some prestidigitatory art so that they can be neither seen nor felt. And this is proved by the authorities and by argument; although it has been treated of before, where Alexander of Hales says that a Prestige, properly understood, is an illusion of the devil, which is not caused by any material change, but exists only in the perceptions of him who is deluded, either in his interior or exterior senses.

And what, then, is to be thought of those witches who in this way sometimes collect male organs in great numbers, as many as twenty or thirty members together, and put them in a bird's nest, or shut them up in a box, where they move themselves like living members, and eat oats and corn, as has been seen by many and is a matter of common report? It is to be said that it is all done by devil's work and illusion, for the senses of those who see them are deluded in the way we have said. For a certain man tells that, when he had lost his member, he approached a known witch to ask her to restore it to him. She told the afflicted man to climb a certain tree, and that he might take which he liked out of a nest in which there were several members. And when he tried to take a big one, the witch said: You must not take that one; adding, because it belonged to a parish priest.[1]

But enough of these tales which slander the serpent's fertility and extoll the manhood of the clergy!

AN INTERVIEW WITH A MODERN WITCH

To the surprise of my readers, I am sure, I now offer an interview with a modern witch. Did I not say just now that witches were the psychic creations of crazed men? Indeed, and I believe that was the explanation in the majority of cases. But according to the interview I now offer, there are covens of witches still in existence. Acknowledging that it is a curiosity of patriarchal thinking to attempt to explain every phenomenon by one inflexible rule, rather than fall victim to that kind of thinking, I recognize that given twelve different instances of witchcraft we may have twelve different "true" explanations. Given that, I think we may still say with certainty that when the witch is stripped, intimately examined, and sado/sexual pleasure is derived from watching her torture, more probably than not she is an innocent woman victimized by hysterical men. And even if she is in reality a witch in the white magic tradition of Margaret Murray's thesis, she is still "innocent" of charges of worshipping the devil since he is a creation of patriarchy.

Further, we have established in this chapter the psychic causes within patriarchy that resulted in the sado-sexual characteristics of the the Holy (!) Inquisition which are so evident in our excerpts from the *Malleus Maleficarum*. Therefore, the presence of a number of witches, whether practicing black or white magic, cannot justify the Church's persecutions if sado-sexual gratification exists in the minds of the persecutors. The Inquisition cannot be whitewashed as a necessary evil to rid the world of dangerous witches, since the actual inheritors of the Mother Goddess tradition practiced a sympathetic magic in order to promote crop and livestock fertility. Because its practice involved no malice or harm to others, this "Craft" was diametrically opposed to the malevolent goings on sought by inquisitors and villagers as characteristic of witchcraft. So innocuous was the white magic of the Craft that their members were seldom suspected, as the following interview attests:

The second surprise about this interview is that the witch is a man! But let him set the record straight. The word witch comes from *wicca,* Old English for a practioner of *wiccan,* sorcery, or witchcraft, so a witch practices the Craft, as it is called, and can be either male or female.

AUTHOR: You've heard the Murray theory that the witches were hand-me-down priestesses of the Great Mother goddess of pre-Christian time. What do you think of it?

WITCH: Well, I'm a living example of one of them. But you have to realize that most of the persons caught and persecuted were not witches.

AUTHOR: Yes, that agrees with my theory. How does one go about becoming a witch or getting into a coven?

WITCH: If you meet someone who tells you they are in a coven, and you are offered the opportunity to join them, then they are not real witches, because the only way you can become a true witch is to be born one.

AUTHOR: How old were you, then, when the Craft was first explained to you?

WITCH: Well, from the time I can first remember, every Tuesday the family would go to grandmother's house—this was in Scotland. All my mother's sisters would congregate there with their children and husbands. We children just accepted it. When you are about the age of puberty, you are sponsered by someone of the opposite sex who teaches you the beliefs and introduces you into the coven. Ideally the coven consists of thirteen people, but there can be more or less, but the most important thing is that there is a balanced polarity of men and women, because the power of the Craft comes from the harmony of sexual forces.

AUTHOR: You agreed to the interview on the grounds that you would say nothing of Craft secrets, but can you tell us anything about sexual practices in the coven?

WITCH: I only met one group that actually performed the Grand Rite in the coven. There is no reason why witches should be any less exhibitionistic than other people, so there are whole groups that perform sex with one another. However, the principle behind it is that there are twelve men and women and the Goddess makes the thirteenth. In my coven, the idea was that you continued to worship the Goddess and the principle of fruition for which she stood when you went home.

AUTHOR: What about so-called modern covens of women only? A number of feminists have been calling themselves witches and attempting to perform magic.

WITCH: Attempt is about all they can do. They do not understand why polarities of all kinds are so important in the universe and here on earth. Until there is a harmony of polarities nothing can happen. That's why there are equal numbers of men and women in the coven.

AUTHOR: So it is a balancing in microcosm of the yin/yang energies in the universe?

WITCH: Yes, to use the Oriental analogy, yes, it is.

AUTHOR: What theory do you have to explain the motivations of the inquisitors?

WITCH: In Scotland, they were not called inquisitors but witch hunters. Witch hunters who came to the towns were judge and jury and received a fee from the Church for every witch they discovered. The property of condemned witches was forfeited to the Church, so by this means the Church increased its land holdings in every country. The lower classes were most frequently the victims because they had the least support.

AUTHOR: What happened if you had a truly religious person who no matter what they did to her would not confess to being a witch?

WITCH: A museum on the Isle of Man contains a device most convincing in drawing out a confession when all other methods had failed. Unlike the diabolical torture instruments, this was utterly harmless; yet utterly damning. In the mythology of witchcraft, it was said that one spot on the witch was insensitive to pain and would not draw blood. The witch-pricker, as it was called, was similar to a stage dagger, the blade receding into the hilt when the flesh was touched. Many's the innocent victim expressed surprise at this, and thought herself to have been a witch all along. Anyhow, even if she didn't confess at this point, they had all the evidence they needed to convict her.

Also, even a tiny mole was enough evidence for the witch-hunters. That was their business, you see. A mole in the arm-pit was regarded as the place where the witch's familiar fed on her, like a tit. The demon that helped her in her craft took the form of a familiar animal like a cat, toad, rat, raven, or owl. But that stuff is all mythology and has nothing to do with the real craft.

AUTHOR: What was the purpose of the rites of the real Craft?

WITCH: Sympathetic magic—to influence nature and life for the good.

AUTHOR: So the Craft is so-called White Magic?

WITCH: Yes, there are laws of nature that if you misuse the power or try to harm another it will come back on you.

AUTHOR: Can you expand on the idea of sympathetic magic?

WITCH: Yes. (Pause) You have to realize that in my country at least—Scotland—the practitioners of the Craft were either farmers or sheep raisers. So if your herds don't multiply or your corps fail, you may die of starvation, at least that was true before the welfare state. So the purpose of the Craft was to insure fertility. There's the story of the professor from Edinburgh University who came upon a coven in the highlands right in the middle of the Grand Rite. Astounded at such a primitive rite he asked them to explain the purpose of what they were doing. Finally he said to one man, "Do ye really believe that your wheat will grow taller, your sheep fatter, and yield more wool, by putting your wee thing into that beautiful lassie's hole?" The man thought a moment and replied, "Well, it cannot hurt, can it?"

AUTHOR: What about the dolls or "poppets" which were found with pins in them? Was that Black Magic at work?

WITCH: Finding one of those in the house led to more members of the Craft being killed than anything else, but it was all a complete misunderstanding of what they were doing.

AUTHOR: Even if someone died after their image had been stuck with the pin?

WITCH: Yes, because the purpose was to heal the sick person. They didn't get sick because of the doll. The doll, or more often a wax figure, with a thorn stuck in it, was serving the same purpose as an acupuncturist's needle. The thorn was a channel for the White Light to be directed to the ailing part of the body in order to cure the person. The mannikin was used as a focus for the visualization, particularly if the person to be healed was far away. Wherever the pain was in the body, the thorn was stuck in there and the White Light, the healing power of the Goddess, was called down by the group.

But if a man died of a heart attack, and the waxen image was found with a thorn in the heart, it was thought that the thorn in the doll had caused the death, and the entire coven was put to death.

AUTHOR: What was done, then, by the coven if one of them was caught?

WITCH: Usually some way was found by bribing a jailer at night to get drugs made from plants to her to deaden the pain or put her out of her misery.

AUTHOR: What are the origins of the Craft in Scotland?

WITCH: In the old days they performed their rites on heaths and were known as heathens. But the Christian mores have influenced even the witches of today, to the extent that they say that the sexual act is more properly performed in the privacy of one's own home. But in the old days there was no shame connected with it; hence, it was performed publicly.

SHADOW ELEMENTS IN THE WITCHCRAFT CRAZE

Thanks to psychiatry and the 20th century's new openness to the unconscious through the channel of dream analysis, humankind is now more aware of the motives lurking beneath the surface of human conduct. Through dreams we are now better able to recognize elements of the psyche that had been repressed because they did not match the sterling self-image of itself which the ego ordinarily posesses. Jung called this process the "realization of shadow". A trick of psychoanalysis which may enable a person to realize or acknowledge the qualities of his or her own shadow is to ask them to describe another person— usually of the same sex—actively disliked by the individual. For example, one may say, "I hate that woman because she's such a social climber, so materialistic, and so stuck-up!" The psychoanalyst may then guide one to realizing that one's vehement reaction can only be possible because there is an unconscious recognition that those same undesirable characteristics are present in oneself.

The shadow usually contains elements antithetical to the conscious ego adaptation; therefore, there can be valuable psychic components in the shadow which may accelerate individual growth if they can be integrated into consciousness. In our discussion here, however, I am concerned only with the negative role of the shadow in relation to the witchcraft craze.

Before an inquisitor is called in, charges of witchcraft have to be made, and that is where the shadow comes in. In his book, *Entertaining Satan,* John Demos, without mentioning Jung's concept of the shadow, noted that a negative identity was projected by entire communities in New England onto individual women who were perhaps ulgy and ill-tempered, and, therefore, vulnerable to the witch-projection. Also, if they had no man to stand up for them and take their part, neither husband, father, son, or brother, then "they were fitted to the role of 'witch' at least in part because they were so profoundly vulnerable".[2] Too, blaming witches for plagues and natural disasters enabled the community to identify the evil in their midst and to give them a sense of control over external circumstances, which were ordinarily controlled by the all-good "God", unless evil intervened.

Certainly there also would have been many elderly, single men in the New England villages, but the projection of evil onto women from Eve's original sin made women fair game for shadow projection. Demos documents that when the early colonists faced real external dangers, such as from Indian attacks, then the anxieties about witches were allayed. The answer, of course, lies in psychology. With real enemies, the shadow projection flies easily to them. "Damn Indians!" Without them, the psyche seeks a sticking-place for the projection of its own nastiness. As Joseph Campbell has so eloquently phrased it in *The Hero with A Thousand Faces*, "we refuse to admit within ourselves.... Rather, we tend to perfume, whitewash, and reinterpret; meanwhile imagining that all the flies in the ointment, all the hairs in the soup, are the faults of some unpleasant someone else."[13]

Thus, many of the women accused of witchcraft may themselves have been accused by women. These cases can be explained by the shadow projection. In the examples of women accused by women of having performed witchcraft upon them, sexual functioning is often impaired by the so-called witchcraft. This again returns us to the scene of original sin in the Garden of Eden, wherein Eve is made responsible for Adam's (all-men's) "Fall," wherein death comes into the world. Whereas the shadow is the explanation for women accusing other women of witchcraft, the anima, or unconscious feminine component in the psyche of man, is responsible for men accusing women of witchcraft. We shall have more to say about this Jungian archetype in our final chapter. But simply put, if one's own unconscious feminine component is contaminated to the extent that women are seen as evil and dangerous, the old masculine bugaboos of sex and death, then eruptions from the unconscious are eventually inevitable in the form of negative anima projections.

The main charge usually made against a witch was that she had cast a spell on an individual, which was the cause of the illness plaguing that person. Or, crops and land had been blighted by the witch's spell. In both cases, the witch becomes the convenient explanation for the disease, whether human or agricultural. Standing behind the disease, and the fear of death, is Eve, the original woman who by her temptation of Adam brought death into the world; therefore, women are dangerous and deadly, and the only safe retreat from them is in the confines of the monastery. Today, as we become increasingly aware of the role of the mind in individual health, we can begin to see that much of the illness attributed to evil spells was actually what I call disease, that is, lack of ease with the body, sex, and life in general. These matters are the subject of our next chapter.

Nastiness is a common characteristic of witches, and the nastiness of the shadow and the unevolved anima is characteristic of an unconscious psychic component that has been shut out of consciousness, but, nevertheless, desires recognition by—and a relation with—the conscious mind. Like the fairytale witches uninvited to christenings, who consequently work mischief on the children, these components of the unconscious psyche behave in unregenerate, socially unadaptable ways when not given their due. In other words, they turn nasty, and can usurp conscious autonomy.

On the world political scene, parallels are apparent to terrorist organizations. And of course, demonstrations outside the convention halls of both the Democratic and Republican parties bear out this theory. For the ruling body of delegates may be likened to the psyche's ego, which thinks itself the only governing body. Outside consciousness, or outside the convention hall, the demonstrators are determined to behave just as nastily and to go just as far in socially unadaptable behavior as the police barriers will permit.

Now if the Great Mother's religions had in the past provided outlets for the shadow, through magic, dance, and sexual rites, thereby promoting psychic stability by involving the whole psyche, both conscious and unconscious, then the outright antipathy of the Judeo-Christian tradition to shadow elements would inflame rather than defuse them, perpetuating their survival, since the shadow resided in both accuser, inquisitor, and victim.

Thus, the more restrictive, puritanical, and dehumanizing the religion, the greater the profusion of witches, since the possession of consciousness by the shadow element is nothing more or less than the psyche's reaction to a too narrow attitude on the part of the conscious ego. And this is verified by history, the 16th and 17th centuries witnessing the greatest number of both individual witches and collective "possessions".

In the 20th century, it seems to me, there was a collective possession by the shadow on a national scale, in the form of the National Socialist Party of Germany, or the Nazis. Hitler spoke directly to the shadow in each German psyche by reviving the ancient scapegoat (the Jew) and addressing himself to the psychially supercharged areas of "Fatherland" and "lost patrimony".

That super-macho society is of interest to us in that the utilization of women was particularly exploitive: breeders of new warriors!

Again, let us refer the historical picture to the question of individual harmony in the psyche. How are we to live to avoid the collective pitfalls of 17th century Salem, Massachusetts and 20th century Germany? Our first defense is realization of the shadow. As long as we believe evil can only exist in others, and not ourselves, then the voice of the polar opposite, the Dark One, will speak as God, invitingly and suggestively, of the need to rid the town, the country, the world, of those evil other persons, whose very lives insult our presence.

Our second defense against shadow possession, the control of consciousness by eruptions from the unconscious, is to "give" the devil his due", so to speak. As the dark, unconscious component seeks relation with consciousness, we can defuse its power by harmonizing opposed and antagonistic elements in an alchemical heirosgamos, or sacred marriage. (See "Eros", the final chapter). For this, we need perhaps a new religion. Modernized in the interest of increased acceptability, the Judeo-Christian tradition has become far too cerebral. As new sects come along demanding personal sacrifices of their followers, and utilizing rhythmic music, bogus miracles, and charismatic leaders, converts fall easily into line: witness Jonestown and various other cults. What humankind needs, more than new governments and new economics, is a new religion, nay, new mythology, that has built-in safety valves for the shadow archetype.

THE LEONARD LAKE CASE

Recently a most diabolical kind of crime has come to light in the San Francisco Bay area. I should like to discuss it here because there is a definite parallel to the kind of crimes committed against women by the inquisitors. The procedures follow precisely those of which we have just read in the *Malleus Maleficarum*. I do not mean to imply that these are imitative crimes, for I am certain that these sadists have never heard of the *Malleus Maleficarum* nor have they studied the lore of witchcraft.* But the parallels are as follows: First, the woman victim is restrained, either by ropes, handcuffs, or legirons, and placed in a confined area, a cell or chamber. Next she is stripped of her clothing; "for in order to preserve their power of silence they are in the habit of hiding some superstitious object in their clothes or in their hair, or even in the most secret parts of their bodies which must not be named."[14]

What hypocrisy! They are writing a manual of instruction for the rape of women, and they are too fastidious and moral to name the private parts!

Next the kidnapped victim and the witch are tortured. Sexual gratification for the inquisitors probably came vicariously from viewing and examining the "secret parts."

The goal of the torture is not only to provide sado-masochistic gratification for the torturer but also to make the will of the victim totally subservient to that of the inquisitor/torturer. "But it might be objected that the devil might, without the use of such charms, so harden the heart of a witch that she is unable to confess her crimes... no matter how great the torture to which they are exposed."[15]

The long-sought confession of the victim denotes the triumph of the inquisitor's will. The modern kidnapper breaks his victim's will in order to make of her a sex slave.

Finally, the end for the hapless victim, whether modern or medieval, is the same, death, for she is otherwise a witness to the indignities her body has borne.

And now, let us face the fact that the crimes were the same, whether committed by kidnapper or inquisitor. Today we recognize, because of the perspective of psychology, that a psychosexual pathology is involved in both instances, but the Grand Inquisitors were honored men, wrapped in a shroud of clerical immunity, and endowed with ultimate license to commit the most barbaric

---

* After I wrote this line, a subsequent newspaper article revealed that the killer was interested in the bible and witchcraft!

crimes against women. In a modern courtroom, they would be given not honor but the death penalty. There were no crimes of witchcraft, except in the hearts and minds of the inquisitors.

The Leonard Lake case involves parallels to the situations of the women victims of Inquisition. Near Wilseyville, in Calveras County, California, police have so far uncovered fragments of human bones—enough to fill fifty bags. No entire skeletons have been found. Most of the evidence of the crimes involved has been derived from videotapes which Lake made. On his property he had built a 14 x 16 foot concrete block building, in which only shelving and workbenches were visible to one entering through the only door. Behind the removable shelves, however, was a wall passage enabling one to crawl into an adjacent room. A door from this room led to yet another room where there was a bed, restraints, and a plastic bucket for the toilet needs of the victims. The rooms were both similar, a two-way mirror evabled one to view the scene in the adjacent room. Lake's accomplice probably filmed the action from the next room because video-tapes were found documenting the following scenes. The reader should realize that the situations of the victims of the witch persecutions contained the same scenario:

Lake brandishing a pistol and threatening to kill two women if they fail to satisfy his sexual needs.

Lake explaining on videotape that he built his secret sex cell so that the kidnapped victims could be indoctrinated into submitting to his desires.

A woman pleading with Lake to return her baby, then being forced at gunpoint to engage in sex acts.

Lake evidently obtained the video-tape equipment—and many of his victims—by answering "for sale" ads in San Francisco newspapers. He then forced one seller and his wife and 16-month-old son to leave with him in their car. Much of the property obtained in this manner was then sold again.

Lake also kept a diary in which he tells of his "Operation Miranda" plan to kidnap women,hold them in his secret rooms, and force them to do his bidding by completely breaking their will. "The perfect woman for me is one who is totally controlled, a woman who does exactly what she is told and nothing else."

One person who knew Lake recalls that he belonged to a bible study group and was especially interested in witchcraft. Maybe he did read the *Malleus Maleficarum* after all!

Let us have a final look at an example from Colin Wilson's *The Occult* which should convince even the most skeptical that for the most part innocent women were fulfilling male sado-sexual projections, and that the witchcraft craze was mostly a male craze and hysteria. Wilson writes, "Franz Buirmann, appointed witch-seeker by the Prince-Archbishop of Cologne in the 1630's, apparently used his position to seduce women who would otherwise be inaccesible. A Frau Peller who refused his advances was the wife of a court assessor. Buirmann acted swiftly; she was arrested one morning and was under torture by the afternoon; the hairs were all shaved off her body and head, and the torturer's assistant was allowed to rape her while he did this. Buirmann, looking on, stuffed a dirty piece of rag into her mouth to stifle her cries.

She was burned alive in a hut filled with dry straw, all within hours. Buirmann had been placed in a position where he could act out sexual-sadistic fantasies. It sounds like an episode from a novel by De Sade."[17]

Indeed it does! But what one cannot forget is the entire female sex was in a position of total vulnerability to such sexual-sadistic abuse, torture, and finally murder, because of the patriarchal structure of the society in which the Church and its representatives, the clergy and inquisitors, had complete autonomy over their lives.

The predominance of female witches makes the put down transparent, revealing it as a male projection deeply based upon the unconscious—and sometimes conscious—male fears of the female sex. Let The Church at last admit to the true nature of the Inquisition: sado-masochistic sexual violence perpetrated against helpless females by the male sex sanctioned by patriarchal doctrine. The females were helpless in that truth availed them not, and their mutilations ended only when they confessed to fantasies (intercourse with the Devil, the size of his penis, etc.) which then earned them death.

NOTE! Never is the Devil's member described as small; it is always huge, and significantly it always gives pain to women. Transparent again is the male fear of sexual inadequacy (size), sado-masochistic fantasies directed at women (it causes pain). Finally, like any rapist or mutilator today, one wants to dispose of the body whose wounds themselves speak the evidence of sexual pathology. So the living bodies are burned, and the evidence of the lust turns to dust. Lust is equated with fire, passion, and the repressions of the Medieval world fanned these flames into funeral pyres for millions of women.

It was undoubtedly the sickest, sorriest time in human history. Sickest still is that the psychic roots persist today.

CONCLUSION

According to the German philosopher Nietzsche, Christianity poisoned Eros. That is say, the unashamed and natural delight that all persons should be able to take in their bodies and their sexuality has been permanently tainted with guilt. Catholicism especially has equated sex with evil, and women with depravity.

What has happened, then, to the Great Mother, embodiment of the sacred life principle itself, since her fall from deification in matriarchal cultures? Our journey from matriarchy to patriarchy has shown that a profound ambivalence took place, in the individual psyches of men, that resulted in a collective, societal ambivalence toward women. On an individual level, the Great Mother as deity = the feminine archetype in the personal unconscious, the *anima,* as Jung named it, Latin for soul. Therefore, it is logical to observe that a change in social structure from matriarchy to patriarchy was brought about in some part by the psychic changes of individual men. In what sense, then, did they become ambivalent?

Because of women's individual link to the greater mystery of nature, her own power to produce life—or death!—women had a numinous, or supernaturally fascinating effect upon men. And because each man—and woman's—life depended on rewards from the Great Mother for survivial, if she withheld the blessings of fertility, then the tribe simply died. So she had both benefic and terrible aspects. Out of this, we may infer, the ambivalence in the male psyche began, reaching its culmination in the witch craze. But first, the Great Mother's spiritual power, radiating to all regions of daily life, became under patriarchy the goddess of love, for some, and the witch, for others, depending upon which aspect of the goddess the males' ambivalent psyches projected. But even as the goddess of love, the totality of the Great Mother's spiritual power of fruition and fertility, vegetable, animal, and human, the very process upon which life on our planet depends, was reduced to a venereal preoccupation; thus the Great Mother became a sex object, extolled either as an embodiment of the virtuous Virgin Mary, or murdered as the dangerous witch/harlot when the supernatural power of the female was experienced as negative and destructive.

The attitude of men towards the Feminine within, in the psyche, creates the projection that is sent out in society, and informs and colors one's attitude toward body and nature, the subject of our next chapter.

CHAPTER V

NATURE, BODY, AND SEX,

There were to have been here two chapters, one on sexuality and the body, the other on nature, but modern man is largely unconscious of the psychic relation between his personal nature (the body) and external nature. In some ways consciousness has deteriorated since the stage of aboriginal man when the ego—as we know it—had not separated from the totality of consciousness in which natural objects and animals were perceived as extensions of one's own consciousness. Now the pendulum has swung to the antithetic position in which man existentially exists apart from his environment and his planet.

Harbingers of a more holistic point of view are known to those readers of *The Secret Life of Plants*. Ironically modern technology provided the means of demonstrating that plants know human thought intents, for a lie-detector device hooked onto a philodendron gave proof of the psychic web connecting all living creatures.

An examination of any one of the matriarchal religions reveals key differences between patriarchy as we know it—Islam and the Judeo-Christian tradition—and the rites of the Mother Goddess. And these differences are crucial to understanding most of the difficulties confronting contemporary civilization. Ecologically we are in a mess, but at the same time the man or woman who has sexual problems cannot see that there is a connection between body and nature.

First of all, in the tradition of the Mother Goddess, harmony with external nature included harmony with the individual body. There were fertility rites in which by symbiotic relation crops flourished and civilization prospered. (When crops fail in matriarchy, additional fertility rites are called for, whereas in patriarchy, at such times one is called upon to practice abstinence!) Naturally this harmony of body and nature promoted individual sexual harmony. One cannot imagine the parishioners of a church of the Great Mother saying, "Well, sex is something we have to have at certain calendar festivals in order to make the crops grow, but we don't like it really. The priestesses say we have to do it though, or risk ex-communication."

An attitude of denigration towards the body, a suspicion, a desire to "tame" wild nature has led inexorably to the denigration of external nature— the whole ecological mess! And if one thinks for a moment that there is no connection, then examine the sex lives of those of your friends who promote and support sound ecological policies, preservation of wilderness, bird life, endangered species, eradication of pollution, care in the use of pesticides, concern with diet and natural foods, and in most cases one will find healthy attitudes towards the human body, and by corollary, sexual lives that are far more harmonious than those of their neighbors who have retained the inherent antagonisms of puritanism towards nature and body.

The division of nature and body, however, is part of a larger, infinitely more tragic schism, that of spirit and nature. Patriarchy, and particularly the Church Fathers of Roman Catholicism, purged Christianity of anything that they thought smacked of paganism or nature worship. Witches were called "heathens" because they worshipped nature on the heath, as our witch has told us. But since man and nature are not in reality separate, being one, this division only served to further dissipate spirit in man. Hence, fallen man, a creature despised by God, housed in a body cleverly designed by the creator as a pleasurable trap to hasten his creation's damnation. As a Hindu once said to a Christian after reading the Bible, "Man hates God, God hates man—very funny religion."

Basically, therefore, there can be no individual harmony between humankind and nature unless there is also harmony between humankind and body. The two are mutually supportive or, as in the Judeo-Christian tradition, mutually exclusive.

Recent statements by the Pope indicate that patriarchy still has a long way to go. Here are excerpts from the San Francisco *Examiner*, February 5, 1981:

POPE TALKS OF BODILY SHAME
Links it with holiness and honor.

Vatican City (UPI) Pope John Paul II said yesterday the shame people feel about their sexual organs helps them maintain holiness and honor.

Speaking in his weekly general audience and citing St. Paul's letter to the Corinthians from the New Testament, the pope said shame about the human body stems form the original sin of Adam and Eve and is part of God's plan for salvation...

'St. Paul's remarks about the less honorable or less presentable parts of the body reflect the sense of shame felt by mankind since the loss of original innocence and the subjection to concupiscence, particularly to the lust of the flesh', the pope said explaining the Biblical passage.

'The parts in question are not objectively less honorable or presentable in themselves', he said. 'They are such only on account of that sense of shame that urges us to surround our body with honor—to control it in holiness and honor.'

'It is precisely by controlling the body in holiness and honor that we overcome the present discord within us', the pope said. 'We restore harmony by purity of heart.'

The pope's message, read in Italian before 5,000 visitors in the Vatican's ultra-modern audience hall, was a continuation of a series of talks he has delivered over the past 14 months on the subject of human sexuality.

He triggered a furor during one of the talks last fall when he said a man could commit adultery in his heart if he considered his own wife in a lustful way.

Well, my comment is that although the pope's talk was delivered in an "ultra-modern audience hall," the ideas remain ultra-regressive, unchanged since the days of St. Paul. Furthermore, the pope is setting himself up as an authority on psychology, which he is not. Following his words, to the effect that harmony can be restored by controlling the body, can be dangerous. For it was this same sense of bodily shame, the obsessive desire to tame the body, and the concomitant fear of fallen women, which had its culmination in the hysteria of the witch craze. In other words, monasticism did not "restore harmony."

Instead of flight from woman, both sexually and emotionally, I am suggesting that this approach is exactly the opposite of what is needed to restore harmony, not only on the personal level, but also on the world scale. For these ideas of patriarchy are demonstrably wrong, as proven by 2,000 years of history, and it is time that more enlightened views were given a chance.

ISLAM AND WOMEN

Nowhere is the put down of women more heavy-handed than in Mohammedanism, or Islam, as it is more frequently known. Unfortunately for women today, this religion outnumbers all others.

The supplanting of the Shah of Iran by the Khomeini was viewed with great consternation by many of the women of Iran, since the Shah had led his country out of medieval practices towards women into a more liberal era. Unveiled at last, and able to attend universities, women breathed the fresh air of modernism; only to be even more cruelly repressed when the Khomeini took power.

For what reasons would women's status be even more diminished under Islam than in Judaism and Christianity? The answer lies in part with the fact that marriage in Islam is a social contract and not a religious rite, thereby limiting women's rights. When learning of executions of wives for adultery, or of teenagers for sexual relations, Westerners react with horror. However, under Islamic law, wives and daughters are merely *property;* hence, if one has utilized your goods the fault lies as much with the woman as with the trespasser, or so saith Islamic law.

Women were married in Islam by contract or capture; thus a legal sanction was given to kidnapping and rape. Women could not inherit property. When the wife of the prophet (Muhammad) died, her property reverted to male kin in Muhammad's family.

Since most of my readers are not affected by Islam, the put down in its *harshest* form, it is not pertinent for us to dwell long on Islam; however, there should be empathy for the millions of women suffering under it.

A few quotations will suffice to demonstrate Islam's severe attitudes towards women.

"Men have dominion over women since Allah has made men superior to women and because men spend their worldly goods on their wives." (Koran 38:34)

"Men possess a degree of superiority over women because Eve was brought forth out of Adam. Thus the superiority of Adam over Eve extends over the whole male sex in relation to the female sex..." (Ibu Arabi Futu-Hat III, 12.13)

"Verily those who believe not in the hereafter do surely name the angels with female names." (Koran 53:29). This line would refer to persons who worshipped the Mother Goddess and gave the diety a feminine name.

And lastly, the sanction for abuse: "Men stand superior to women in that God hath preferred the one over the other... Those whose perverseness ye fear, admonish them and remove them into bed-chambers and beat them..." (Koran 4:38)

THE GAIA HYPOTHESIS

The winter of 1981-82 set records for the coldest weather of the century in most of North America. As I am writing now, updating this chapter, the same thing has happened in January 1985—new record lows from Canada to Florida. At the same time, the five year period preceding this winter is remarkable for cold winters, blazing summers, and in the far West, drought in the late seventies, and then floods and landslides in the winter of 1981-82.

Analyzing this weather phenomenon from a purely patriarchal point of view, that is, rationally, and even mechanistically by resorting to charts with isobar graphs, etc. the conclusion reached may suggest no startling trends.

From the opposite point of view, which, indeed, is the point of view of this book, one comes away with the conclusion that Mother Nature is very angry, perhaps even bent on eliminating man from the planet. But the contention is ridiculous, from the point of view of science, because a fallacy is involved, attributing a human-like awareness (Mother Nature) to planet earth. Nature, says science, is chaotic, and cannot act with concerted self-interest. Or can it?

To support what he calls the "Gaia hypothesis," scientific evidence has been gathered by James Lovelock and published by Oxford University Press. Before we proceed with Lovelock's hypothesis, we need to understand the background of the word Gaia, a variation of Gaea, the Greek Earth Mother:

In the beginning, Hesiod says, there was Chaos, vast and dark. Then appeared Gaea, the deep-breasted earth, and finally Eros, 'the love of which softens hearts', whose fructifying influence would thenceforth preside over the formation of beings and things...

The only divinity with well-defined features is Gaea, the earth. According to Hesiod it seems likely that Gaea, from whom all things issued, had been the great diety of the primitive Greeks. Like the Aegeans and like the peoples of Asia, the Greeks must doubtless have originally worshipped the Earth in whom they beheld the Mother-Goddess. This is again confirmed by the Homeric hymn in which the poet says: 'I shall sing of Gaea, universal mother, firmly founded, the oldest of divinities.'

Gaea, 'the deep-breasted', whose soil nourishes all that exists, and by whose benevolence men are blessed with fair children and all the pleasant fruits of earth, was there at one time the supreme goddess whose majesty was acknowledged not only by men, but by the gods themselves...

Gaea the omnipotent not only created the universe and bore the first race of gods, but also gave birth to the human race![1]

According to Lovelock, in his Gaia hypothesis, the "Earth's living matter, air, oceans, and land surfaces, form a complex system which can be seen as a single organism and which has the capacity to keep our planet a fit place for life. ... I have frequently used the word Gaia as a shorthand for the hypothesis itself, namely that the biosphere is a self-regulating entity with the capacity to keep our planet healthy by controlling the chemical and physical environment. Occasionally it has been difficult, without excessive circumlocution, to avoid talking of Gaia as if she were known to be sentient. ... The notion of Gaia, of a living Earth, has not in the past been acceptable to the main science stream and consequently seeds sown in earlier times would not have flourished but instead would have remained deep in the mulch of scientific papers."[2]

Gaia, then, is the collective intelligence of all the planet's kingdoms: mineral, vegetable, animal, and human. That intelligence, therefore, regulates conditions for all life. But human consciousness does not seem to be aware of its contributory role in this great scheme of things. Still concerned with "taming nature" and dominating the planet, this same patriarchal attitude seeks to make of Mother Earth a submissive female prone to a dominant male consciousness. Yet such an attitude has created an imbalance felt throughout all Earth. And a reaction has commenced, most apparent in what appears at first to be merely a change in the weather from hospitable to inhospitable for man.

In our discussion of the religion of the Mother Goddess, we have seen that there was a harmony with nature, and as a corollary, there was also a harmony with personal nature, the body. We have discussed the sexual rites of the Mother Goddess, necessary for promoting the harmony with outer nature. Even now as our relation to Earth's weather begins to indicate an ominous change, so too, the sexual diseases of the body appear in new and potentially devastating forms, (AIDS, Herpes II), as if a vengeance is to be wreaked upon us not from above at the hands of an angry patriarchal god, but from below, the unconscious of man. Stressful conflicts within the psyche manifest as conflicts in the body (dis-ease) in which the immune system is immobilized, and, therefore, incapable of combatting the disease. Viruses seem to be similar to the insect population in their ability to be able to stay one jump ahead of science.

GAIA IN THE GARDEN

In Greek myth there is an interesting parallel to the Eden story of God's antagonism to the serpent, consort of the Mother Goddess, the patriarchal gods of Mt. Olympus attaining victory over the Titan offspring of the Great

Mother. Gaia's last union had been with Tarturus, which we may think of as synonymous with the depths of Earth, or a Greek parallel to hell/Hades. Her offspring was Titan, usually depicted with three human heads culminating in intertwined serpent coils. Being a product of the depths, Tarturus is an apt antagonist for Zeus, god of light and mountain heights, and as such symbolic of patriarchal antipathy not only to darkness and the world below, but also to to the offspring of the Mother Goddess. In terms of Jungian psychology this myth corresponds to the antipathy of the conscious mind (light) to the unconscious (darkness). This snake-god offspring of Earth also has a relation to the cosmic scene of 4,000 B.C., when Draco was atop the World Axis/Tree, and the sun had entered Taurus, an earth sign.

The battle of Zeus and Typhon is epic indeed. Entwined in the coils of the monster, Zeus is rescued by Hermes, who as guide of souls to the underworld mediates between light and dark worlds. Renewing the struggle, Typhon is ultimately conquered by Zeus' thunderbolts, products of the sky, or light-world. The "taming" of nature, therefore, begins with the conquest of Gaia's children, the Titans. As we shall see, it now may be that man needs taming. This is perhaps yet another manifestation of Mother Nature showing who is really boss.

Our ecological policies today also seem to reflect the desire to tame, conquer—even kill—Mother Nature. And so, Nature in return appears now to take an avenging form like the Furies, hunting down and destroying the interloper—Man.

Is it mere chance that our increased concern with ecology has coincided with the new concern with diet, aerobic exercise, and physical fitness? I think not. Query any joggers or bikers you know and you will find real antagonism to policies that pollute the air and poison the earth. Smog is a notorious example, but a less well-known pollution comes from the smoky stacks of Canada and northern New England, contributing to the phenomenon known as "acid rain," which is killing fish in northern lakes and streams, and poisoning vegetation. By analogy the smoky stacks of industry are nothing less than giant cigarettes, polluting the lungs of the Earth's atmosphere.

In mythology, Moon and Venus symbolize the Mother Goddess. Planetary exploration has so far revealed that neither is hospitable for life. The example of Venus bears examination. At 800° F the surface is so hot that lead melts, a thick cloud cover retaining heat by the "greenhouse effect." Since the industrial revolution in the nineteenth century, our planet also has begun to develop a greenhouse effect from the burning of fossil fuels, releasing carbon dioxide into the air, which then puts a lid on some of the heat normally radiating out into the atmosphere. The long term effect of this may be the melting of the polar ice caps, with a commensurate flooding of coastal areas, wherein resides the greatest population concentrations in the world. Envision New York, Washington, Boston, Miami, Chicago, San Francisco, Los Angeles, Tokyo, and London, all submerged!

But the problem of our relation to our planet, to Mother Nature, is simply that we do not have a formula or a time-table as to when we must stop in order to avoid setting in motion the falling dominoes that may one day result in a climate as hot as Venus' and a world unable to sustain life in any form.

EARTH'S INTELLIGENCE

What level of awareness can we attribute to Mother Earth? Let us hear again from James Lovelock:

> Among several difficult concepts embodied in the Gaia hypothesis is that of intelligence. Like life itself, we can at present only categorize and cannot completely define it. Intelligence is a property of living systems and is concerned with the ability to answer questions correctly. We might add, especially questions about those responses to the environment which affect the system's survival, and the survival of the association of systems to which it belongs... If Gaia exists, then she is without doubt intelligent in this limited sense at least.
>
> With creatures who possess the capacity of conscious thought and awareness, and no one as yet knows at what level of brain development this state exists, there is the additional possibility of cognitive anticipation. A tree prepares for winter by shedding its leaves and by modifying its internal chemistry to avoid damage from frost. This as all done automatically, [we assume] drawing on a store of information handed down in the tree's genetic set of instructions. We on the other hand may buy warm clothes in preparation for a journey to New Zealand in July. In this we use a store of information gathered by our species as a collective unit and which is available to us all at the conscious level. So far as is known, we are the only creatures on this planet with the capacity to gather and store information and use it in this complex way. If we are a part of Gaia it becomes interesting to ask: To what extent is our collective intelligence also a part of Gaia? Do we as a species constitute a Gaian nervous system and a brain which can consciously anticipate environmental changes?
>
> Still more important is the implication that the evolution of homo sapiens, with his technological inventiveness and his increasingly subtle communications network, has vastly increased Gaia's range of perception. She is now through us awake and aware of herself...
> This new interrelationship of Gaia with man is by no means fully established; we are not yet a truly collective species, corralled and tamed, so that the fierce destructive, and greedy forces of tribalism and nationalism are fused into a compulsive urge to belong to the commonwealth of all creatures which constitutes Gaia. It might seem to be a surrender, but I suspect that the rewards, in the form of an increased sense of well-being and fulfillment, in knowing ourselves to be a dynamic part of a far greater entity, would be worth the loss of tribal freedom.
>
> Perhaps we are not the first species to fulfil such a role, nor possibly the last. Another candidate could be found among the great

sea mammals, which have brains many times larger than ours... Perhaps one day the children we share with Gaia will peacefully co-operate with the great mammals of the ocean and use whale power to travel faster in the mind, as horse power once carried us over the land.[3]

FINDHORN

From scientists deducing an intelligence, or regulating consciousness, in nature, we proceed now to an adventure involving communication with this consciousness. Our story concerns an RAF squadron leader, his wife and three sons, and a gifted psychic who had left a position with the Canadian Foreign Office to take up residence in a trailer park in a remote coastal area of northeast Scotland. Peter Caddy, tall and athletically robust, had once walked two thousand miles from Kashmir to Tibet, through the Himalayas, as an initiate a school of spiritual adepts. His wife Eileen had had a clairvoyant vision of seven cottages, gathered around a flourishing vegetable and flower garden. Their friend, Dorothy MacLean, favored the Sufi religion, in which one works at ordinary tasks, never flaunting spirituality, finding fulfillment in a natural oneness with all life.

Findhorn began with a small garden in fine, sandy soil and gravel, in which nothing grew naturally except spiked grasses, peculiar everywhere on earth to coastal areas bounding cold seas, yet the horticultural results of the Findhorn experiment have astounded the world. Floral, fruit, and vegetable gardens of such beauty and abundance that they have been visited by persons from all over the world.

In 1975, Dorothy MacLean, the gifted Findhorn medium, appeared with me in a seminar, "The Evolution of Consciousness," and it was then that she read to us her message from a tree, that is from, one part of Gaia, or the Great Mother, Earth.

MESSAGE FROM A TREE

"I'll read out a message I had from a tree. This is from the copper beech deva. I contacted it after a period of attuning to a very small flower bordering the garden. This will explain the very first line:

'Our firm tone contrasts with the piping voices of the small plants. You have need to feel the steady strength of our flow of forces. All of you can gain much by partaking of our balance and flow, especially at this time when people rove a changing land of lost values. All life needs a firm foundation, and our radiating strength can invoke in you a similar force which is too often dormant. You have touched on yet another reason for the need of large trees. We channel a type of force which has a steadying influence on life. Truth tells you to build your foundations on rock, which is what we do, and what we unconsciously remind you to do. Man does not realize that among other things, his natural environment corresponds to and therefore can bring out, some part of his own make-up, and that he is influenced by his environment in many subtle ways. Here too the great trees have a mighty part to play and you are bereft of some part of yourself and of your heritage when you denude the land of large trees. Now come closer, resting in our strength and becoming aware of the smaller notes we play. Be aware of the flutter of leaves, the bright sheen of color, the sunshiny softness of spring, all connected in some way with the birds, the insects, the elements. A large tree is a family, a country to explore, and a place of beauty. It stands, giving out to all and sundry a refuge for many. It stands proud, reaching to the sky and deep into the earth, enduring. It stands as a symbol of a particular perfection of God. Let it stand and you will come closer to God'.

But the secret of Findhorn's prosperity was even more amazing than its manifest results. According to Peter, Eileen, and Dorothy, they had entered into a sort of spiritual partnership with forces which controlled the growth and fruition of the vegetable kingdom.

Today, Findhorn is a prosperous community of persons who have gone there to learn the lesson of living in harmony with nature. The proof of Findhorn is the pudding. Without an inner soul, psyche, or spirit—call it what you will—in nature, and without the kind of communication between it and humankind which took place at Findhorn, Findhorn would have failed. Pragmatically, the flourishing growth there is impossible because of adverse soil and growing conditions. It was made possible only by the fact that the gap between humankind and the inner soul of nature was bridged. As we have said, it is a return to a time when humankind lived in harmony with Gaia, the Mother Goddess, and as such the Findhorn community is an example of what hopefully the future may bring as mankind rediscovers the relation of individual psyche and the planet's soul.

Findhorn is unique in that it demonstrates evidence of communication between humankind and Gaia, or the Mother Goddess, represented by what Dorothy MacLean calls devas, nature spirits nurturing plant growth from a plane of being that is itself non-physical, interpenetrating and sustaining the physical plane. Scientifically, we may speculate electro-magnetic properties to this plane which enable it to link up with the animal, vegetable, and mineral kingdoms on earth, and perhaps throughout the universe.

Every material object appears to have a particular frequency of vibration which is caused not by the material of the object, but by a more subtle body of unknown properties. In his visionary book *The Nature of Substance*, Rudolf Hauschka states that life cannot be interpreted in purely mechanistic terms, since life is not a product of chemicals and elements, but an intangible which precedes the elements; consequently, matter is a precipitate of life. The same theme has been sounded in the Seth books of Jane Roberts, and appears again in the posthumous volume *Dreams, "Evolution," and Value Fulfillment,* to be published in 1986 by Prentice-Hall, and quoted here thanks to her husband Robert F. Butts, and to Tam Mossman, her editor: "The world formed out of what God is. The world is the natural extension of divine creativity and intent, lovingly formed from the inside out—so there was consciousness before there was matter, and not the other way around."

Such theories correlate with world mythologies in which the Mother Goddess Sophia, Inanna, descends the World Axis/Tree from an unmanifest, spiritual dimension, in order to manifest on earth as the divine in matter. Surely now the example of Findhorn and the wisdom of the devas has opened our minds to new dimensions in nature. Despite his technology, modern man cannot tame nature, the Mother Goddess. The time of retribution is at hand. As the Gaia hypothesis has warned us, she will insure her needs and environment in spite of man. We live in harmony with Her and natural law, or we perish. Earth sustains Herself.

It is perhaps best now to attempt a kind of scientific formulation that will explain the invisible web linking All as One. Plants have neither mouths nor ears; how then do they broadcast and receive. The answer seems to lie in what I call the "Vibrational" Theory. Every living thing has a particular frequency of vibration which seemingly is not caused by the material matter of the object, but instead by a kind of electromagnetic surround or aura. Thus this "electricity" picks up what the rest of the planet (including humankind) sends out, and in turn broadcasts itself.

According to Rudolp Hauschka, "the elements as we know them are already corpses, the residue of life forms. Though chemists can derive oxygen, hydrogen and carbon from a plant, they cannot derive a plant from any combination of these or other elements."[4]

Therefore, he questions is it "not more reasonable to suppose that *life existed long before matter and was the product of a pre-existent spiritual cosmos*?" (Italics mine)

Our drawing of the Vibrational Theory, presents a simplified explanation of the interrelations. In experiments, Hauschka discovered that "plants could not only generate matter out of a nonmaterial sphere, but could 'etheralize' it once more, noting an emergence and disappearance of matter in rhythmic sequence, often in conjunction with phases of the moon."[6]

Furthermore, Bird & Tompkins in *The Secret Life of Plants* cite numerous examples of experiments begun in the 19th century and leading up to the present in which plants are "able to transmute, in alchemical fashion, phosphorus into sulfur, calcium into phosphorus, magnesium into calcium, carbonic acid into magnesium, and nitrogen into potassium'. "[7] Indeed, in some cases, plants seem capable of synthesizing from "thin air" (the cosmic radiations from deep space) chemicals not available to them in the soil in which they are growing. From this evidence, we must postulate another body capable of such wizardry, interpenetrating the material body of the plant.

As we know, the very life of the early planter peoples depended upon the fertility rites of the Mother Goddess and her priestesses. To the uninitiated eye, such ceremonies were sympathetic magic that could not have been very effective in speeding germination and instilling growth in the community's crops. However, experiments completed by Louis Kevran *(Biological Transmutations)* indicate "that powerful energies are at work in the germination process of seeds which synthesize enzymes, probably by transmuting

VIBRATIONAL THEORY

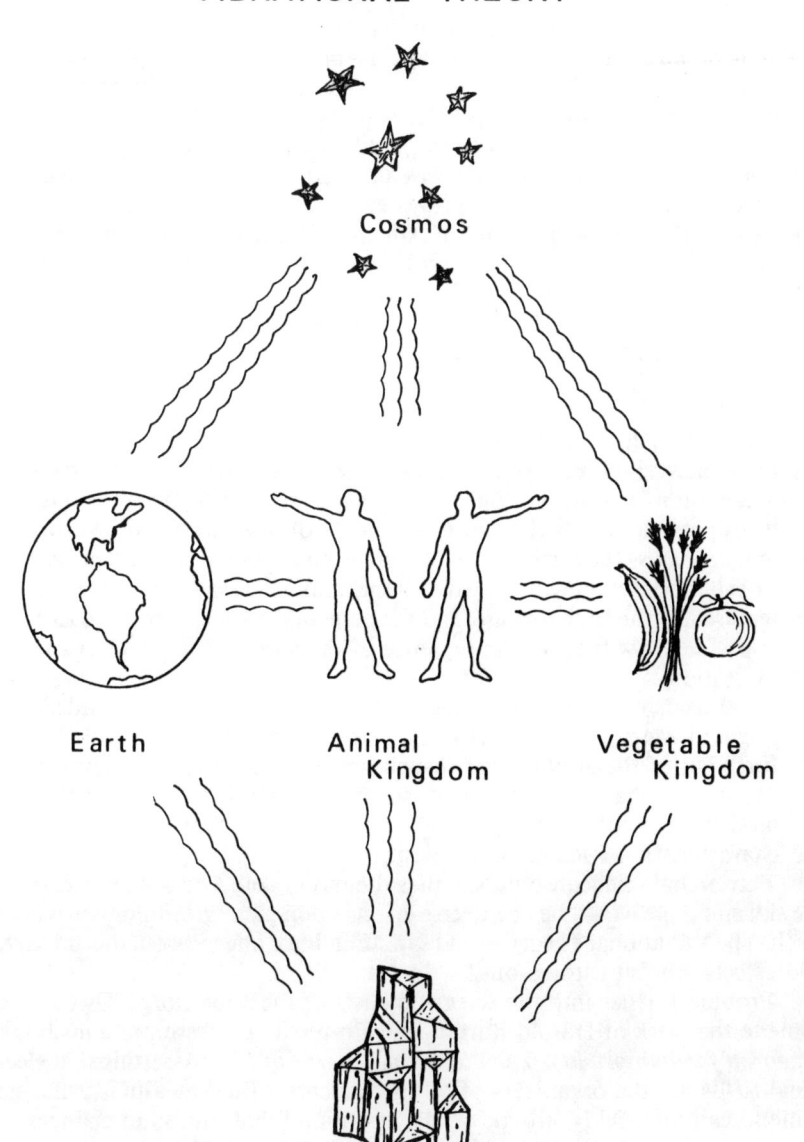

Cosmos

Earth

Animal Kingdom

Vegetable Kingdom

Mineral Kingdom

matter within them. His experiments have also convinced him that lunar forces are extremely important in germination, though botanists have long asserted that only warmth and water are required."[8]

The importance of lunar forces again reminds us of the role of the moon in the religion of the Mother Goddess, in which the sun was seen as blighting growth, whereas the moon's light furthered growth:

> The moistening power of the goddess depended not only on her control of the rainfall, for she was also believed to produce the dew. In Greece, the Moon Goddess was called the All-Dewy-One, and a dew service was held for her in Athens, when dew maidens danced about the statue of the goddess. Dew is a symbol of fertility and a bath of dew was often prescribed, late in the middle ages, as a love charm. In short, as Plutarch says: 'The moon, with her humid and generative light, is favorable to the propagation of animals and the growth of plants.'
>
> Ishtar, the Babylonian moon goddess, was connected with springs and dew, and bore the title All-Dewy-One. This epithet takes on a new significance for us when we recall how hot and dry Mesopotamia is. In the cold North a sun is needed for fertility, but in tropical countries the sun is an enemy of vegetation, while rain and dew cause the earth to bring forth the green things. So the temples of the moon goddess were often in natural grottos, where a spring represented the source of life, and the perpetual greenness of the oasis in the desert witness to the presence of the moon goddess, giver of vegetation...
>
> Like Ishtar, moon goddesses from whatever region were regarded as guardians of the waters, rivers, brooks, and springs which gushing forth out of the ground, were usually held sacred to the goddess of fertility; probably because they so aptly symbolize that invisible hidden power of 'bringing forth from within' which is the peculiar characteristic of feminine creation'.[9]

Patriarchal science would say that the moon could be obliterated from the sky and there would be no adverse effects upon plant growth on the planet earth. The Vibrational Theory would say, "Eliminate one factor in the universe, and effects are felt throughout."

Probing further into the scientific basis of the Vibrational Theory, we come to the work of Harold Burr, a Yale University professor, and his book *Blueprint for Immortality: The Electrical Patterns of Life*. Asserting that electrical fields are the organizers of all life systems, "Burr measured what he came to call 'life-fields' around seeds, and found that profound changes in the voltage patterns were caused by the alteration of a single gene in the parent stock. Even more interesting to plant breeders was his discovery that it is possible to predict how strong and healthy a future plant will be from the electrical diagnosis of the seed which produces it."

"...Burr charted the life fields of trees on the Yale campus and at his laboratory in Old Lyme, Connecticut, over nearly two decades. He found that recordings related not only to the lunar cycle and to sunspots, which flare up at intervals with many years between them but revealed cycles recurring every three and six months that were beyond his explanation. His conclusions seemed to make less suspect the long-mocked practices of generations of gardeners who claimed that their crops should be planted according to the phases of the moon. ..."

"Burr's life work... indicates that the organizing field around the 'bodies' of living things anticipates the physical events within them and suggests that the mind itself... can, by modulating the field, affect positively or deleteriously the matter with which it is held to be associated."[10]

The implications for 21st century medicine are astounding. Not only have we the potential to revolutionize agriculture—and so insure the planet's food supply—but also when medicine recognizes that changes in mind as (positive or negative emotions) can affect the body's health, we will be closer to attaining true health; for then science may cease questing agents of disease (viruses) and recognize that the agents are always potentially present, but they are activated and dangerous only when the body's "field" is altered by mind.

Our next area of investigation involves solving the question of how this phenomenon is possible, that is, through what medium does the mind influence and alter bodily health?

KIRLIAN PHOTOGRAPHY

That plants, as well as animals and human beings, have fields of fine sheaths of subatomic or protoplasmic energy which permeate the solid physical bodies of molecules and atoms was a centuries-old allegation by seers and philosophers. This extra dimension or "aura" depicted in ancient iconography around the bodies of saints, with golden halos, around their heads, has been referred to by persons gifted with extrasensory perception since the beginnings of recorded history. By laying film or plate in contact with an object to be photographed and passing through the object an electric currect from a high-frequency spark generator which put out 75,000-200,000 electrical pulses per second, the Kirlians [Russian scientists] had come across a way of photographing this "aura"—or something akin to it.

Leaves from plants, sandwiched with film between the electrodes of their device, revealed a phantasmagoria hitherto restricted to clairvoyants, a micro-universe of tiny, starry points of light. White, blue, and even red and yellow flares were pictured surging out of what seemed to be channels in the leaves. These emanations, or forcefields round a leaf, became distorted if the leaf was mutilated, gradually diminishing and disappearing as the life was allowed to die. The Kirlians were next able to magnify this luminescence by adapting their photographic processes to optical instruments and microscopes. Rays of energy and whirling fireballs of light appear to shoot out of plants into space![11]

In *Psychic Discoveries Behind the Iron Curtain* (1970), there is a chapter entitled "Science Probes the Energy Body." It is of extreme relevance to our thesis that the body contains a preformative spiritual body. Since the publication of the above title, hardly any research has been done in the West on the information contained therein. This is highly ironic in view of the fact that Russia is manifestly anti-religious; nevertheless, spiritual implications may be derived from the Russian discoveries of the "Biological Plasma Body."

According to the Russian scientists who made the discovery, all living things from plants to humankind have a second body of "some sort of elementary plasma-like constellation made of ionized, excited electrons, protons and possibly other particles. But at the same time, this energy body is not just particles. It is not a chaotic system. It's a whole unified organism in itself. It acts as a unit, and as a unit the energy body gives off its own electromagnetic fields and is the basis of biological fields."[12] That is to say, the bio-plasmic body seems to possess an organizing consciousness.

"An American neurologist found he could pick up traces of the electrical field pattern of the missing limb of a salamander. Other scientists have taken a blob of protoplasm that should grow into the arm of a fetal animal and placed it in leg position. A leg, not an arm grows, again implying an organizing field. ..."

"In the photos shown us by Soviet scientists, we saw that if part of the physical body of a living thing is cut away, the bioplasmic body remains, whole and clearly visible in a high frequency field. When this energy body itself disappears, the plant or animal dies."[13] Thus if the soul or spirit puts on chemical clothes when taking on a physical body, it does not die with the body, but leaves the physical body behind before transforming to another level of energy/consciousness. An awareness of this on our part changes one's attitude towards death—and by corollary—towards life also. Such an awareness reinforces the belief that we must live in harmony with nature and our bodies, and the denigration of either reduces humankind and nature alike.

How then does one revitalize the more subtle energy body upon whose health the grosser physical body evidently depends?

William Tiller, departmental head of Material Science at Stanford University, became the first American physicist to be invited to Russia to investigate Kirlian photography. Tiller speculated that the radiation or energy coming out of a leaf or a human fingertip actually might be coming from whatever is present prior to the formation of solid matter. This, says Tiller, "may be another level of substance, producing a hologram, a coherent energy pattern of a leaf which is a force-field for organizing matter to building itself into this kind of physical network."

"Tiller thinks that even if part of the network were cut away, the forming hologram would still be there."[14] Tiller's theory is correct according to evidence supplied by the authors of *Psychic Discoveries Behind the Iron Curtain*. They were presented with two Kirlian pictures which appeared to be of "the same leaf except... there seemed to be a line down the middle of the right side of the leaf. Beyond that line the sparkling outline and veins seemed airier, the background fluffier."

" 'This is the same leaf as the first picture,' the young scientist explains. 'The actual leaf itself has been cut. One third of it has been removed. But the energy pattern of the whole leaf is still there!'

"'In other words, we were actually seeing the 'ghost' of a part of the leaf--a phantom counterpart of pure energy.'

"'What happens if you cut away more than a third of the leaf?'

"'Then the leaf dies and the whole 'energy body' of the leaf vanishes.'

"'If a human being loses a finger or an arm or has a leg amputated, does he still retain this 'counterpart body'--a sort of ghost of the finger or leg?'

"'Yes,' the scientist nodded.

"From what we'd seen, the Soviets appeared to have evidence that there is some sort of energy matrix in all living things, some sort of unifying invisible body or luminescence penetrating our physical bodies."

How then does one revitalize the more subtle energy body upon whose health the grosser physical body depends?

According to further Russian experiments, surplus electrons of inspired oxygen are converted into energy that the bio-plasmic body utilizes. We have also known that persons who exercised the most were the most energetic and conversely those who exercised not at all were ennervated and "logy." However, we must qualify this by saying that those who pursue the largely sedentary discipline of Yoga are deriving great benefits since Yoga involves a patterned breathing designed to recharge the Prana or Vital Energy. Further, the above discovery dovetails nicely with what we shall have to say in recommending aerobic exercise, in which large quantities of oxygen may be inspired.

THE ENERGY BODY AND ACUPUNCTURE

Dr. Mikhail Kuznich Gaikin, a Leningrad surgeon, gazed intently at the myriad patterns of lights sparkling out of Kirlian's hand and his own hand under the impact of high-frequency fields. Dr. Gaikin had read about the Kirlians in the *Literary Gazette* in 1953. Something about the picture accompanying the article set an idea ticking in him. . . .

The pattern of lights he saw in the human body reminded Gaikin of something he'd come across in China . . . 'An energy we call Life Force or Vital Energy circulated through the body on specific pathways,' the Chinese told him. 'This Vital Energy can be tapped at seven hundred points on the skin that were mapped out thousands of years ago.' The Chinese inserted fine needles at those points to correct imbalances in this supposed primary energy flow, and thus apparently cured disease.

The Kirlian pictures coupled with the knowledgeof acupuncture lead perhaps to a new perspective on some kind of precognition. Every organ in the body, according to acupuncture theory, communicates its condition via the energy pathways to the skin in the form of energy patterns. . . .

So far, coming from left field, the ideas of acupuncture seemed to tally with what the Kirlians had observed experimentally. It was bizarre. And the parallels went even further. The Kirlians had found that emotions, moods, thought all seem to have a drastic effect on these energy pictures of ourselves.

In Chinese medicine, they learned, you are always viewed as a whole—a concept which includes body, mind, and environment. The Chinese say that both habitual states of mind and sudden moods reflect in the Vital Energy. According to them, it is this energy that links the mind and the physical body. This is the *modus operandi* of psychosomatic illness, the means by which the mind affects the body. A negative depressed state of mind acts on the Vital Energy like a toxic substance, they say, and will eventually manifest itself as illness. . . .

It may have been more than moods that caused changes in the lights flaring from the Kirlians' hands. Acupuncturists believe Vital Energy in the body links man with the cosmos. If there is a change in the universe and environment, a resonance is produced in the Vital Energy of the human body which in turn affects the physical body. In this way the body adjusts to changes around it. The Vital Energy, the Chinese say, is affected by a host of things: the seasons, cycles of the moon, tides, thunderstorms, strong winds, and even levels of noise. Supposedly an illness and its treatment can be affected by any of these changes in the environment. Eventually the State University of Kazakhstan affirmed that the bioplasmic body is affected by changes in the atmosphere, just as acupuncture theory predicted![6]

And so we have scientific evidence for the Vibrational Theory. Far from existing existentially, like a spider at the center of a web, humankind responds through its bioplasmic body to changes from sun, moon, and other forces in the cosmic sphere, and to the thoughts and moods of others in the social environment. Our relation to the microcosmic world of viruses and sub-atomic particles is little known as yet, but when it is discovered it will fit undoubtedly into the Vibrational Theory on the other end of the scale.

NATURAL HEALTH

Health appears to be the natural condition of the body, dis-ease being just that, a disturbance of the natural harmony between he bioplasmic body and a surrounding network of vibrations. Ultimately this dis-ease may manifest as a physical disease. No area of human endeavor is more important to us than health, and the richest man would gladly give all his money if he could be saved from a fatal disease. Psychiatry has been the first new science of the 20th century to give us clues to the effect that the old mechanistic theory of germs and viruses was inadequate to explain the complexity of factors governing individual health.

Furthermore, we have applied the same warlike patriarchal policies of overkill to combatting human disease as we have to overdosing Earth with chemicals, so that She must compensate from the soul level to restore balance. But the chemical, mechanistic approach to medicine does not work any better than the same method when applied to ecology. Once seen as the planet's panacea for destroying insects, DDT's overkill led to the poisoning of earth and sea. So too, chemical medicine has demonstrated that truly for every action there is a reaction. The body reacts to the medicine, and often throws up new symptoms, that must be treated just as Mother Nature's insects evolved and adapted in spite of our chemical attack. We have come a long way from the time when disease was thought to come from the spells of witches, and that charms and magic could ward off illness; but although we intellectually accept the concept of psychosomatic medicine, we cannot make the connections on the personal level between disease and our own psychic dis-ease. Just as Findhorn's flourishing gardens in the face of "impossible" soil and climatic conditions demonstrated the proof of the soul in nature, so too "impossible" cures and psychic healings demonstrate the response of the physical body to more subtle and yet vital energies to which the physical health is untimately beholden.

THE BODY, NUTRITION, AND HEALING

Evidence continues to mount that healings defying medical probabilities occur every day. The scientific community labels these "spontaneous remissions" in order not to have to change its concepts governing the body's potentials. Therefore, the healing is not accepted, but seen as commensurate with a change in the illness, which conveniently "happens" at the time of a healing.

At the same time, evidence also increases that no one can heal another who does not want to be healed; therefore, the agency for the healing seems to lie within the sick person, the healer acting as a catalyst. Thus, each one of us seems to possess a Gaia-like power for regulating our lives towards sickness or health. Why, one may ask, does one choose illness and another health? Surely if we had a choice, no one would be ill. The answer seems to lie in the psyche, and the reasons are usually inaccessible to the conscious mind; however, in the illness, the symptoms of the disease, or in the area afflicted, we sometimes perceive a symbolic language at work, the psyche using the disease as a metaphor of a deeper distress.

The role of diet in health has come into its own in the latter half of the 20th century. For our mothers and fathers, sugar was seen as a healthy, energy-promoting food. Since then we know that for every action in the body, there is a reaction, and sugar induces lassitude and depression after its initial "high." Its role in heart diseases is also coming increasingly to the fore. We know now that our carbohydrates should come from natural sugars in fruits and vegetables.

Diet and the products of the earth are the realm of the Mother Goddess. We have listened to Father for too long. In the form of the doctor who knew best, we came to believe that medical science had a cure or pill for every disease. Now we find that the "cures" induce reactions or new diseases that the body's protection cannot handle in the face of too much chemical doctoring.

One of the most amazing advances against heart and lung disease is entirely "natural" and, therefore, worthy of our consideration in a chapter on nature and the Mother Goddess. Nathan Pritikin has an institute in Santa Barbara which reduces the effects of heart and lung disease through diet and exercise. Indeed, he has heart patients jogging within a week or so of recovering from heart attacks! The principle is the same as that employed by competitive runners. When the arteries are narrowed or clogged, the heart has to work harder, wearing out sooner. Pritikin's diet reduces cholesterol so drastically (and sodium is all but eliminated to reverse hardening of the arteries) that the pulse lowers significantly, blood pressure comes down, and the patient is then ready for a jogging program to begin strengthening the heart.

When a man of 65 can outrun a boy of 25 in a race of four or five miles, no one can argue with the methods that have made the old man young again. The New Age harmony with the body, the joy in exercising the body, having the body as a friend again rather than as the traditional antagonist of the Judeo-Christian tradition, has its historical root in the religions of the Mother Goddess: harmony with nature = harmony with body. Pritikin's diet is so "natural" that it perhaps provides a clue to the fact that our diet like our religion may have changed for the worse when patriarchy supplanted the natural religion of the Mother Goddess.

The period of 4-2,000 B.C. was the time of planters; crops such as grains, vegetables, and fruits were main staples of the diet. We shall never know for sure, but I believe cancer was unknown at that time. (Since the time that I wrote the preceding line in the mid-1970's, a new medical science have evolved called paleo-pathology, which is simply understood as autopsies on mummies. I am grateful to Dr. Dean Edell for providing me with data from the studies of Dr. Michael Zimmerman, who made autopsies upon well over a hundred mummies from Alaska to Egypt. He found no evidence of bowel, breast, or lung cancers. Clearly the diet during the time of the Great Mother was preferable to our own.)

When man began to herd and eat animals, cancer may have begun. We know that the pig was one of the animals sacred to the Mother Goddess, but was the pig eaten? Judaism set prohibitions against eating pork because it had been the animal of the Goddess whose religion it supplanted.

Roughage in the colon cleanses it, as we are being told, and the foods of the Mother Goddess are perfect for the body, whereas the eating of charred meats promotes cancer. Perhaps we should listen to the Goddess once again.

Now that we have rediscovered in this New Age the mortal value of diet and healing, we can realize the tremendous power of women in the cultures of the Mother Goddess; she held the literal reins of life and death in daily, personal matters involving the family.

In the religious rites—in her roles as priestess—she assured the annual salvation of the community through the magical reappearance of the food supply.

Woman cooked, fed, healed, and brought forth the family. Basically man was merely a walking sperm bank, from which woman required a periodic deposit to insure future generations. Man was an appendage of the community, so useless that he developed with his fellows the game of warfare to while away his time, and then sold woman on the idea that he ought to have the upper hand to provide protection from the other societies, which under matriarchy had been inherently peaceful! Thus it is that the game or toy that man created as plaything now occupies the major part of most nations' annual budgets.

FOOD VALUES

A vegetable stands in the same relation to humankind as does humankind to earth, or Mother Nature. When we consider medicine, healing, nutrition, and overall health, the Vibrational Theory comprises a kind of Unified Field theory ranging from the planet's health (ecology) to human well-being, to an individual plant's health.

Suggested reading that supports this theory is *The Secret Life of Plants*, by Tompkins and Bird, truly a book of wonders. The authors cite the work of George De La Warr, an English civil engineer who has developed equipment capable of measuring the frequency of plants and has established the relation between human thoughts and emotions in furthering or blighting growth. Accordingly, every living plant has a critical rotational position (CRP) relative to the earth's geomagnetic field, and within its CRP the plant has a unique pattern of radiation surrounding it (the aura of mystics?). The authors cite an experiment involving the "aura" extending outward some twenty feet from a large oak tree. Its interaction with the human aura expands the latter significantly, indicating a transference of energy from the vegetable kingdom to humankind. Have you hugged a tree today? Indeed, the energy levels of the very foods that we eat contribute dramatically to our own energy levels, which may be crucial in determining overall health.

Tompkins and Bird discuss a device for measuring the vibrational level of foods developed by Andre Simoneton. As a young engineer during World War I he worked with physicist Louis de Broglie, who established that every particle, down to a photon of light, has a specific wavelength. Simoneton measures foods in angstrom values. Naturally, the higher the angstrom vibration, the higher the vitality of the food, and we may infer, the more beneficial for our bodies. In this way we live off Gaia's body and are nourished by her.

Normally human beings have a vibrational wavelength of 6,500 angstroms. Arbitrarily, in order to classify foods, Simoneton has defined four categories, commencing with "dead" foods, those which possess no angstrom value. They include bleached white flour, refined white sugar, and margarine and preserves. Secondly, radiating at 0-3,000 angstroms are cooked meats, sausages, and organ meats. The pig was one animal sacred to the Great Mother, which may explain patriarchy's prohibition against it. Most persons who wish to justify this edict choose to attribute profound medical foresight to the founders of patriarchy. Be that as it may, pork soaked in brine and smoked over a wood fire attains a high radiance of 9,500 to 10,000 angstroms.

In the next category of radiations comes foods in the range of 3,000 to 6,500. These include fresh eggs, which, however, should be nearly eliminated from the diet because of their role in contributing to high levels of cholesterol in the blood. Cooked fish and boiled vegetables also fall in this category.

In order to raise one's own vitality, foods should be chosen which fall in the category of having angstrom values higher than 6,500. Fortunately, most fish, fruit, and vegetables when eaten raw are much higher. The only exception to the rule of eating foods raw in order not to destroy their vitality through cooking is the lowly spud. Radiating at 2,000 angstroms when raw, it rises to 7,000 boiled, and 9,000 when baked.

The long lives of many Italians may be explained by the radiations of olive oil, 8,500, and fresh garlic juice, also 8,000. Pasteurized, it coagulated like blood, its angstrom value dropping to zero. Frozen fruit and vegetables maintain the level of vitality at which they were frozen. Raw milk when fresh has a value of 6,500, losing 40% of its radiation within twelve hours, and 90% at the end of a full day. Instead of milk, the meal may be washed down with a good red wine, radiating at 4,500. Baked wheat bread rises to 9,000 angstroms.

Next we shall discuss a dietary phenomenon which indicates that patriarchal science is only now catching up to the radiance of the Great Mother's diet, as we have outlined it so far. Incidentally, all figures for angstrom values may be found in Chapter 18, "Dowsing Plants for Health," in Bird and Tompkins' *The Secret Life of Plants*. According to Simoneton, the best source of protein would be shellfish, crabs, oysters, clams, ect., because they are usually eaten raw and vibrate at up to 9,000 angstroms. However, up until now medical science has advised avoiding shellfish because of the high levels of cholesterol which they contain. However, now it has been discovered that four ounces of shellfish contain about half a gram of omega-3 fatty acids which actually lower blood cholesterol.

Here's how it works. Until recently most research had been done on only the omega-6 fatty acids, those which predominate in the poly-unsaturated vegetable oils. However, results just in from tests on volunteers reveal that an omega-3 fish oil, eicosapentaenoic acid (EPA for short) is up to five times more effective at lowering blood cholesterol. And the fish which has the highest amounts of this fatty acid?—salmon. According to figures released by The Center for Science in the Public Interest, Washington, D.C., only four ozs. of canned salmon contain 3.3 grams of omega-3 fatty acids.

Now let us analyze the effect upon the blood of a quarter pounder at MacDonald's, and 4 oz. of shrimp or salmon. In the latter you get only 0.1 to 0.2 grams of saturated fat, whereas the Big Mac will give you 50 times as much, about 11 grams, which eventually will be converted into artery-clogging cholesterol. But whereas the meat source of protein has no side benefits, the 3+ grams of fish oils derived from the salmon meal go to work like a vacuum cleaner in the bloodstream, sweeping up low density lipoproteins (LDL) that carry harmful triglycerides and cholesterol directly into body tissues. Furthermore, the omega-3 fish oils raise the level of high density lipoproteins (HDL) which clear cholesterol from the arteries, carrying it to the liver where it can be excreted.

Heretofore, we had the evidence of the Eskimo and Japanese races who ate large quantities of fish and had a low incidence of heart disease. These races fish the cold marine waters surrounding their islands. But why are the beneficial omega-3 found only in a few species of cold-water fish? The more saturated that an oil is, the faster it solidifies. The old can of lard that grandma kept for cooking was solid at room temperature because it was not poly-unsaturated, as are most cooking oils. However, fish oils are the most unsaturated oils —at least twice as unsaturated as vegetable oils, meaning that they do not harden at even very low temperatures. The effect upon the fish is like an anti-freeze, preventing blood and organs to function normally. Inside the human bloodstream, the omega-3 oils cruise like sentinels of the healthy heart, seeking out and destroying clumps of artery-clogging cholesterol.

EXERCISE

Lastly a brief note on the effect of exercise upon the body. It goes without saying that everyone knows that a muscle that is not strengthened tends to function less efficiently and that goes for the heart also. However, since the tragic death of Jim Fixx, jogging's high priest, those who hate to exercise have made a case for the sedentary life, albeit erroneously. But here are some interesting statistics to consider. In a study made over 12 years on 6,000 men and women with normal blood pressure at the Institute of Aerobics Research in Dallas, Texas, those who were less fit had a 52% greater chance of developing hypertension. Further, it is now definitely known that cholesterol-cleansing HDL's are increased by aerobic exercise. In a study made at Stanford on a group of sedentary men who took up jogging, their HDL levels increased 16% compared to another group that did not run.

Just how exercise increased HDL levels in the blood has been something of a mystery, but an article in *Science Digest*, July 1983, presents some very interesting material.

You surely know that it's healthy to exercise, but you may not know exactly why this is so. Now, a team of Houston scientists have pinpointed a biochemical mechanism that may provide the answer.

According to Josef Patsch of the Baylor College of Medicine, a regimen of vigorous exercise, such as jogging, raises the blood level of a chemical called high-density lipoprotein (HDL). Patsch and his colleagues recently found that people with high HDL are better able to clear fats from their blood than are people whose HDL level is low. This cleansing ability is important because a buildup in arterial walls of a fat called cholesterol reduces the supply of blood to the heart, increasing the chance of developing coronary heart disease.

What's the source of HDL and what does it do in the blood?

One theory goes as follows: A couple of hours after a meal, chylomicrons—particles made up of various fats, including cholesterol—appear in the blood. An enzyme, also in the blood, partially digests the core of these particles, leaving a remnant that is carried to the liver for further digestion. It is thought that, as a result of the exzyme's action, certain components are freed from the surface of the chylomicrons; these combine with another blood chemical to make HDL. Whether the HDL then scavenges cholesterol from arterial walls or simply serves as an indicator that fat is being broken down is not known.

In addition, it's not clear how exercise increases the HDL. But Patsch's research shows that the effect is short-lived. If a person becomes less physically active, his HDL level will return, within three to four weeks, to what it was before exercising.

Says Patsch, "It takes several months to increase the HDL level but only a short time to lower it. So exercise," he says, "should not be used as a handy medication, to be taken only when needed. It should be a lifelong habit."

Just before we are to go to press with this book, some new information has arrived in the mail with the September, 1985 issue of *Science Digest*, a magazine which I recommend for the variety of its interesting articles:

> Remarkable findings have resulted from studies of maximal oxygen consumption (*VO2max*), also called aerobic capacity—the body's ability to utilize oxygen. This is the yardstick of fitness most often used by physiologists. Chronological age can be meaningless. Many fit 60-year-olds have higher *VO2 max*'s than do sedentary 20-year-olds... And a sedentary 60-year-old who hasn't reached his potential can improve his *VO2 max* as much as a 20-year-old can.

Says cardiologist and world-famous runner George Sheehan, "We have learned that aging is a myth."

Sheehan is entitled to exaggerate. At 61 he ran a marathon in just over three hours—a personal record and an excellent time for a 30-year-old.

About a seven-minute mile pace. Running one and one-half miles at an eight-minute-mile pace is regarded as aerobic fitness. Dr. Sheehan runs faster for three hours!

VO2 max is typically determined by a treadmill test. As the treadmill speeds up and its slope increases, the subject's inhalation of oxygen and exhalation of carbon dioxide (the by-product of fuel burning) is measured to determine how much oxygen has been processed.

Physiologist Michael Pollock, now the director of cardiac rehabilitation and sports medicine at Universal Services in Houston, conducted research on aging and exercise at Mount Sinai Medical Center in Milwaukee. Twenty-five competitive runners, all over 40, were tested on the treadmill in 1972 and again in 1982 to see how their *VO2 max* had fared. Their average age is now 62. Fourteen of the runners had continued logging the same number of miles but had cut back on speed. They experienced a 10-percent reduction in *VO2 max* in 10 years. The other eleven had maintained the same distance and pace; they experienced no drop. "This finding indicates that if you maintain your training you can significantly retard declines in *VO2 max*," says Pollock.

Interestingly, all twenty-five runners were more fit than the average 20-year-old.

> ... sedentary 60-year-olds can increase their *VO2 max* by more than 30 percent if they follow a 12-month exercise program that includes walking, jogging and cycling.

The scientists are only proving what Sheehan has known for years. "We are masters," he says. "We have time to make our bodies into works of art. I tell my audiences, 'I look inside and I don't see wrinkles or a tired heart. I see an unspent youth.'"[15]

GAIA'S EMANATIONS

There is an area of influence upon us which has been largely overlooked except for a few visionary thinkers such as John Michell, author of *The New View Over Atlantis*, among others. While we may begin begrudgingly to acknowledge cosmic influences from beyond earth, those influences from within earth, Gaia's own emanations, have been neglected. Michell, discussing Guy Underwood's *The Pattern of the Past*:

> In the course of his work he made the remarkable discovery that the entire geographical arrangement of prehistoric Britain coincides with the lines and centres of the subterrean influence. Every stone circle has at its centre a strong source of energy, referred to by Underwood as a blind spring, and the individual standing stones match the paths and spirals of underground streams, cracks or other features associated with intensified magnetism. Underwood distinguishes between three different types of current, one emanating from underground flowing water and two others, aquastats and track lines, whose nature is not altogether certain, but which frequently follow the course of old tracks, linear earthworks, ancient banks and boundaries. The current that runs along these lines is everywhere related to the traces of prehistoric engineering, to lines of standing stones and earth ridges. Its course, therefore has evidently remained constant for thousand of years although, according to Underwood, the direction of its flow varies with the phases of the moon.[17]

Elsewhere in his book, Michell implies that there is a connection between the human body and that of earth. "The occupation of the first man, Adam the gardener, is not without significance, for the formal gardens that surround the temples of the ancient world extended far beyond their apparent boundaries, and in every district the local inhabitants tended their part of the earth according to its astrological character. In the eyes of the philosophers of that time the earth was a living creature and its body, like that of every other creature, had a nervous system within and relating to its magnetic field. The nerve centres of the earth, corresponding on the human body to the acupuncture points of Chinese medicine, were guarded and sanctified by sacred buildings, themselves laid out as microcosms of the cosmic order, the universal body of God."[18]

By now we have begun to see the magnificence of the correspondences between the macrocosm, the microcosm, and humankind on the body of the Mother Goddess, the mesocosm. According to the authors of *The Secret Life of Plants*, bioplasma, common to all living things, is the medium whereby we may communicate with plants and receive the influences of the cosmos.

"... Dr. Anatoli Podshibyakin, a Kiev electro physiologist, had discovered that bioplasma ... instantly reacts to changes on the surface of the sun even though cosmic particles, ejected by the sun, take about two days to reach earth. ... If there is a change in the universe and environment, say the para-psychologists, a resonance is produced in the vital energy of the human body which in turn affects the physical body. It is through his bioplasmic body that para-psychologist, believe a man can be in direct contact with a living plant."[19]

Heretofore, we have discussed Findhorn and the contact there between humankind and the vegetable kingdom. Evidently the emotional climate is the most crucial environmental element for both plants and humankind alike, for the bioplasma reacts to emotions, transmitting invisible signals to the physical bodies of both. Obviously, negative emotions charge the atmosphere in a way that is ultimately injurious to well-being. We have all worked in situations (usually small offices) in which some one there was hostile to us, so that the time spent there was dreaded. Conversely, an atmosphere of friendliness makes us welcome our time at work. So-called "green-thumb" person are not necessarily superior gardeners; more probably they are radiating love and encouragement to their plants.

John Pierrakos, a New York psychiatrist, has done extensive experimental work in the area of emotional climates, particularly by investigating the response of the bio-plasmic body to various emotional stimuli. "The energy field of plants can also be severely affected by disturbed patients," says Pierrakos. "In some experiments with plants conducted in my office with Dr. Wesley Thomas, we found that a chrysanthemum's field contracts markedly when a person shouts at it from a distance of five feet, and loses its blue-azure color, while its pulsation diminishes to one third. In repeated trials, keeping live plants more than two hours daily near the heads of screaming patients (a distance of three feet away), the lower leaves started falling down and the plant withered within three days and died".[20] One wonders, therefore, if the collective anxiety and violence on the planet is not doing as much as chemical pollution to poison Gaia's atmosphere. Recall Dorothy MacLean's remark in the "message from a tree" that trees are like the skin of the earth.

Dr. John Pierrakos' research has further implications for the relation of humankind as a mesocosm between the mineral kingdom's microcosm and Earth's macrocosm. He found that the number of pulsations per minute of the human energy field indicated one's overall vitality and well-being. The higher the frequency, the healthier the individual. Energy flow, or bio-plasma, commences in the area of the navel and moves down toward one leg, then rises in an inverted L towards the opposite shoulder, whereupon it reverses again down the back, the total pattern resembling a figure 8.

"The same kind of energy field observable in humans is seen by Pierrakos macrocosmically over the ocean with miles-high fountains of radiation bursting forth from narrower bands of pulsation below. Since the amount of activity in this earthly aura plotted by Pierrakos against the time of day reveals the lowest ebb just after midnight and the highest shortly following noon [paralleling the human aura], this directly correlates with Rudolf Steiner's account of how the chemical ether is exhaled and inhaled by our planet."[21]

The theory that emotions or mind can influence other living things beyond an individual's body also has been investigated under laboratory conditions by Dr. Bernard Grad of Allan Memorial Institute of Psychiatry at McGill University, Montreal, Canada. Grad worked with a healer named Oscar Estebaney, watering seeds with a solution sealed in vials which Estebaney had held. These seeds sprouted at a rate which was far greater than that of the control seeds given ordinary water. Taking the experiments a step further, Grad utilized both normal and mentally disturbed person. Publishing the results in the *Journal for the Society of Psychical Research*, Grad concluded that negative emotions such as anger, depression, or anxiety, result in impeded plant growth, whereas efforts to infuse the solution with thoughts of well-being or love led to a dramatic fruition of growth. Given these conclusions, we must again relate them to our personal relation to the planet, its vegetable "skin", and the cosmos beyond. In the light of the above information, the "Mysteries" of the Mother Goddess are mysteries no more. The rites, initiations, chants, and dances had a specific purpose, to harmonize the individual with the natural harmony in nature. The Vibrational Theory holds true, as does the discoveries of the impact upon the bioplasmic sheath—vegetable, animal, and human. So patriarchal science has at last supplied the knowledge that is needed to realize that a planet populated by persons of violence, anger, hate, depression, and anxiety is ultimately a doomed planet in the sense that Gaia will not tolerate the continued existence of a species harmful to all her creatures, and to her plants, forests, and the air itself.

This chapter, then, explores the individual's relation to his personal body and to the collective body, Gaia, the Mother Goddess. Just as love and harmony are in order in relation to both, so in our next chapter we shall explore the relation of love in regard to masculine and feminine elements, not only those of the sexes in society, but also those of masculine and feminine archetypes within each psyche.

The following words of Marcel Vogel make a fitting conclusion to our discoveries, "A thought is an act of creation. It is what we are here for, to create, to bring into being ourself by means of thinking. The way a thought can be observed and measured by a simple life form, a plant, shows a wonderful relationship between man and plant. When we love, we release our thought energy and transpose it to the recipient of our love. Our primary responsiblilty is to love."[22]

I am going to close with a poem of homage to the Great Mother, Demeter, or the White Goddess, muse in man when she descends from on high, and personal anima when she ascends to consciousness from below. However she is seen as coming to man, when she comes she is inspirational, and like Demeter, she redeems Eden.
If we recall our discussion of the Eleusinian mystery, when Kore/Persephone was abducted to Hades, Demeter withdrew from the earth the touch of her fertile hand, causing a terrible drought to descend upon the land, withering the green earth. Every woman is potentially the living embodiment of the goddess in the eyes of her lover, and her parting from him is like Demeter's leave-taking from the earth, a withdrawal of the fertile, natural world wherein love resided.

ON PARTING

Take with you the mountain
On which we loved that day.
We were so high the sky cradled us
As we coupled in the blood sun
Of summer, and I did not see
The great, dark bird silently fall
Upon my shadow with murderous beak.
Roll up like blue parchment the sea
We lay so long beside to hear it tell
With sighs the vows of our tongues.
Forget not the moon that knocked
Upon the window pane as we slept,
Each within a separate, deathless dream,
Wrapped in a mummy shroud of moonlight,
Till the moon spilled silver coins
Upon the carpet, and we awakened,
Forsaking all dreams for each other.
And pack up with you a mirror,
Carrying it there like a man frozen in ice,
My reflection, for legends say
That the soul of a man lives therein.
Seeing mine now, mirrored in glass,
I know the man not. The eyes are empty
Of Paradise. Or was it that my eyes
Were alive, lived only in yours?
Unravel the wind and string it
In your bag, and there let it wind
The colors of the yellow West Wind,
The white North, with a snow beard,
The green East, and the maddening
South Wind that lovers die by.
Unravel the wind and string it
Like a lutesong in your bag
Till he come howling out
To dance for you my pain.

And carry with you, finally, in your womb,
Our child, stillborn on the bier of our fears.

CHAPTER VI
EROS

Except for psychopaths, who seem to be immune from caring about others, everyone has known the feeling of having been devastated by love. Greek mythology recognized that not even Zeus could escape his arrows. Commonly he is called Cupid, but I shall use the name of Amor or Eros. He is the son of Aphrodite, goddess of love, a primordial form of the Great Mother because she dwells at the bottom of the sea. When we are "in love", or have "fallen in love", it is like falling into the sea, or the unconscious, because the normal direction given to consciousness by the will and ego has been negated. At such times we are capable of dying or killing for love. Being in love is not the same as loving, which entails a conscious, willful caring for the other person, and regard for their welfare. We love our children, for example, but are never "in love" with them. When someone who is in love is thwarted by the object of his desire, he may begin to passionately hate the other person as easily as he had fallen in love.

When we fall in love, we shoot out an arrow of psychic energy from the quiver of our unconscious. When this energy finds a person worthy of our projection ("worthy of our love"), then the energy flies back to us like one of Eros' arrows and we are zapped. But it is not the quality of the other person who has made us fall in love, but the *quantity* of psychic energy projected by ourselves. We are the cause of our falling in love, and, in a sense, have fallen in love with ourselves. To me, this is the most fascinating area of Jung's psychology, and one which we shall investigate in this chapter, for within it lies the secret pathway to individual harmony, which must come first, and then comes collective harmony between the sexes.

Basically there is not only an outer war between the sexes, but also a personal war of masculine and feminine waging within each one of us. The unconscious archetype of the opposite sex (to consciousness) creates and personifies the personal war of the sexes within each one of us. This inner conflict requires resolution, truce, the alchemical *sacred marriage*, before an individual's outer, social war with the sexes may be resolved harmoniously. Also encompassed in the opposites of conscious and unconscious, are good and evil, light and dark, up and down, hot and cold, etc., which are also represented in our earliest mythology, and as such, are reflections of our psychic development. To be human is to be divided. Other animals do not have this problem. It is the price paid for attaining higher consciousness. The psychic cause for our awareness of the opposites and our sense of separation is the separation of consciousness from the unconscious (which began in Eden).

Jung's visionary intuition was to recognize that alchemy was not a chemical process but an esoteric psychology disguised as such. The secret key to this ancient psychology is that each person has within the psyche a man or woman of the opposite sex. Recognizing the truth in this, Jung gave these figures the collective name of archetype, and individually called them *anima*, for the soul in man, and *animus*, for the spirit in woman. Since they are not obvious to the conscious mind, and can only be observed in dreams or by the affects they have upon our lives, Jung had to posit both a *personal* and a *collective* unconscious for the "place" where they resided in the psyche.

The resolution of opposites is attained in alchemy by a sacred marriage, or, as it was known in Greek, *hierosgamos*, wherein not only masculine and feminine were married, resolved, but also *all* pairs of opposites. This "marriage" produces the gold which Jung termed Selfhood, our divine potential.

If the reader will imagine for a moment a triangle, he or she will have an idea of what I mean by "Triune Consciousness", a third state of consciousness which is the resolution of two previously opposed kinds of consciousness, masculine and feminine, and also conscious and unconscious. Triune consciousness is higher and greater than any form of opposed consciousness because it harmonizes the opposed forces, creating an offspring that is a blend of both. The "third" is like the child of the hierosgamos, a tiny mannikin that appears in the glass retort at the end of the alchemical process. Or he is an androgyne composed of both the masculine and feminine elements of his father and mother, who are King Sol and Queen Luna, sun and moon, apt symbols for both patriarchy and matriarchy.

The ways of bringing about the sacred marriage in our individual lives shall be the main concern of this chapter, and Eros, the god of love, is the key to our attaining that resolution of opposites, as we shall see. Before proceeding, however, I should like to mention the practical result of Triune Consciousness as I see it. It is a higher consciousness because it harmonizes oppositions, but also because it *blends* all opposites, so that one element fertilizes another, and in so doing creativity is born in the mind, a new thought, whereas when the opposed elements were separated, no such thought was possible. If we recall again patriarchal and matriarchal consciousness, and the characteristics of each, we must recognize that each excluded elements from the other which may have had valuable potential. For example, in this book, the point of view is matriarchal, but I utilize the scientific method of patriarchal consciousness to enable my reader to perceive the spiritual superiority of matriarchy. This is the advantage of the printed word, and the modern technology that can make an author's words accessible to the entire world.

If the reader accepts, therefore, my thesis that Triune Consciousness breeds creativity, one may ask how important is creativity to one's life? You may think that its importance is limited to so-called creative people, artists and writers. Certainly in the day-to-day job of the average person there is precious little call for creativity. Unfortunately, that is true. We are on the verge, however, of a new society at the turn of the century in which people will have as much free time as work time during a week. Unions are now pushing for the 30-hour week, and we may see companies increasing productivity by means of six-day weeks in which workers each have three shifts of eight, nine or ten hours, per week; thus, three to work, four "free". What we do with our freedom, however, is crucial to what we become, not only as a nation, but also collectively as the human race.

Even now antennae are sprouting like mushrooms all over the country, offering choices of hundreds of TV channels from orbiting satellites. I think it is significant that as gifted a man as Joseph Campbell does not watch TV. I believe it was Marshall McLuhan who alerted us to the fact that the transmissions from our screens lull us into an alpha brainwave state, so there is a certain perniciousness in sitting idly by while our brains turn to jello.

It must be obvious after reading the last chapter that I advocate aerobic fitness over the sedentary life. But what we do with our time returns us to the importance of creativity. Marcel Vogel has told us, "It is what we are here for, to create, to bring into being ourself by means of thinking". The goal or apex of Triune Consciousness points towards creativity. Naturally we recognize that our lives are more abundant because of creativity, but does it have significance beyond the personal sphere?

I think so. I believe the evolution of human consciousness *depends* upon creativity, and that all consciousness throughout the universe evolves—or perishes—because of creativity. The question is how ? In the last chapter I postulated that matter formed from spirit, "so there was consciousness before there was matter, and not the other way around," according to Seth. (See previous chapter).

If matter is the result, or precipitate of an intangible which we call spirit, then it takes precedence over matter and—most importantly—does not depend on matter. If this thesis is correct, and we have no way of proving or disproving it, then a corollary thesis is probable, that our thoughts are similarly free of dependence upon our brain cells; so that new creative thoughts create new cells in the brain, and these new cells reflect new thoughts. By a synchronous, simultaneous process, new cells are made and new kinds of thinking come into being, whereby we evolve.

EROS AND CREATIVITY

To be creative, you have to like doing what you are doing—care about it—and this is where Eros comes in. An analogy may help us to comprehend the deeper meaning of Eros. Eros, the winged god of love may be omnipresent, everywhere, because of the speedy way his wings enable him to get around. His quiver of arrows and his tiny bow also lend themselves to symbolic analysis, for when they hit the mark they make a connection between the marksman and his target, the object of his arrow. It is this sense of connection which conveys the real meaning of Eros, psychic relatedness. If we recall again my stress on RELATION in regard to the feminine principle, then we may begin to realize the deeper implications of Eros.

On one level, Eros functions as an erotic impulse towards another person. On another it is the caring, nurturing impulse a mother may feel towards her child, a gardener for his prize flowers, or a beekeeper for his bees, or an artisan for his craft. In these cases, the arrows have been shot out of the psyche, and have landed on the objects of their affection. The kind of *caring* which imbues Eros is the essence of the feminine principle, and it is the natural facility of women, according to the Jungian women who have written the books that stimulated my mind. Oddly enough, it is not Eros alone which wrote their books, but the animus, the unconscious archetype which came to realization in conscious, to discrimination, knowing, and to the *meaning* enabling these women to write their books. Their lives and their books are evidence of the hierosgamos, the marriage of conscious and unconscious, masculine and feminine. No male writers on Jung can rival them, and their words have such compelling force in revealing the complicated labyrinth of Jung's psychology because of the added revelance to our own lives which their Eros confers.

In my own case, in writing this chapter for you, the reader, it has been particularly difficult not to slide easily into the masculine facility for knowledge and meaning, conveyed by the word Logos. Some one hundred pages had already been prepared for this chapter alone, comprising the choicest quotes and explications of animus and anima and the nature of the hierosgamos. But this approach does not hit the mark. Instead an intellectual shaft dipped in the magic blood of Eros, given as a gift by my own anima, flies truer and sticks to the mark. Thus, I wish not only to convey concepts, but also to create a special relation with my reader, so that facts and theories are not meaningless, but become *meaningful*.

Eros is not naturally easy to come by in men, and its development is in direct proportion to development of the anima. At the same time, woman must work at developing Logos,and her animus is the guide for that. But before we explore this new area, which is the essence of the hierosgamos, we should pause to contemplate that the great truth of Jung's psychology was that he revealed that for every individual, consciousness requires the creative fertilization in psychic marriage, of the unconscious partner of the opposite sex, the animus in women, and the anima in men.

Since the artistic product is the creative offspring of the marriage of conscious and unconscious, we can see the blend of meaning and caring at work in the painting, the poem, the ceramic work, or the novel. In the field of writing we can clearly see the arrow of Eros, for possibly one in a thousand writers make a living from writing, and yet they go on with it. This is Eros' role in one's life; to make one care enough about something to go on doing it. Eros, therefore, is the essence of the feminine principle. But how has the feminine principle fared in the thousands of years since the first rough picture of the Great Mother was scratched on a cave wall?

According to Esther Harding, author of *Women's Mysteries*, the *feminine* principle is:

> . . . in spite of the feminist movement and the masculization of modern women, the mainspring of women, controlling both her physical life and her inner psychological being.

The same feminine principle, or Eros, functions in man as well as woman. But while in woman her conscious personality is under the guidance of this principle, in man it is not his conscious but his unconscious that is related to Eros. His conscious personality being masculine, is under the masculine rule of Logos. In the unconscious, however, he is given over to the 'other side.' There his soul, which mankind has consistently regarded as feminine, rules. This feminine soul of man is the anima. The nature of his anima, and his relation to her determine the nature of his relations to women and also his own inner relations, to that spiritual realm over which his anima rules.

A discussion of the nature of the feminine principle and the Laws which govern it is of vital importance to both men and women today, for . . .the care and tendence of the life-giving springs, which lie hidden in the depths of nature, have been disregarded. For these sources of spiritual and psychological energy can only be reached, or so the myths and ancient religions say, through a right approach to the feminine essence of nature, whether this functions in inanimate form or in women themselves." [1]

In the religion of the Great Mother, rituals were performed designed to place humankind in proper relation to body, nature, and the divine goddess herself. But this divinity is at once an outer reality (Gaiea) and also an inner psychic component of humankind, best described as Eros. It is because the goddess resides in the psyche of humankind as Eros, that her divinity is so true. That is to say, on an unconscious level there is a compelling need to worship the principles of nature and spiritual harmony which are embodied in Eros. To be in proper relation to the Eros principle signifies that personal weal and woe have been transcended; therefore, a *religious* experience—in the grandest sense—has occurred. For woman, her soul is always involved in the Eros experience, for Eros is the essence of her soul, as we have said. Therefore, a sexual encounter that does not involve her soul, or core of Eros relation, is always a prostitution of love for woman.

To a woman who is true to her basic self, *un*relatedness is the touchstone of abomination. She must never forget that *un*related sexual intercourse much as she may enjoy it, festers in her belly, and that spiritual and intellectual achievements which are destructive of life cause the air which she breathes to stink. These are the the things she must remember and of which she must constantly tell the animus, if he is to guide her aright through the maze of a masculine culture whose walls are lined with precepts. It is only if he knows her truest feelings, feelings upon which she takes her irrevocable stand, that he can be relied upon to throw his light on what is relevant to *her*, relevant to the situation, relevant to the living moment.[2]

. . .but for a woman physical union with the soul apparently ignored makes her acutely unhappy. We all know this. But her distress may I believe be mainly due to her own lack of awareness that no man can truly meet her body without also encountering her soul because, as she is identified with soul, her body and her soul are indivisible.

I think it is indisputable that women recognize their own soul quality the moment they think about the matter, but this brings us back to the part of my talk to which I have already alluded: they cannot really focus upon such a thing to the point of being able to see it and realize its meaning without prior development of thier masculine side, so that the Logos development of a woman is the essential first step towards her becoming really conscious of her own soul images.[3]

In retrospect, when we think about the ecstatic rites invoking the Great Mother, and the ritual sexual intercourse, which involved the entire community in a participation mystique with the soul in nature, it would seem to me that this lingers as a kind of archetypal memory in the unconscious of modern woman, so that she seeks relation with this soul of the Great Mother in every act of intercourse. But unless the man has in turn made connection with his own soul, the anima, the woman is doomed to experience intercourse that 'festers in her belly.'

Too, it is the sense of this other presence which the female invokes in intercourse that causes men to fear the sexual power of the female, and to arouse their hysteria, wherein they see cloven-footed, horned devils copulating with willing witches, psychic recollections, dimly sensed, of the ritual intercourse in the rites of their ancient forebears.

There are, however, in practice today similar rites. I am referring not to the Black Masses of Satanic cults, nor to modern covens, but to the practice known primarily in India as Tantra, a sexual yoga. It is my thesis that Tantra has descended from the rites of the Great Mother, and, therefore, goes back to at least 7,000 B.C., and symbols painted within the Paleolithic caves (c. 20,000 B.C.) have startling correlations to current Tantrik representations. The sexual symbology in alchemy probably has *its* origins in Tantra as well; consequently, parallels abound to the hierosgamos. Tantra is a union of body and divine, matter and spirit, humankind and nature. It is utterly foreign to Western love, because it is so highly conscious unlike Western love, which is involuntary, one 'falls into it.' The devotees love not the personalities of their sexual partners, but the living embodiment of the divine manifest in their partners.

Whereas the Judeo-Christian tradition views nature and body as fallen* since Eden, Tantra begins with very positive assumptions about life and one's relation to nature, body, and sex. Assuming the relation of the divine to humankind to be benefic, else the divine would not have created humankind, Tantra's attitude towards the universe, world, and body is that being good they are fit for enjoyment. Our bodies, being the means for experiencing the joys of this world, are to be enjoyed to the fullest. The life-negating aspect of patriarchy is absent, along with all the accompanying, devastating, psychological effects. Joy need not be postponed to a future life, but experienced *now*. The *now* experience of joy and ecstasy is the experience of the divine. When in God's name did we begin to buy the Big Lie that God could be attained through only the most negative emotions and practices: guilt, sorrow, and mortification of the flesh?!

Since Eros is the key to the hierosgamos, which itself unlocks the barriers to harmony between the sexes, it must be evident that Tantra develops Eros, not only in relation to others, but in the sense of a psychic relatedness to the entire universe. Further, Tantra utilizes the energy of sexual ecstasy to promote greater harmony between the divine and the individual in order that one may experience

---

*Theology: The lapse of mankind into a state of natural or innate sinfulness through the transgression of Adam and Eve.

himself as divine. Hence, also absent is the separation of Creator and creation which pervades the Judeo-Christian tradition, conferring a sense of insignificance, inferiority, and sin. Defenders of the faith would say that I am speaking of the "old days," and that more enlightened attitudes prevail today. That is true, but we are tracing the threads of the inherent guilt that has made us the psychological messes which we are today, and those threads inevitably wind back to Eden and to sexual guilt.

But beyond the disparate attitudes towards the body, Tantra and the Judeo-Christian religion have further contrasts. Ritual use of words is called prayer in the latter, and mantras in Tantra. Prayer invokes God, in seeking blessings and boons from the power of the divine without; however, a Tantrik mantra is designed to set up harmonious vibrations of energy between the individual's subtle—or bioplasmic—body and the surrounding cosmic energy. The field of energy can then be utilized by the Tantrika to activate the divine within. If the subtle body has a parallel in Christianity, it is the soul; yet we are taught that our souls are God's property. Beyond the expression that something may be "good for the soul," there are no practices in the Judeo-Christian religion equivalent to the practices of Tantra that are designed—almost scientifically, one might say—to produce specific effects on the subtle body. Tantra has never required the advanced technology of science in order to photograph or prove the reality of the subtle body, *since the practices of Tantra that involve the subtle body produce proven effects upon the physical body*. Furthermore, the success of Chinese acupuncture further validates the subtle body's effect on the health of the physical body. Tantra would say that the physical body is naturally healthy if the spiritual—or subtle— body is in harmony with the cosmic energies enveloping it.

Most of us are familiar with the *chakras* or energy centers of Kundalini yoga. These *loci* of specific kinds of energy begin at the base of the spine and move to the "crown" of the skull. This energy is thought to be a sleeping serpent that must be awakened in order to activate the energy potential of each center. It is beyond the scope of our chapter to explore Kundalini; however, in Tantra the subtle body contains channels of creative energy which all of the rituals of Tantra are designed to utilize for the pleasure *and spiritual development* of the Tantrika. Indeed, pleasure and spiritual evolution are not thought to be mutually exclusive—as in the Judeo-Christian tradition—but rather one promotes the other.

Again the serpent rears his head, and once more we may reiterate what we said earlier of the serpent consort of the Great Mother in the Near East: that the object of veneration of an earlier religion becomes the object of denigration in the religion which supplants it.

Perhaps, even in the India of 4,000 B.C., those who looked at the heavens saw the same configuration of Goddess, serpent, and tree that were known in the Near East. Tantra also identifies the tree or celestial pole with the human spinal chord, further cementing the concept that the worshiper is at the center of the universe.

The Tantrika who sits down to carry out his ritual and yoga begins by settling himself at the centre of his own world. He first visualizes the earth, with its continents and seas, as an immense plane disc—a mandala—spread out around a collossal central mountain pinnacle, the mythical Mount Meru, which resembles a high peak of the Himalaya. Around this disc he sets out the circling orbits of the planets and the apparently revolving constellations, perhaps visualizing them in the form of anthropomorphic deities. To him, the heavens, which provide our human reckonings of time, are a significant function of the creative faculty in which he shares, and to survey them can lift his mind to a sense of the immensity of what he both worships and is. The Tantrika takes a deep interest in astronomy and astrology, and always studies time-charts of the significant events in his life. Many works of Tantrik art relate to this whole essential first phase of ceremonial, and provide the basis for the Tantrika's visualizations.

In the next phase the Tantrika identifies the inner central column of his spine (called Sushumna) with the axis at the centre of Mount Meru, so that he experiences himself as the centre around which the whole circuit of his world revolves. Cosmos and man are identified.[4]

The icons and images of Tantra (called yantras) are conceived to enable the Tantrika to identify his-or-her self with the divine. Women have a superior role in Tantrik practice because the female principle is part of the divine creative principle, as it is in the biology of life. All yantras are essentially feminine.

Therefore, Tantra focuses its attention and meditation on the female as the most direct approach to the intuition of truth. It uses many female icons, including lotus-flowers, the strange natural form of the coco-de-mer which resembles the female genitals, caves and natural clefts or hollows in stones and trees, downward-pointing triangles, and representations of the female vulva itself.[5]

In our chapter on witches we saw the destructive, sexual anima image which the inquisitors had projected onto their victims. Completely at the opposite pole of anima development, the Tantrika projects a positive image of the Goddess onto his partner, whereby he approaches "the intuition of truth." An individual's projection, whether as witch or goddess, is conditioned and colored by the context of one's religion; therefore, the Judeo-Christian tradition must be held accountable for the negative projection put upon women.

Tantra stands as an enlightened precursor of Jungian psychology in that its practitioners are completely aware of their projections. They are not unconscious, as in the anima possessions of the witch hunters. The Tantrika's awareness of his projection of the image of the Goddess onto the women he encounters in his daily life is possible because of an interesting aspect of Tantrik cosmology. The "subtle snake Kundalini," as Rawson puts it: . ."is each man's own Goddess-world-projecting function."[6]

Tantra holds that our impression that things exist outside ourselves is really the result of an encounter between fields of energy.[7]

But as Tantra's philosophy is never merely abstract, it states even these philosophical propositions [the original creation of the universe, or Genesis, in biblical terms] in terms of human and erotic symbolism which keeps them directly in touch [eros] with human experience. At the summit . . .are the male and female principles, which are called Shiva (male) and Shakti (female energy). The latter has been projected from the former as the first stage of creation. The image is analogous to the dot and downward-pointing triangle of yantra diagrams. The pair are so closely embraced that neither is fully aware of the other as distinct; and Shiva, the principle of self and complete identity dominates. Shakti is said still to 'have her eyes closed,' in total bliss, because she has not awakened to the state of separateness.[8]

It is this sense of oneness that the human Tantrik couple seek in sexual embrace, not only with one another as the resolution of the sexual pairs of opposites, but also a oneness of their subtle bodies and individual consciousnesses with the cosmic energies and harmonies.

In Tantra's cosmology myth, the next phase is an awareness of separation. "The two face each other; but the fact is that this separation, and the separation which follows, are all the work of Shakti, who was projected expressly for this purpose."[9] That is to say, the divine plan is that humans may conceive of themselves as separate from the divine, and also separate as sexes, without the original unity that the myth tells us is our heritage. But for us today, the psychology of C.G.Jung restores our other half, the contrasexual archetype in the unconscious, anima for men, and animus for women, thereby creating the potential for primal wholeness. As we shall see, the life problem is to "awaken" the sleeping partner, and to attain wholeness again by integrating some part at least of the unconscious archetype into consciousness.

In the previous chapter, we discussed male dis-ease with the Great Mother in the form of nature. Now let us move on to two other male dis-eases, *social* dis-ease with women in the outer world, and *psychic* dis-ease with the inner women, the anima. A man's relation to the inner woman determines the nature of his relation to woman in the outer world. At the same time, a woman's relation to her animus determines the quality of her relations with men. This is why the hierosgamos is the key to defusing the war between the sexes, and to restoring harmony on the world scene.

I acknowledge that the previous chapters have provided a wealth of ammunition for feminists, or anyone, for that matter, wishing to perpetuate conflict. This is not the intent of this book. Social harmony is wholly dependent upon individual psychic harmony, of which outer harmony is but a mirror; therefore, the means to attaining it, which this chapter expounds, have ramifications for the future of the the entire planet. Having recognized ecology as the life of our planet, we are addressing our collective consciousness outwardly in attempting to resolve the threats of annihilation posed by a poisoned environment, starvation, and nuclear warfare. On paper at least, we are all united against such threats to human life. On a much deeper level, where psychic realities influence our conduct in an unconscious way, we maintain antagonist positions that obviate the solution of our world problems because we have not realized that they are but mirrors of our individual psychic problems.

The greatest individual challenge to men and women everywhere is the resolution of the warring elements within, the pairs of opposites which are encompassed initially in the grand structure of the psyche, conscious and unconscious. C.G. Jung has gone further than any other 20th century figure in unraveling the mysteries of the psyche by mapping for us the previously unexplored terrain of the unconscius mind. In this respect he is worthy of being called the century's most important thinker.

The threat to ourselves, hanging like a sword of Damocles above the gateway to the 21st century, posed by starvation, a poisoned environment, and nuclear war, does not come from the environment, or Gaia herself, nor from the atom, but from ourselves. We have found the enemy, and he is us, as the saying goes. Which brings us to that other grand pair of opposites, good and evil. Our cause is always good, and anyone who opposes us is evil, it being our nature to always convert the other guy, whether he likes it or not. However, as Jung has said, "There is no cure and no means of improving the world that does not begin with the individual himself."

THE HIEROSGAMOS

The goal of alchemy, the mystical marriage, or *hierosgamos*, is also the goal of Tantra, so we may assume we are on firm ground in comparing them. At the same time, this resolution of opposites is also the goal of Jungian psychoanalysis, of which Selfhood is the end product. A Self is no longer divided by oppositions of conscious and unconscious, male and female, good and evil. And what man or woman in harmony with his own archetype of the opposite sex within can war with men or women without?

We are at an important crossroad in our evolution, as the 20th century nears its end. First of all, in relation to nature, Gaia , the divine woman without, but also in relation to our individual psychological and sociological roles. The role of men in society has remained relatively unchanged since the onset of patriarchy, and men today require drastic changes in the interest of developing their Eros capacity for relation. But an area of major concern involves the questioning of woman's natural aptitude for Eros, and the re-evaluation by feminists of the feminine principle itself. Here let us hear from Ann Belford Ulanov in her excellent book *Receiving Woman*:

> A receiving woman rejects the partial version of herself in the old stereotypes of the female, such as the hausfrau or helpmate; also the new stereotypes—feminist, political activist, career person, and nothing else. A woman receiving all of herself carries within her the conviction that you do not come to yourself either by subtraction or by abstraction. To call feminine only those qualities of compassion and nurture traditionally associated with women omits essential pieces of a woman's reality—power, intellect, aggression. To take away from a woman her vaunted softness and interiority, leaving only capacities for anger and a warrior-like boldness, equally distorts her reality, abstracting and concentrating on one kind of element to define a much larger whole. A receiving woman *would* really receive all of herself, and not settle for less.
>
> Hard-line feminists abstract woman from her own particular life at the dependent, vulnerable core of human being. They attack any image of the female that significantly differs from the male or from the

symbolism that clusters around the masculine mode of being. They reject what they derisively call the "special nature" of women, even labeling their own sisters "soft" feminists as opposed to their preferred "hard" feminism. Soft feminism recognizes differences between the sexes and fights for equal standing for the female in society. Hard feminism repudiates any distinguishing of qualities of woman as a mere perpetuation of stereotyped sexual roles. The unconscious assumption is that sexual differences must translate into sexual discrimination against women. Those who hold this view blame woman's suffering exclusively on the political injustice systemic to society. Any psychological component in the fear of the female and what she represents is ignored as if inquiry into such factors might reveal more than their egos could take.

Stereotypes, old or new, place woman in a passive position, defined by abstract prescriptions, to which she must conform or risk attack by the stereotyping group. Many women are beginning to understand that they can no more be determined in their inmost selves by the old benevolent patriarchy than by the new malevolent sexism. New stereotypes are no less coercive than old ones. No great distance exists between "All real women marry and bear children" and "All real women know that men are sexists and rapists at heart." These opposing views are simply two sides of the same coin. In both, woman is a passive victim determined by forces outside herself that she may resist, but is all but helpless to change. Some feminists take up this position of woman as victim so vigorously that their conviction of woman's capacity for self-determination is belied. It may reflect in displaced form their own psychological struggle with forces within themselves. In this view woman is left angry, wailing even, but stuck where she is, using up all her energies to get free from powers larger than herself.[10]

Beneath the tiers of influence of our parents and the culture around us, there lies, according to Jung, an autonomous a *priori* existence of the unconscious out of which ego functioning emerges. Beneath the animus of a woman's personality there lies a primordial spiritual force that drives us toward articulation of meanings. This considerable force arises from the deep collective layers of a woman's unconscious and can lead her to receive her own Self (for Jung the center of the psyche), which for women often manifests itself in unmistakably female form. We must receive into consciousness this deep impulse toward meaning as the basis for constructing a sense of values in relationships with others.

Any woman whose thought matures will develop a capacity to think for herself—to put together bits and pieces of insight in a disciplined way. This frees her to receive spontaneous intuitions of her point of view from beneath the surface of her life. She comes to connect her lived experience with some conception of its meaning and the spirit that informs it. She thinks with her own authority, rather than as an intellectual groupie who merely copies whatever outside authority declares to be true.[11]

One of the most hilarious satires on intellectual groupies "copying whatever outside authority declares to be true" was Cyra McFadden's *The Serial*, a novel which ran in serial form in Marin County's *Pacific Sun*. Kate Holyrod is a young (35-40) married woman, college-educated, who has just learned that Carol one of her best woman friends, has "come out of the closet," announcing that she is bi-sexual. Kate is to have lunch with Carol, but being totally outer-directed, Kate is so concerned with the statement her clothes will make to Carol that she has been unable to dress for the luncheon. In desperation she finally calls her friend Martha.

"I can't go through with it," Kate told Martha on the phone. "I'm freaking. I can't even dig on what to wear, you know? I've been standing in front of my closet for hours, practically, just sort of staring at my clothes."

"So what's the problem?" Martha asked. "Okay, so you're having lunch with Carol. And Carol's come out. I still can't see why you can't even figure out what to put on your bod."

"Well, I thought if I wore my tap-dancing shorts, Carol might think I was coming on or something. And if I wore my Diane von Furstenberg, she might think I looked establishment and get negative vibes. And then I put on this yellow sundress . . . you know my yellow sundress?"

"Sure," Martha said. "Dynamite."

"I'd forgotten about the neckline," Kate said. "It's terrifically low, you know? I thought Carol might think I was trying to make, like, a statement."

"Kate," Martha said wearily, "why don't you just wear your French jeans? You look terrific in pants. Really."

Kate let out a little cry of alarm. "I can't wear pants," she said. "I don't want Carol to think I'm latent or something."

"Look," Martha said, sighing, "it's quarter to twelve now, right? And you're supposed to meet Carol at Le Bistro at noon. So you're gonna have to get your act together and move on out. Wear your caftan. Carol can't pick up any signals if you're a coupla boy scouts in a pup tent."

"Oh, wow," Kate said. "You're right, you know? You oughta be a therapist or something. I mean, you have these incredible insights."[12]

THE TYRANNY OF THE INNER MALE

Kate is such a divided person that she vacillates between one "thought" and another as to what her friend Carol will think of her. But basically she is not thinking, only parroting animus opinions which agree with the consensus opinions of her peer group. Kate is also losing her feminine facility for eros relation, psychic relatedness. She should be able to tell Carol that as her friend it does not matter that she has come out of the closet. But her feeling function has been usurped by the animus, and her eros falters.

When woman's talent for relation falters, the animus takes over her thinking, supplying "a lot of ready-made opinions which form an unknown, unseen foundation for her mind and are never questioned by the woman herself." [13]

In order to bring the sexes together in harmonious relation, it is first necessary to begin on the individual level, as we have said. Man's problem is with relation, but his anima, the feminine unconscious element, when brought into partial consciousness in the wedding of the hierosgamos, supplies the eros needed for relation. Man needs to come out of his head and into his heart else there cannot be a real relation.

In woman's case, the aptitude for relation is naturally present as the eros essence of the feminine principle. When relations go wrong, when woman goes into her head (coldly, distantly judgmental) when the situation calls for a heartfelt reaction, then the woman has fallen under the tyranny of the inner man.

Permit me now to present the reader with a montage of Jungian women's writings, on the theory that a collection of women's writing on animus opinions is better than one man's opinion.

In The *Inner World of Man*, Frances Wickes has provided us with an excellent exposition of the animus:

> It is necessary, therefore, to study the real nature of the masculine image—the Animus—which appears in women's dreams and which often speaks with the voice of authority, the Jehovah voice. It is only through studying this image that she can see where the final authority for her life is invested—whether she is ruled by an unconscious masculine image or whether, as a conscious woman, she directs her own life, and under that direction develops the values of her masculine side.... For the image of the Animus, like that of the Anima, is built up from within and from without; from without, by any man who influences a woman's life—father, brother, lover, friend, teacher— or from the ideas about men which she may receive from other people, from the mother's attitude, the opinions of women friends, or through stimulation by or identification with the Animus of another woman; from within, by connection with the embryonic masculinity in her psyche, and with the archetypal images in the collective unconscious.
>
> The most obvious form of Animus identification manifests itself, as we have already said, in opinions. An Animus-ridden woman argues, not in order to discover truth, but in order to overcome her adversary. She passionately defends her opinions (the children of her Animus) in the same intensely personal way that a biological woman fights for her children, not because she has considered the merits of the case, but because they are hers. For the negative Animus would rather be right in an argument than in a human relation; and argues for the sake of domination, not for the discovery of truth. So, in herself and others, the Animus-ridden woman destroys the potentials of creative thought.
>
> The opinionated woman may use her opinions to build up a satisfaction with her own limitations. She then takes refuge in generalities. She judges the opportunities that life gives her in accordance with those generalities, and so feels superior in refusing life unless it comes to her in pre-conceived and static form. Also, in her generalized opinions about other people, she judges all acts in accordance with her code, not in their relation to the inner motive and the

life values of a given situation. And so, while she may live adequately enough within the limits which the Animus prescribes, the chances of evolved thinking or feeling are rather slim.

For when the "idea" is pre-conceived and unconscious, it takes on the character of mere opinion. It loses those qualities of differentiation and discrimination which are attributes of directed thought. As unconscious feeling is emotional and undependable, so unconscious thinking is opinionated and generalized. The woman dominated by the Animus tries to fit everything into an arbitrary pattern thus limiting the potentials of life, instead of nurturing them. [14]

In her book *Striving Towards Wholeness*, Jungian analyst Barbara Hannah tells of Jung's experience at a dinner party, which illustrates how the animus forms a woman's mind. Jung sat next to a woman whom he had not met before:

She talked to him unceasingly, airing her views on philosophy, expressing a great deal of knowledge of her subject and mentioning exceedingly abstruse ideas. Then she suddenly stopped and asked him, "How do my ideas strike you?" He asked in reply if she really wanted to know. When she assented eagerly, he said, "You do not think." "Not think!" she exclaimed. "Why, I have been speaking of some really profound ideas." "Quite so," he replied, "but I could have read it all in an encyclopedia." "But that is how my mind works, it all comes into my mind like that, ready-made as it were." "But I should like to hear what *you* think about it all yourself." Deflated, she murmured, "But then I should have to *think* about it!"

It is very hard work for most women (there are, of course, exceptions) to find out what they really think, just as it is difficult for a man to find out what he really feels, because the animus automatically feels for the man. Therefore the first task for a woman—after the personal shadow has been faced—is to deal with her animus opinions. [15]

But in these days, the animus by no means stops short at the woman's mind; he weaves his opinions most disastrously into her own field of relationship. There is certainly a connection here with the fact that women have succeeded in establishing their own economic independence of man and have entered so many professional fields that have heretofore been reserved for men. This, in itself, is a great achievement and a necessary step on woman's way back to her own wholeness, but it has undoubtedly, one hopes only temporarily, complicated her relationship to man. There are far fewer women than there were formerly who find their whole interest in life only through men.

Emma Jung once commented on this situation in a seminar, stressing the fact that women who are completely submissive to their husbands have become very rare. She asked the question: "But where is this complete submission? It is a typical feminine quality." She came to the conclusion that it is now, in very many cases, turned towards the animus. The woman secretly, and usually quite unconsciously, submits to the ruling of her animus, just as she used in days gone by to allow her decisions to be made by her husband. This, of course, has strengthened the power of the animus over her to a most undesirable extent and has made it imperative that she learn to know of his empirical existence. [16]

But before the woman can *know* of his empirical existence, ironically she must have the animus' help, because knowledge, meaning, etc. are qualities of the Logos, which the animus personifies. Basically she is in a psychic bind, requiring the animus' power of discrimination to discern where his opinions leave off and her real thinking begins. According to Jungian analyst Irene de Castillejo:

> For such discrimination needs the help of the animus himself, the very fellow who appears to be causing the trouble. There is only one way that I know of grappling with the difficulty. The woman must use every endeavour to give him all the data she can find. Animus opinions are based on insufficient knowledge of facts: 'the majority is always right', 'where there is a will there is a way', 'psychology is not to be trusted', or any other half truth. So also, in an inner dialogue, what the animus tells her will be a valueless generalization unless she gives him all the facts; above all, the facts of her feelings, their intensity, their object.[17]

To sum up this analysis of the animus by Jungian woman writers, we come to a very odd conclusion, indeed. That is, the most outwardly aggressive women, militant, if you will, the most antagonistic to men *per se* are in reality the most submissive to men, i.e. the collective animus opinions manifesting from the unconscious man within.

This phenomenon is what I deem the tyranny of the male within. It signifies that within the psyche the ruling feminine principle has been overturned, and the masculine unconscious has usurped the conscious feminine autonomy. No one has ever expressed this more dramatically than Esther Harding:

> ... in their endeavor to escape from the dominance of the male, inherent in our patriarchal civilization, women themselves disregarded the effects of their own rhythm and tried to resemble men as closely as possible. Thus they fell once more under the dominance of the male. This time it was not under the male without, that is under men, but under the rule of the male within. They lost touch with their own feminine instinct and began to function consciously, through the masculine qualities of the animus.[18]

When we consider the effects of animus opinions, then we begin to see the devastating role of the animus in disrupting the woman's relations. Unfortunately, animus possessed women have little or no awareness of the effect of their behavior on others. Psychic relatedness, indeed the whole feminine principle, has been sabotaged. This inner tyrant now has her all to himself, because her possessed state exasperates and alienates all who would be close to her. Although her career may prosper, her feminine receptivity has taken a back seat, the rationalization then being, 'one must make sacrifices for a career.' But the sacrifices are her friends and lovers, devoured by the negative animus as surely as human sacrifices upon the altar of Moloch.

A metallic note in a woman's voice or some physical rigidity will announce his presence; it may be a stiffening of the shoulders; a slight twist of the lips or rigidity of the whole body. Words are powerless to remove him. Only action can do—an affectionate gesture, a playful shake or even a cup of tea. [19]

What Irene de Castilljo is indicating is that once Eros has forsaken women, then only Eros from another can bring back the god of relation. Trying to talk a woman out of her animus possessed state is futile because she will "stand by her words." Oftentimes, arguments between lovers are only concluded by the Eros of the bedroom, where words are not necessary, nor can their meaning be mistaken.

The "metallic note" in the voice, or the "physical rigidity" not only announces the animus' presence, but also the departure of the woman's eros, for she is no longer about to *relate* thru conversation, but is primed to defeat through bombast. For Barbara Hanna, "An extreme but very typical example was provided by an aunt of mine who was in the middle of an emotional argument with my father. He said reflectively, ''Well, I think. . . .?' She interrupted: "And I don't agree with you!'" [20]

To further her animus growth, and to develop her thinking, woman needs to avoid collectives, where slogans bounce off the walls like ping pong balls. A woman has as much chance of developing original *thinking* in a "Women's Building" as a man does of developing eros *relatedness* in a whore house.

Woman needs to sit alone with her thoughts or a book, preferably in nature, and reflect upon the ideas she reads or hears expressed by others. She needs to ruminate upon the words, playing them back *through Eros relatedness* against her own individual experience. If she does this, then the animus cannot play her false. And lastly, she must open the natural channel of communication for the unconscious, her dream life. She must attend to the dreams the animus presents, for here consciousness lies down, sleeps, and does homage to the unconscious.

Finally, let us hear from the master himself. In *Two Essays on Analytical Psychology*, C.G.Jung states:

If I were to attempt to put into a nutshell the difference between man and woman in this respect, i.e., what it is that characterizes the animus as opposed to the anima, I could only say this: as the anima produces *moods*, so the animus produces *opinions*, and as the moods of a man issue from a shadowy background, so the opinions of a woman rest on equally unconscious prior assumptions. Animus opinions very often have the character of solid convictions that are not lightly shaken, or of principles whose validity is seemingly unassailable. If we analyze these opinions, we immediately come upon unconscious assumptions whose existence must first be inferred, that is to say, the opinions are apparently conceived *as though* such assumptions existed. But in reality the opinions are not thought out at all; they exist ready made, and they are held so positively and with so much conviction that the woman never has the shadow of a doubt about them.

Like the anima, the animus is a jealous lover. He is adept at putting, in place of the real man, an opinion about him, the exceedingly disputable grounds for which are never submitted to criticism. Animus opinions are invariably collective, and they overide individuals and individual judgments in exactly the same way as the anima thrusts her emotional anticipations and projections between man and wife. If the woman happens to be pretty, these animus opinions have for the man something rather touching and childlike about them, which makes him adopt a benevolent, fatherly, professorial manner. But if the woman does not stir his sentimental side [appeal to his anima] and competence is expected of her rather than appealing helplessness and stupidity, then her animus opinions irritate the man to death, chiefly because they are based on nothing but opinion for opinion's sake, and "everybody has a right to his own opinions." Men can be pretty venemous here, for it is an inescapable fact that the animus always plays up the anima—and *vice versa*, of course—so that all further discussion becomes pointless.

In intellectual women the animus encourages a critical disputatiousness and would-be highbrowism, which, however, consists essentially in harping on some irrelevant weak point and nonsensically making it the main one. Or a perfectly lucid discussion gets tangled up in the most maddening way through the introduction of a quite different and if possible perverse point of view. *Without knowing it, such women are solely intent upon exasperating the man* and are, in consequence, the more completely at the mercy of the animus. "Unfortunately I am always right," one of these creatures once confessed to me.[21] [Italics mine]

HOW TO MARRY THE UNCONSCIOUS ANIMUS

The task, therefore, is for woman to separate herself from her opinions in order to develop her thinking function through more fully developed discrimination. In part she needs to step outside herself in order to obtain objectivity. After the initial step in animus development of analyzing dreams, speaking directly to the animus (particularly before sleep) and asking for a communication, message, or sign; then it would seem to me that by taping some of her more *heated* conversations, in which she is particularly *certain* of her ideas, she would be able to discern in retrospect that the logical underpinnings of her argument were slender indeed. The married woman, who had not pursued further education because of the exigencies of raising a family, might return to classes in later life. And if she is at all interested in developing intellectually so that instead of merely holding opinions she is capable of objective, rational thought about herself and the persons in her life—as well as world issues—then she should select courses that require the discipline of writing a composition in which there is a progressive exposition of idea. Further, at this stage she needs to cultivate friends who can provide intelligent conversation, who will catch her up if she strays into inferior opinionated thinking, for often animus women collect friends who reinforce their own opinions. The marriage of consciousness with the unconscious animus involves a blending of these two opposites, wherein masculine and feminine are wedded, the Eros relatedness of the feminine principle, and the Logos qualities conferred by a more highly conscious animus. Beyond the methods of taping and composition, which I have just delineated, there are other helpful means which enable consciousness to communicate with this unconscious archetype. Here is a good exercise to utilize which does not require the aid of a therapist or counsellor. In order to examine one's opinions, a woman may make a list of the logical steps she followed in order to arrive at her opinion. Often as not she may find herself staring at a blank pad, the reason being that she had not thought out her opinion at all, but that it came to her unbidden, as it were, by the animus.

Or, as an alternate method, she may ask a friend to converse with her as follows: "Please go through the steps you followed to arrive at your opinion." When the woman begins to hedge with phrases such as, "You know," or, "Well, they say," then her friend must respond with, "No, I don't know, you haven't said." The problem is to attempt to discern where collective animus opinions leave off and where creative, *individual* thinking begins.

The most tell-tale clue to an animus possession is the voice in the head, heard commenting in a negative way about the woman's conduct, her relations, or her desire for action, to create, or to go to school. Frequently if the woman has a negative, animus possessed mother, then the animus takes up where the mother leaves off in making self-defeating comments about the woman. In respect to art or writing, the animus voice can effectively stifle any attempts on her part through the words, "What's the point in doing it. It wouldn't be any good anyhow." As I have said before, it does not matter whether the product of creativity has any merit; what counts is the creative process, a necessary step in the marriage of consciousness with the unconscious.

There are those who have erected a wall between conscious and unconscious minds. In order to enable the animus to come through (or the anima, for that matter), I can suggest yet another exercise. Before going to sleep at night, address the animus directly, saying, "I have just read of your presence in my unconscious. Tonight, while I sleep, I shall be grateful to you if you come to me in a dream, which I would like very much to remember in order to learn more about you." Every time a woman has tried this, she has received a significant animus dream. To me this supplies the empirical evidence needed of the validity of Jungian psychology.

Women psychotherapists have learned the value of speaking directly to the animus, not only for their patients, but for themselves as well. The question most often asked is why does he so often behave in such a negative way in invading consciousness?

Barbara Hanna, in a paper on the animus, quoted his answer to this question. He told her that he understood nothing of her world, but that he could not bear a vacuum, so he always slipped in when a vacuum occurred. He told her that he needed to know about our world as much as we needed to know about his, and that it is a woman's business to enlighten him. In my own talks with the animus on this point he has expressed a similar idea, using the particular imagery in which he has shown himself to me. He has explained that he, the torchbearer, is an autonomous spirit whose sole concern is shedding light, focused light, light for its own sake. He has no feelings towards us, neither good nor ill, he has no feelings of any kind. Feeling is a human prerogative. He has no interest in us one way or another except, and this is vitally important, that he needs us for his very existence, for it is only in the human mind that he can dwell. He needs a human being to see the light he sheds. But shed his focusing light he must. To me, this is who he is.[22]

SLEEPING BEAUTY
OR
'WAKE ME UP, BABY'

On March 24, 1974, at the University of California Medical in San Francisco, I gave a seminar with Joseph Campbell entitled "Mythology Actualizes Reality." The theme of the seminar was that one's individual myth or myths brought to pass the events in his-or-her life through one's belief system. Therefore, it was highly necessary to scrutinize the myth in order to become aware of our own hand in so-called outer events.

During that day I passed out 3x5 cards and asked the participants to name their favorite fairytale. My suspicions were confirmed. Ninety percent of the women over 40 named "Sleeping Beauty."

Let us examine the significant elements in the tale of "Sleeping Beauty." Her salvation comes from without, having no role whatsoever in deciding her own fate. Absolutely nothing she can do will free her from the enchantment. Her fate is in the hands of the Prince.

This tale has a close parallel to the collective myth foisted upon women by society. When I say "society," we must realize that it consists of men *and* women; therefore, there has been an unconscious acquiesence on the part of women. Why? The answer lies in the nature and role of the animus in a woman's life. Before we answer this, the collective myth of Sleeping Beauty is worth attention. Until marriage woman is in a kind of limbo or so the myth goes. Let us hear from one of the women in the seminar, a Southern "belle." "Particularly in the South, where I was brought up, we were taught that a man would make us happy. So all any girl ever thought about was *when* she would get married. We were all in a a state of *waiting* for a man to fulfill our lives."

This presents the Sleeping Beauty myth projected onto collective society, and as such it epitomizes abject passivity, helplessness, and utter dependency.

"My father said, 'What good does it do to send you to college? You'll only get married when you get out of college anyhow.'"

The education of the female is to be undertaken only if—horrors!—a career is contemplated. Those who might fall into the "career-girl" category did so frequently because they were not "good prospects" for marriage because of "looks." A father who had such a girl "on his hands" might then undertake her education as an investment to "get her off his hands." Was it really assumed that women were intellectually inferior? As a matter of fact, in the grade school and high-school levels, women are better students.

Why then the reluctance to educate the female? In the collective myth of

Sleeping Beauty, women fulfilled the passive roles set for them as intellectual inferiors, hence, the less education the better.

Obviously the collective myth of Sleeping Beauty was believed by most women; otherwise, it would not have been accepted. At its core lies the assumption, by men and women, that a woman's life is fulfilled by a man. Oddly enough, this is true, but not in the way that society assumes. Paraphrased, we may say, a woman is *completed* by a man, the corollary being true as well.

Before I lose most of my militant readers, let me say that the man who completes a woman's life is not a flesh and blood man, but the animus. This brings us now to the acquiesence of women in the collective myth of Sleeping Beauty. An interesting process is involved in the awakening of a higher consciousness and awareness in the female psyche. The masculine archetype, the animus, may be thought of as sleeping, since he resides in the *unconscious*. As a Jungian therapist has told us, "it is a woman's business to enlighten him." However, the unconscious is conscious, but not in a way that is readily accessible to the conscious mind.

We are presented, therefore, with an image of a Sleeping Prince, residing in the feminine psyche. In part, woman's life quest will be to discover him and "kiss" him awake, that is, bring him into partial awareness in the conscious mind. Why? Because he is the carrier of components that are not naturally hers, but which can be with his help; hence the idea of completion. All this is just as true for a man, the unconscious feminine archetype supplying him with the factors he requires for achieving totality. The fairytales "The Frog Prince" and "Beauty and the Beast" complement our investigation of Sleeping Beauty, for they tell us about the animus. In both "The Frog Prince" and "Beauty and the Beast", the animus is represented by figures repugnant to feminine consciousness. The hateful *appearance* of frog and beast represents the unevolved level of the animus within the psyche. In other words, he is a low creature because he has remained undeveloped; and he is hateful, and often dangerous, because consciousness has rejected and refused to recognize him, just like the witches of men's negative anima projections.

As Sleeping Beauty was enchanted by unconsciousness, so beast and frog are under enchantments. The spell is broken by relationship, Beauty's compassion for the dying Beast, and the Princess' kiss. The transformation is instantaneous, the Instant Prince being a motif of fairytales. (What modern society could really use is a prepackaged Instant Prince who could be dropped into water and instantly materialized.)

At any rate, the same transformation of the animus commences when recognition and attention are directed towards the archetype, although the Prince, as in "Sleeping Beauty," may not appear for many years. At that stage in the woman's development, the actual appearance of a flesh and blood mate is not all that important anymore, simply because she has made the inner marriage with the masculine component, and her life *has* been fulfilled by the gifts of new consciousness which he has given her.

She is now active, where she had been passive; she is independent, where she had been dependent; and she is whole, where she had been half.

She needs no man, and needing none can give herself, whereas in desperation of need, no one can freely give of themselves.

Now a paradox appears. The natural endeavor of woman lies in the arena of relationship. But as her intellectual and creative powers come to the fore through enhancement by the animus, her new personal autonomy liberates her in her personal relationships. She now is more free. By this I do not mean that she is more promiscuous, although that choice is hers as well. Let us say, she is now easier. Relaxation comes to mind, but also grace. Her relations are stylish. Her choices in men are stylish. They must be her intellectual and creative equals. Her life is lived with a flair.

She has a secret which preserves her if her romances turn rocky. She knows that her beloved is always with her, that he and she cannot be separated, for they have consummated the marriage of conscious and unconscious. Left to herself, she embraces solitude as abundantly creative, the time of communion with "her man," the animus. He is also her best friend, as a lover should be. Also she can "talk" to him.

Let us return to our Southern Belle, who waited like others of her era for a man to make her happy. Her biography is as follows: Her father was a strict disciplinarian, her mother a martyr. A *man came into her life* who shared her love of dancing, and she married him. My italics stress this phrase because it demonstrates The Sleeping Beauty syndrome. One must wait for the Prince to come. The alternate, highly conscious way of viewing the Prince's appearance is that he will appear (in so- called real life) after he has been actualized from the so-called unconscious plane. In a way of speaking, he is her creation.

At all events, our Belle marries her suitor, but a pall comes over the marriage. He refuses to take her dancing and begins to manifest the repressive, authoritarian qualities of the father, whom she sought to escape by marrying her husband. What's happening is a lesson in the way in which the "unconscious" (so-called) archetype dictates behavior to masculine partners. Naturally the woman's animus had been conditioned—in part—by the father's repressive personality. The unconscious messages were conveyed to the husband, and he began to act in the mold of the animus.

As the years wore on—twenty, in fact—it became impossible to tell the difference between father, husband, and animus. The briars had grown up to close like a trap. Where was the Prince now? Still asleep, of course. But Belle was lost in her own dream of Sleeping Beauty.

As anyone knows who reads fairytales, something has to happen to break the enchantment. In this case, deliverance comes through a Jungian analyst, who starts hacking his way through the thickets of enchantment.

The woman soon gets a divorce, and the husband moves into a government (service connected) retirement home, where his meals are cooked and served on time, the dishes promptly disposed of, the beds made, his clothes cleaned and pressed (No more ring around the collar!), and his every need catered to. There we get a glimpse of the husband's myth—Mama. Army, Navy, or Marines as Big Mother ! But I don't want to dwell on the husband's problem, since this is his wife's story. At any rate, our Belle is beginning to live at last, and her animus is coming out of his long hibernation. A final, funny note to our happy ending. Belle receives a letter from her ex. He's hooked up again with some old service cronies, and they are going out to dance halls. He adds that he had forgotten how much he enjoyed dancing. Remembering all the times she had tried to revive the memory of their first year of marriage, Belle has a good laugh.

The ironical import of the "Sleeping Beauty" tale is that the Prince, as animus, is asleep in the unconscious until awakened (or enlightened) by the woman's consciousness. Thus effort, not passivity, is required on the part of the woman.

ANIMA EFFECTS ON MEN

When we spoke of the way in which positive animus development could endow the woman's life with a new purpose and meaning, and confer upon her thinking, objectivity, reflection, and logical, sequential conclusions, it may have seemed to the reader that I was implying that these qualities were characteristic of men. But men are as often anima possessed as women are animus possessed. What are the tell-tale signs?

Certain men, however, seem to be dependent, almost like women, on the changes of their inner feelings. A curious inversion of the masculine and feminine parts of the psyche has taken place in such men. The rational, Logos, functions have been relegated to the background, while the feminine part of the psyche, which is usually concealed, comes to the fore and forces their changing moods into undue prominence. This change results from domination by the anima, the feminine spirit in man, which, however, should not rule the conscious but the unconscious. Consequently the domination by the feminine spirit has a peculiarly unpleasant quality. For such men are not ruled by changes in the nonpersonal Eros, but by moods and whims which have as their chief characteristic that they are exceedingly personal. Domination by the anima produces a curious womanish quality, a dependence on personal likes and dislikes, on moods and feeling tones to the exclusion of all capacity to react with adequate feeling in accordance with any judgment of fact or the validity of an impersonal truth. This situation is a travesty of the woman's submission to her inner law of change.[23]

In *Contributions to Analytical Psychology*, Jung defines the anima. "Every man carries within himself an eternal image of woman, not the image of this or that definite woman but rather a definite feminine image. This image is fundamentally an unconscious hereditary factor of primordial origin and is engraved on the living system of man."[2]

A man's life is even more dependent on woman than is woman's life upon man, as we have seen from our study of matriarchy. Without mother to nurse and protect, infant man perishes. In nature we witness in all the species the same protection of the young, often even from the father who seeks to devour his own offspring. Frances Wickes tells us:

> Man's nature is attuned to woman. He presupposes her existence in his life as mother, sister, early love, wife, inspiration—and also as problem.
>
> Inborn in his nature is another woman—the feminine side of his

own psyche—who, from the beginning, brings him intuitions of things beyond masculine ken. She too moves in him in intuitive perceptions of feeling situations, in mood and in creative inspiration.[25]

The man's own growth and transformation depends directly upon the development of the woman within. His completion as a human being cannot happen unless the anima develops. The ego's growth, and the transformation of the conscious mind, do not happen first, followed by anima development. Rather, the anima evolves, with the consent of consciousness, subsequently bringing about a new relation of conscious and unconscious, out of which a new *totality* is born, whereby one has been irrevocably changed.

Like an embryo stirring in the womb, the anima moves in the unconscious, indicating by mood and dream her presence to consciousness. She is the High Priestess of eros relation; hence she comes to instruct about relation.

The anima is a personification of all feminine psychological tendencies in a man's psyche, such as vague feelings and moods, prophetic hunches, receptiveness to the irrational, *capacity for personal love, feeling for nature*, and—last but not least--his relation to the unconscious. It is no mere chance that in olden times priestesses (like the Greek Sibyl) were used to fathom the divine will and to make connection with the gods. . . .The anima (the female element in a male psyche) is often personified as a witch or a priestess-- women who have links with "forces of darkness" and "the spirit world." [26]

As with the animus, the anima archetype is generally classified according to four levels of meaning, and her development is indicated by progressively higher levels, indicating the upward tendency of an unconscious archetype's desire for light/consciousness. In order to determine the level of a man's attraction for a particular woman, and the commensurate level of his own anima development, I have found that the four levels may be equated with the human body. In the accompanying drawing, a line is drawn across the figure's navel, indicating that on the first or primary level of attraction, the focus is below the navel, centered on the sexual organs. The man craves a sexual relation with the woman. This is not bad of itself, because anima and animus development usually proceed consecutively through the four levels. Something of value is conferred at each level. If we put down the erotic impulse of a purely sexual attraction to woman, we risk comparison to the Church monastics whose repressions culminated in the witch hysteria. Too, a purely sexual attraction is entirely natural. *Initially* there is nothing wrong in a man or woman looking upon another as a sex object.

Psychic problems occur when the anima—and the man—do not develop further. If a man has not experienced an erotic attraction to the female, it is doubtful to me that he shall one day evolve to the wisdom of Sophia at the highest or fourth level. His "wisdom" would not encompass the Goddess' beauty, and therefore, would have a hollow ring.

Biologically and temporarally we tend as a species to move through four stages equivalent to the levels of the anima, which apply equally to the animus, of course. At puberty our sexual drives are strongest, so the first level may be associated with one's early years, the teens, and perhaps the twenties.

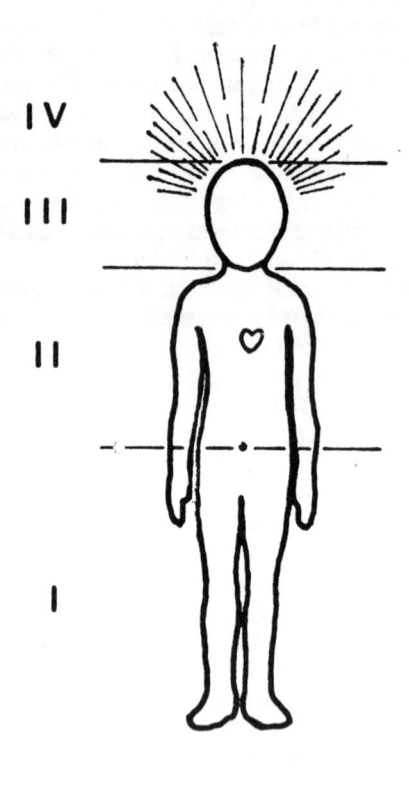

Figure 8

In my book *Tales for Jung Folk*, I present a primer for the four levels:[27]

1) The animus/a appear as seductive sexual figures, or as objects or animals to which the dreamer finds himself attracted. Often the figure arousing the dreamer is elusive, but just as often some sort of sexual relation is consummated. Now on this primary level, sexual release is all that is sought. Yet such dreams beyond puberty and the teen years, may indicate that the dreamer views the opposite sex as sex objects, serving the purpose of sexual release, but with whom there is no real relation as *persons*.

2) The second level contains much of the sexual attraction of the first level, but now love comes into the picture, and with it caring, for now such dreams reveal the psyche's desire for its other half, completion through relation. Animus/a dreams of Mr. or Miss Right have a profound effect when recalled upon awakening. One is still in love, but with whom one knows not as the dream vision begins to vanish in the light of day. And when we fall in love, life becomes like a dream vision, the world illumined by enchantment. Such dreams indicate that the

dreamer seeks fulfillment not from within, in the realm of the Self, but from another person without; hence such longing is usually doomed.

Here I must interrupt myself to comment that a man may be fixated by a woman's breasts, as is so often the case in our *Playboy* culture. Personally I have not found that large-breasted women are the best of lovers; however, I do not interrupt myself here in order to stroll down Mammary Lane. My point for the man with the breast fixation is that even though his attraction is focused above the waist, it does qualify him for the second level of anima development.

3) Continual failure and disenchantment may lead to a partial centering in the psyche, which may end the period of waiting for another to set the life right. Thereupon, one may begin to dream of men or women who *inspire*, releasing creative energies which the psyche had squandered earlier upon sexual relations. The man's muse or the woman's teacher may reconnect the conscious mind to unconscious sources that begin to fulfill the Self's urgings toward higher development.

I should add here that as the fires of "being in love" begin to burn down with age, one begins to move more towards conscious loving. In other words, love becomes more conscious in the man or woman because of the increasing consciousness of animus and anima. Any successful marriage will evolve from first level eroticism, to second level caring, and thence to a relation in which each one stimulates the other, so that they cherish one another's company. This third level corresponds with the head because words, ideas, and intangibles inspire and accelerate change and growth.

Disenchantment, however, is not a necessary prerequisite for consciousness to proceed to the third level as a result of the corallary animus/a development. Sometimes one leaves behind the previous levels in changing partners, but most often the current level should *incorporate* the previous levels. Thus, the old married couple can have a jolly good sex life (1st), still be 'in love' romantically (2nd), but also cross-pollinate one another on a daily basis. For example, the wife may be trying her hand at writing a novel, with daily feedback from the husband, while he has taken up weaving intricate designs into throw rugs, as my father did in his retirement. Here we see traditional roles reversed, signifying not only that the couple help one another, but also that the animus' marriage with consciousness is promoting the woman's creative growth through writing, while the anima also stimulates the husband's creative growth through eros relation to fabric, texture, design, and patient completion at the loom. Women who write and men who weave? Why not. Any offspring of the sacred marriage is possible.

I am put in mind also of the creative way in which my father worked with Gaia. Hybridizing new varieties of roses, Copper Lustre and Vanity Fair, he knew Gaia's inspirations. But more basically, while pushing a wheelbarrow of horse manure one has one's nose pushed, so to speak, in the recognition that the inspirations of nature must be fertilized by hard work. Laboring at her typewriter to bring to birth the Great American Novel, the wife in my previous ancedote might add, "Ain't it the truth!"

4) The final stage of animus or anima development, although rarely attained, confers *wisdom*, a knowledge of personal relation to our world and universe, and our own unique place in the scheme of things. And, ultimately, this level is the end of projection, for whatever guru we may have instructing us now warns that the projection is to be fully withdrawn, that the divinity we see in them is to be found in none other than ourself. Thus animus and anima guard the last threshold to Selfhood, for until we have passed this portal we cannot find divinity within, individuation, or total integration of consciousness and unconscious archetypes. As long as this crucial archetype is projected, like Sleeping Beauty we await rescue from without. But oddly enough, when we have found our purpose in life, are deep in creative endeavors, and aware of our particular relation to the world, then Fate (aha ourselves!) brings along Mr. or Miss Right just when we no longer need them. Not needing their love, we can give our own in an unconditional way, thereby insuring the success of our relation with them, although unable, perhaps, to resist a final question: "Where were you when I needed you.?!"

Significantly, the fourth level of animus/a development transcends the body, indicating that a flesh and blood person is no longer the object of our projection. Generally, too, when one attains this level of consciousness one recognizes the nature of projections and how they have functioned previously in the life.

The fourth level remains more a potential than a map of actuality, for few attain its lofty heights. In *Man and His Symbols* von Franz tells us:

Finally, in his fourth manifestation, the animus is the incarnation of *meaning*. On this highest level he becomes (like the anima) a mediator of the religious experience whereby life acquires new meaning. He gives the woman spiritual firmness, an invisible inner support that compensates for her outer softness. The animus in his most developed form sometimes connects the woman's mind with the spiritual evolution of her age, and can thereby make her even more receptive than a man to new creative ideas. It is for this reason that in earlier times women were used by many nations as diviners and seers. The creative boldness of their positive animus at times expresses thoughts and ideas that stimulate men to new enterprises.[28]

ANIMUS/A IN FILMS

When it comes to seeing the effects of animus/a in action, no where is there more fun than at the movies. Here we can experience love and loss without coming away with the permanent scars that usually go with the experience in 'true' life. But the movies often become truer than life in presenting textbook studies of the havoc wreaked by animus and anima. For years *Wuthering Heights* has been cited as a study of Emily Bronte's own anima. When it was made into a film with Sir Lawrence Olivier, the animus qualities of Heathcliff became ever more apparent. For readers who may be interested, Barbara Hanna has analyzed the novel in *Journey Toward Wholeness*.

My own favorite film on the animus is a French film, "The Story of Adele H." Perhaps it is the truth of its accurate depiction of the animus that makes it such a fine film, or perhaps it is the portrayal of its star Isabelle Adjani. To me she is without doubt the finest actress in the world today, and I say that with full awareness that she is a second and third level anima projection for me. And as to last year's (1984's) best film being "Amadeus," I invite my readers to catch her act in "One Deadly Summer," my idea of last year's best film. This was also a French film, so you may not get a chance to see it again unless you live in one of the larger American cities.

In "The Story of Adele H," Adjani plays the daughter of Victor Hugo, France's most prolific and popular author of the 19th century. Hugo's olympian influence has had a profound effect in forming her animus along the guide lines of the 3rd level animus. When she becomes animus possessed in her love affair, the animus manifests in her feverish *writing*, not creative, but in the form of letters and notes to her lover.

The most moving film ever made on the anima, in my opinion, is Albicocco's "Le Grand Meaulnes," or in its sub-titled English version, "The Wanderer." The film first came out in the mid- 1960's, but I have been lucky to catch it at little theatres in London the last two times I visited there. The film is based upon the novel of Alain-Fournier, killed at St. Remy, France, during the First World War, at the age of 28. No other film captures as eloquently the poetic, dreamlike quality of the love experience. Albicocco used special lenses that made the moments at the lost chateau diffuse, as if under water, or occurring in the unconscious. I also think it is the best film ever made, but that is only personal preference.

As my readers become more proficient in comprehending animus/a, evidence of the effect of these archetypes will be more apparent, not only in their own lives, and in the lives of their friends, but also in works of art such as film or plays. The 1950's film version of the opera "The Tales of Hoffman" lends itself to analysis because all four levels of the anima are presented in the four women Hoffman seeks and loses. Hoffman is a poet, and as the film commences, he is entertaining university students with the "tale of his three loves." He has sent a handkerchief to his current amorata, embroidered with the words, "I love thee. Hoffman." She is a ballerina performing in a nearby hall that very night, but his gift and message is intercepted by a man, portrayed by the actor Robert Helpmenn, who is his antagonist in each of the other three tales. As the students in the rathskeller settle about him with pipes and steins he begins the first tale.

On the lowest anima level, woman may be but a flesh and blood Barbi Doll to be undressed by the man to give him sexual release without challenge or the complication of relation. By the guile of a maker of magical spectacles, and a cleverly automated life- size doll, Hoffman falls in love with the goddess as doll. His anima projection is shattered only when the doll runs out of control, breaks, and the head comes off.

The second level of the anima is demonstrated in Hoffman's affair with Guiletta, a beautiful Venetian courtesan. Here sexual desire is transformed by love, and Hoffman loses his soul to her, which is symbolized in the film by the loss of his reflection as he views himself in a mirror.

Art and inspiration are present in Hoffman's third affair, with an opera singer, Antonia, who must never sing again or risk death, due to some exotic illness. Here the statue of her mother comes to life and begins singing; Antonia joins her in a deathly duet and dies.

When Hoffman has finished his last tale, his new love enters accompanied by his antagonist. Her name, Olympia, suggests the divine heights to which the anima can transport the creative artist.

Now quite drunk, Hoffman appears unfit to her, and she leaves wrapped in the black cape of his shadowy antagonist. But as Hoffman stares into the middle distance, one is aware that these tales he has told comprise his art, his work, and that in a sense he has transcended anima projection and found a personal harmony with an inner anima of inspiration which has given him the "Tales of Hoffman."

At one point, Hoffman sings of "three souls in one soul." We recall that the word "anima" means soul in Latin; hence the anima is the the "soul of man," or "the soul *in* man." Also he sings of the one face which is always before him, which signifies his anima quest.

I had a close friend whose entire life was an anima quest. During a period of his life when he was a college professor, his life bore a close parallel to the 1930's film "The Blue Angel," starring Marlene Dietrich and Emil Jannings. As the film begins a Herr Professor type is ruling his class with an iron hand of severe discipline and cold intellectuality. But the order of this all-male world is disrupted by an erotic postcard of Lola Lola, a cabaret singer. And my parallel story involves a man who has the highest gradepoint average in his college class, and now finds his pursuit of a higher degree disrupted by an unrequited love. He has only a few more weeks of study to endure in order to procure his M.A. degree, but so smitten is he that he loses all initiative and becomes totally passive and depressed, because his love is not returned. He lies on his bed, staring at the ceiling, refusing to eat or go out.

Our Herr Professor visits the club of Lola Lola. Never having permitted the Eros element to enter into his life, and totally buffered against the irrationality of the unconscious, he is easy prey for Lola Lola. He is made a clown in her travelling show, and his subsequent life is progressive—and appropriate—degradation.

In the parallel tale, the young man is unfit to take his final exams, and through the grace of his professor is granted "incompletes." The incompletes have a symbolical value, for his own psyche was incomplete without the anima development.

Because the young man had such a brilliant record, he is given a fellowship to teach at another university, where he will be a Ph.D. candidate. But there he falls in love with one of his Freshman students, and ceases all scholarly work towards his doctorate. The sad tale ends with neither M.A. nor Ph.D. completed, and his being washed-out of university life. Eventually, all at sea, he goes to sea, (as a merchant seaman), becomes an alcoholic, and dies in middle age.

We cannot say women killed him, but certainly his negative relation with his anima destroyed him as certainly as the drink. If the animus signifies meaning, the anima signifies an image. Men who are alcoholics or drug addicts are very often obsessed with the elusive dream image. The real world is too harsh for them.

As a final note on films, I originally prepared an entire chapter on "The Wicker Man," which came out in 1979, I believe. Suppose a group of persons had persisted in worshipping the Great Mother even unto the present. What sort of confrontation could we expect if patriarchy discovered them? This is the theme of the film, and it is extemely well-executed.

Edward Woodward stars as the virgin "Christian copper," whose foil is Christopher Lee, Lord Summerisle. Woodward is better known for his role in "Breaker Morant," but I rank him as the world's best actor.

Regretfully I had to drop the chapter on "The Wicker Man," but the reader who cannot see the film (some VCR rentals stock it) may be interested in reading the novel of the same name on which it is based.

Yet another director who deals with the anima projection is Bill Forsyth, particularly in his films "Gregory's Girl" and "Local Hero." Again, these films—like "The Wicker Man"—require more time than we can devote to them here, so I shall say no more than, "Go see them!"

DEPRESSION AND THE ANIMUS

What could be more unpopular in an age of sexual equality than to insist that the psychological differences between men and women are as fundamental as their physical ones? Science writer Maggie Scarf, however, wonders what else could explain some lopsided statistics: for every man suffering from depression, there are two to six times as many women. Scarf studied case histories, observed women under treatment in psychiatric clinics and interviewed scores of others in her search for an answer. Now, in a powerful and disturbing book called "Unfinished Business:Pressure Points in the Lives of Women," she announces a conclusion that has aroused the ire of feminists—but may evoke the shock of recognition from many other women.

Scarf's thesis is that women are vulnerable to depression because emotional attachments are much more important to them than men. In many cases, she says, women define themselves almost exclusively by their relationships to others. When these bonds break—through death, divorce, or children leaving home—they often suffer depression. Some say they would rather kill themselves than live alone.

The *Newsweek* article goes on to delineate the reasons for the greater importance of attachments in women's lives to emotional bonding in female babies, a trait that evolved as part of female biology from primate behavior, and "eventually found its way into the female genetic code."

These apparent differences raise a troubling possibility: that emotional bonding, once a key to survival, is making women's lives more difficult in today's feminist era. Women are caught between the demands of their genes, urging them toward marriage and family, and a society sending them powerful new signals to be independent. While Scarf also admits that men also suffer from depression, she says that the condition is usually triggered by failure in their profession, not in their personal relationships. It might seem logical that women who follow men into the marketplace would be less vulnerable to depression. Not so, says Scarf. The working women she studied were just as depressed as those who stayed at home, reinforcing her unsettling conviction that mood is a function of biology.

Here we must raise again the chicken or egg question: which came first, the biology or the psychic causes ? If we say the latter, as I believe, then the primitive emotional bonding by infant primates to keep their mothers close by was *psychic* in origin, and the depressive moods of modern women have a cause in the animus archetype, as we shall see later in this chapter after we have demonstrated the four levels of development of the animus and anima in women and men with specific reference to their effects. Characteristically, depression is a dead giveaway to animus repression/possession, just as a plague of witches is an indication of anima repression/possession in the lives of men.

"I freaked out when I started interviewing people and it was coming out this way," says Scarf. "I said I can't write this because people are going to see it as a sexist statement." . . . And in every case, she says, the root of depression was the disruption of crucial attachments. . . . Bonds: Scarf concluded that a woman's depression is related to specific phases of her life. At key points, all women must make and break a series of emotional bonds. If they fail to do so, if they become emotionally stranded, their 'unfinished business'' almost inevitably leads to depression. The adolescent girls Scarf interviewed were concerned about separating from their parents. Women in their 20s focused on balancing the desire for a family with the demands of a career. And at mid-life, women had to confront the loss of their roles as wives and mothers. Contrary to Scarf's expectations, she discovered that menopause is more an emotional issue than a hormomal one. "I thought I would find menopausal depression keyed to hormone loss," she admitted. "But that was the one thing I didn't find." In fact, says Scarf, women in their early 30s suffer far more depression than those going through menopause.[29]

To a Jungian analyst reading the article, the animus related causes of depression are mainfest; however, nary a Jungian term creeps into the article. Women are ruled by the Eros principle, psychic relatedness; therefore, attachments are ruled by Eros, the mysterious force which attracts human beings to each other,or as unaccountably drives them apart. The masculine principle rules work and achievement; hence, it is thoroughly predictable, according to the Jungian model, that depression in men "is usually triggered by failure in their profession,"as Scarf tells us. When a relation ends for a woman, whatever the causes, she is thrown back upon herself and becomes depressed because she has no longer any sense of value or self-importance in her own eyes, and because she sees no way out unless or until she finds a new relation, wherein her natural facility lies.

This is why Jungian psychology becomes so important in understanding and treating depression, not externally with drugs, but by initiating a new relation with the man in the unconscious. The necessary quality which the animus can bestow to abate the depression is conscious objectivity about the woman herself and her relations, so that she can end them rather than clinging to them hopelessly when they do not suit her needs or fulfill her. This objectivity is no more nor less than the ability to take a step back, as it were, to be able to appraise a situation or person without being swept away.

Furthermore, if we examine the biographies of particularly creative women, when asked if depression ever plagued them, they respond with remarks such as, "I had no time to be depressed," and "I was too busy creating." Creativity, then, is its own antidote to depression; yet one rarely if ever creates while depressed, so the pattern should be clear to us. The animus carries with it *libido*, or psychic energy, normally utilized by consciousness. If repressed because consciousness has not acknowledged the animus, psychic energy drains back into the unconscious, with depression being the *effect* upon the conscious mind.

Creative women, therefore, have tapped the animus power that frees them from the sleep of unconsciousness. In a kind of reversal of the "Sleeping Beauty" roles, the animus "sleeps" in the unconscious until awakened by the woman. He can be prince or devil depending upon how he is regarded and treated by the conscious mind. But if the woman makes no attempt at relation with him, then he lies below, robbing her of her precious psychic energy, and compelling her towards depression.

Feminists may be shocked at the idea that their completion as women depends upon a man of sorts, even if he resides in their own unconscious. Or they may feel—as did our monks—that any contact with the opposite sex is contaminating, even in the form of an archetype. Unfortunately such an idea reveals an imbalance in attitude not on the side of feminity but masculinity! When possession by the animus takes place, the woman behaves like an inferior man, or rather boy. She is full of half-baked opinions, has many "crushes," frequently on members of her own sex, and is antagonistic towards authority and responsibility (growing up). Feminists are staunchly behind the position that except for physical characteristics all differences between the sexes are socially conditioned. The Jungian concept of innate sexual differences constitutes the rankest kind of sexism, therefore; but our next survey goes even further in substantiating the Jungian model pertaining to psychic differences between the sexes. "Why Should A Woman Be More Like a Man?" asks Carol Gilligan in the title of her article from *Psychology Today*.[30] In the following excerpts I have italicized certain words which correspond to the Eros principle of relationship for women, and the Logos principle of achievement for men.

> Women not only define themselves in a context of human relationships, but judge themselves in terms of their ability to care. Woman's place in man's life cycle has been that of *nurturer, caretaker, and helpmate, the weaver of those networks of relationships* on which she, in turn relies. . .
> Citing Daniel Levinson's study of males at Yale, in which their lifetime goal is to realize their Dream, a vision of "*glorious achievements*," she notes that "Relationships, whatever their particular intensity, play a subordinate role. . . . As a tentative generalization we would say that *close friendship with a man or woman is rarely experienced by American men*."
> In yet another study, *women achievers found that they measured* "Their

strength in terms of attachment ('giving to', 'helping out', 'being kind', 'not hurting',). *These successful women do not once mention their academic and professional distinctions when describing themselves as women.* If anything, they regard their professional lives as *jeopardizing their sense of themselves*, and the conflict that they encounter between achievement and care leaves them either divided in judgment or feeling betrayed."

Proceeding further Carol Gilligan and Susan Pollak write that they collected data on 88 men and 50 women in an undergrad course on human motivation. "*We found that the men saw more danger in situations of affiliation than in situations of achievement, and described danger as arising from intimacy.* In contrast, *the women tended to perceive more danger in situation of competitive achievements than in situations of affiliation, and were more likely to associate danger with isolation.*"

Whereas men were quite willing to sacrifice wives and sweethearts for their Dream (which explains how men can rely on their wives as helpmates in the early part of their careers and then quite callously reject them and seek new wives when on the brink of success), "women's sense of self becomes very much organized around being able to make, and then maintain, affiliations and relationships. . . .[and] eventually, for many women the threat of disruption of an affiliation is perceived *not just as a loss of a relationship but as something closer to a total loss of self.*"

"The differences found in this study suggest that men and women may experience attachment separation in different ways, and that each sex correspondingly perceives a danger that the other does not see—*men in connection, women in separation.*"

From what we have seen of the role of the contrasexual archetypes, it is obvious that *completion* for men and women may be attained when men and women can approach without trepidation those areas where they have the least facility and meet on a common ground of sharing their lives with one another.

HOW TO TELL TRUE LOVE FROM PROJECTION

In writing the above caption, I am deliberately leading the reader astray, for the projection of animus and anima is bound up with every person to whom we are attracted. It is all a matter of degree. When the archetype overwhelms consciousness, then we are really in trouble because the ego can no longer steer a course for us, as in the cases of Adele Hugo, and the Herr Professor in "The Blue Angel."

The feeling of love at first sight certainly indicates the presence of projection, but it is what we make subsequently of the relation that counts. Every relation must evolve; otherwise it withers, like an unfertillized plant, and dies. But the needs of man and woman are almost diametrically opposed, as we have seen from the previous studies. Woman fears isolation, and man fears intimacy. From this revelation we must realize that neither sex can be psychically completed by another person. Since their psychic goals do not dovetail, they are not always one in purpose when together.

Man may come to woman for sex, whereby she gains intimacy. A most interesting study revealed that women often had sex in order to gain cuddling, which along with intimate conversation is often a greater intimacy than sexual intercourse, particularly if the male, in his goal-oriented way, is proceeding on all pistons to the end of it, without regard for "play", or the woman's personal satisfaction. Then after the orgasm, the man's mind may drift inevitably back to his world of achievement, whereupon winged Eros has to take a hike out the window.

Interestingly enough, however, if the man were like the woman and craved intimacy as much as she, then neither one would grow or develop, because both would remain in that idyllic Eden state of post-coital bliss, and their marriage would be merely an ongoing self-reflection, each giving back the other's image in narcissistic preoccupation. Thank god, then, for the pairs of warring opposites, we may say.

But having different goals as to what they want out of life and relations, both partners come to realize that the other cannot fulfill them. With this recognition is the beginning of growth, for then one feels a vague longing for completion, which completion can only come from the sacred marriage with the inner archetype. When that has occurred, one can go back into the world and have more fulfilling, enriching relationships, which is the extravert reward for introversion.

When the vague longing first comes, however, one must never, never seek to assuage it by more sex, more relationships, more extravert behavior. This is particularly true for women, because if a man has a bad experience he may *naturally* return to his world of achievement, whereupon the anima will commence her spinning, compensating through dreams and intuitions, the imbalance with consciousness.

But woman will *naturally* turn to another relation, fearing isolation, and fulfilling her natural Eros. This is when she needs to fight against instinct in order to be able to sit alone and invite "the other man" into her life, the animus within.

In addition to the methods I mentioned earlier for enabling the animus to come through to consciousness, particularly helpful is speaking outloud to him of your desire to receive whatever he has to offer, just before descending to his level in sleep. Also, drawing and painting are useful. Often he will draw a picture of himself for the artist. The evidence of the drawing should be adequate rebuttal to those who contend that the archetypes do not exist, that they are a product of Jung's mysticism. I should like to recommend to the reader two books in which the patients painted their dreams during analysis. Both texts present the paintings—some in color—and both authors' commentaries are incisive. The first is Frances Wickes' *The Inner World of Man*, and the second is Gerhard Adler's *The Living Symbol*.

Each one of us must pay particular attention to the levels of our projections. If our relationships become re-runs of previous affairs, if we feel emotionally "ripped off" each time, if destructive scenes characterize each relation, then it is time to step inside the vicious circle of external events to the eye of the hurricane, where the archetype waits, wherein we may discover what is wrong with the inner relation to the animus or anima *that is creating the outer problem.*

There are no exercises or methods that I know of for helping a man to develop his Eros. Woman is more complete, more a totality. By the methods mentioned she can call up the animus from unconsciousness, but man requires the initiation of a woman. To initiate, to take in. Woman takes man into her body, thereby opening *him* to his own woman within. Each initiation that man receives from woman is dual in nature, not only erotic sexually, but also Erotic. Thereafter each experience of woman should produce a new relation with his anima. Within she climbs ever higher towards the light, whereas without, in the world of experience, he commences the ascent of the Tree of Life that reaches ever higher to the Throne of Iananna, for the Eros relatedness which man receives as a gift from woman (within and without) is the life and soul of man. As a man moves to progressively higher levels of anima development, he may each time have a sexual experience of woman, since the new level of anima development incorporates previous levels, but the gift each time received from the woman's initiation may be greater in value than the experience before. Above all, a man must become aware of the level of his projection, in order to anticipate the direction in which he should be growing.

THE PROJECTION

When I began my readings in Jungian psychology years ago, I discovered that many of the writers utilized fragments from fairytales in order to clarify an archetype. Marie Louise von Franz has become famous for this, with many most interesting studies, such as *The Feminine in Fairytales, Shadow and Evil in Fairytales, Interpretation of Fairytales*, and *The Psychological Meaning of Redemption Motifs in Fairytales*. In 1973 I began to have some very interesting dreams that I found I could complete upon awakening by the "active imagination" process. Subsequently I would write down the dream and fantasy as a story. When I realized that each story illustrated a different archetype, I published the collection under the punning title *Tales for Jung Folk* (1983). I included a primer to go with each story, explaining the archetype involved. Since most people are almost completely unconscious of their projections, I think it may be worthwhile here to share with the reader part of the primer for—and a few lines from—the story called "The Crystal People":

Once upon a very long time ago there was a race on earth called the Crystal People. They looked very much like you and I except in the center of their foreheads there grew out an inch or two a cluster of beautiful crystals.

If you were up close to these people, you could see little tiny figures in the crystals, a king and queen perhaps, or a wise old man or woman. And all of them seemed to have at least one disagreeable figure, dark and shadowy, which when called to the attention of that person was always denied. Why that was so, I could not say, except that no one would want to admit to having such a nasty character in the middle of his head.

Now the very strange thing about these people was that you could tell what they were seeing only be examining the little figures in their heads. What happened was this. As they turned to look at someone or something, one of the little figures in the crystal would fall into place at the center, from which a light of brilliant intensity emitted. So at the same moment that the object was seen, the light fell upon it, cloaking it in the garb of the king or queen, or the nasty shadowy person, turning a boulder into a troll, or a weeping willow into a stick-riding witch, hair trailing down clouds as she flew on a mission of witchery.

Strangest of all was the way these people fell in love, for seemingly the most important figure for this was an image of the opposite sex that each possessed in his or her crystal. Oddly enough these tiny figures when projected outward became larger than life. Too, they were not always ideal objects for love, since some of them seemed to find attractive what others found unattractive. . . .

So it seemed that whatever quality a man or woman deemed important for his or her own fulfillment, he was sure to project a figure onto his beloved that embodied that quality, whether from past or future. How this was possible I cannot say; yet as these images contained gods and goddesses from the race of men, there were also great figures of imagination from the race of men, and stranger figures, whom I did not know, but whose meaning came to me by the feeling they gave.

In "The Crystal People," I have removed the archetypes from the unconscious and placed them "out-front," so to speak. In this manner we are able to observe the effects of the projection of the archetypes. Our way of seeing others is conditioned by the specific qualities of our archetypes. For although the quantity of the archetype is the same in each of us—a prince is a prince is a prince is a prince—the *quality* of that archetype is unique for each of us; thus by merely observing another person, in effect we have projected our quality of the archetype onto that person.

Since there cannot be a strictly objective observer, Heisenberg's Uncertainty Principle in physics is paralleled by Jung's awareness that merely looking is highly subjective, clothing the object or person in the qualitative garb of our own archetypal projections. Good, evil, love, hate—these qualities we assign to people at first meetings, often even before a word is spoken. "I hated the man at once." Or, "it was a case of love at first sight." Such strong reactions *before* the other person is known at all indicate that the unconscious archetype has been aroused by the other person and its *quality* projected onto him.

My story is perhaps an unconscious take-off on the Grimm classic "The Frog Prince." In that tale, we may recall, the prince had been turned into a frog by some spell or enchantment by a witch. From the point of view of Jungian psychology, the projection-making quality of the unconscious is a kind of enchantment, for the other person taking the projection appears to be someone he is not. When two persons establish an intense relation based upon such a projection, we can predict that they are headed for trouble, since neither sees the other as he or she really is, and "disenchantment" is sure to follow.

Jung's psychology, which may have seemed mystical and impractical in regard to the Self, becomes quite down-to-earth in regard to the give and take of the war between the sexes. Indeed, I would say that Jung's most important contributions to psychology are in the area of sexual relations.

One purpose of Jungian psychology is to make us aware of our projections in order to be able to see others as they really are, for in many cases we find ourselves disappointed because others do not fulfill our *expectations* of them. Thus, a kind of disenchantment takes place, and we blame other for our unfulfilled expectations, saying, "You are not what I thought you were."

RETURN TO EDEN

The war in humankind between conscious and unconscious is a reality of life, the price paid for the separation of the ego from the Eden of unconsciousness. All other pairs of opposites are but pale reflections of this one great conflict, including the external war between the sexes, and the grander war among nations. Certain esoteric teachings recognized this truth long ago and sought to reconcile the opposites in order to consummate individual psychic harmony. As to whether or not they also saw this process as a means to world harmony I cannot say, but it follows that they did. The teachings of which I am speaking are Tantra, alchemy, and Tarot. Jung's great intuition was that the secret of the resolution of problems arising in human relations lay in alchemy, and with great practicality he made it the cornerstone of his psychology. The consummation of psychic harmony was seen as a mystical marriage, heirosgamos, wherein a new being, the "child" of the marriage, transcended the polar opposites.

Within the psyche, each of us must wrestle with our angels, shadow and animus or anima, who first appear to be devils in disguise, but can provide the liberated psychic energy to enable us to scale the heights to higher consciousness. The Tree of Life is that which we climb, and against it rests a ladder of levels of animus and anima. At the summit is the Self, our own divinity.

A WOMAN'S BIG DREAM

As I slept the Serpent came unto me and laid his head upon my breast. Gazing deeply into my eyes he said, "Woman, your time has come."

Not knowing his meaning, I raised my head and peered into his eyes. Within each was a whirlpool of stars that converged towards a center of light that swirled faster and faster. And as I gazed, I felt my spirit being drawn out of my body towards the tiny, receding brilliance that danced at the center.

"Where are you taking me?" I said.

"We are going home," he replied, gliding from my bed.

I followed after. He moved so swiftly I had to run to keep up. Finally he entered a cave, dark, and cold, but I followed fearfully.

As I entered, the path where I stepped became illuminated by a veiled woman holding a torch that gave out a green light. When I had passed her, another light shone out of yet another color. As I progressed on the path, there was always a veiled woman ahead holding a torch.

"Why are they veiled?" I asked the Serpent.

"Because it is not yet time for their beauty to be revealed."

We had gone down in the cave for a very long way when we began to climb for an equally long time.

I said to the Serpent, "To where does the path lead?"

"To the place where the Sun sets in the West and the moon rises in the East."

At last we came out in an open place, illuminated only by starlight. Strange were the stars, and unlike any constellations I had seen before.

Then I saw that from where we stood water flowed out of the ground from a crystal spring. But the water was alive, leaping, bubbling, from the center of the pool. And rainbows of every color arched over the laughing water. I could half hear the voices of children talking merrily in many languages.

The sky, azure blue at first, darkened to deep purple. All nature was expectant.

I said to the Serpent, "What is to happen?"

And the Serpent said, "The miracle of birth."

I knew it was to be my birth, and I began to cry because it felt so beautiful to be born.

Then in the West I saw a great King in the sky with a golden crown, and he began to descend. I saw his feet, then his legs, drop behind the horizon. And as he descended a beautiful silver crown, completely round like his golden crown began to rise in the East. Beneath the crown rose the head of a woman, and she looked across the sky lovingly at the king, and their eyes met, and the rays from their crown reached out, touched, and intertwined.

Then at my feet the earth began to shake, and I trembled, holding to the serpent. The crystal water parted and a green vine, twisting like a serpent, emerged from the waters and began to climb to the sound of singing, many women's voices, as if all the women in the universe were singing at once, many songs in many tongues, but all interwoven like a tapestry. The King and Queen in the sky smiled, closed their eyes, and gradually their lights went out. Then did the vine thicken and become like a tree, always climbing, its base ever widening so that the serpent and I had to move ever farther away.

The tree climbed higher and higher, until it seemed to attain the very roof of heaven. Then did its crown unfold and spread, unfurling stars like blossoms across the face of night. Then did the stars also take shape and form, merging to form the body of a woman so splendid that I felt humble to look upon her. Her feet touched the earth, but a gown of stardust enfolded her. Her hair blew all around her, as it wafted on the nigh wind. A halo of white light surrounded her, and her diadem was spiked with stars.

Then her hands descended to the serpent and me, beckoning. And the Serpent, like the tree, began to climb, encircling the tree, and growing with each fold until he filled the sky with the Woman and the Tree. Then she looked down and her eyes filled mine, and her love filled my being. Then I knew that she was me, and I was her.

CHAPTER VII

SOCIAL HARMONY

I had thought to conclude this book with the previous chapter, but two things have prompted me to add yet another chapter. First, when Dr. Dean Edell had read some of the manuscript, he asked me if I knew about the circumcision of 74 million women. Aghast, I did not; yet count myself as one who is particulårly alert to abuses of women. When he kindly provided details for me, I felt that the least I could do was to provide my readers with the information.

Secondly, I have had some preliminary feedback on the manuscript from women, most reactions being quite enthusiastic. Be that as it may, some reactions have been unfavorable, but for quite predictable reasons. The kind of thinking—or lack of it—falls into a pattern of stereotypical thinking which does more to prevent social harmony than anything else I can call to mind. Therefore, I should like to investigate it relevant to the animus in this chapter.

The reactions to the manuscript that in part prompted this last chapter went something like this. "You should not have written this book!" (This I expected from defenders of the Church and patriarchy, but not from women).

"Why should I not have written the book?"

"Because the Jungian Theory is wrong."

"Why is it wrong?"

"Because the only psychological differences between the sexes are the result of psychological conditioning."

"What about the contrasexual archetypes of the unconscious?"

"They don't exist. Jung was a mystic. He paid too much attention to dreams and not enough to real life."

Calling someone a mystic these days is a severe put down—only the epithet "fascist" is worse. The foregoing response ignores the evidence of Jungian psychology, and the evidence presented in this book, ninety per cent of which has been provided by women. Further, anyone who says the archetypes do not exist has to ignore the evidence of his or her own unconscious, *which will always provide a complementary function to consciousness if one will but listen.*

But since dreams are the expressions of the unconscious, the means it uses to make itself known, if the archetypes are rejected then the validity of dreams has to be rejected. This puts us back an hundred years or more when dreams were put down as "nothing buts..." A bit of bad beef in the evening meal, etc.

ANTAGONIST OPINIONING

Having come this far, I must acknowledge that the previous chapters have provided a wealth of ammunition for feminists, or anyone for that matter, who wishes to perpetuate on the social scene the war between the sexes, and on the interior, psychic scene, to wallow in their own inabilities to reconcile inner masculine and feminine components. But perpetuating the war was not my intent and purpose. This last chapter is crucial to the thrust of this book because it points the way not only to a new social harmony between the sexes, but also to an individual psychic harmony of which the outer harmony is but a mirror. Indeed, social harmony between the sexes *cannot* be attained until individual harmony proceeds it. Therefore, the means to attaining it, which this chapter expounds, has ramifications for the future of this planet. Having recognized ecology as the life of our planet, we are addressing our collective consciousness outwardly in attempting to resolve the threats of annihilation posed by poisoning the environment, nuclear warfare, and starvation. On paper we are all united against such threats to human life. On a much deeper level, where psychic realities influence our conduct in an unconscious way, we maintain *antagonist* positions that obviate the solution of our world problems because we have not realized that they are but the mirror of our *individual* problems. Ours is the era of "one man's—or woman's—opinion is as good as another's." The more stridently the opinion is expressed, the greater the number voicing it, then the more attention it receives in the way of media coverage, which further spreads the opinion. Soon still others adopt it as their own, particularily if it is simple-minded enough to lend itself to sloganeering. The considered opinion then becomes lost in stereotypical thinking. This is mob rule at its worst, and is on the increase through the fault of the media, particularly television, whose cameras race about from one demonstration to another, without exercising the slightest self-control or judgment in their creation of the "event". One almost gets the impression that TV orchestrates the protests, the more far-out the better! This procedure only leads to even more outrageous demonstrations. Greek *demos* means "the mob." Such antics are indicative of democracy's Achilles heel.

We need to be able to recognize the animus opinion, and to analyze it for what it is worth. We have learned from our discussion that vehemence is a good indication of an animus opinion, because the conscious mind is not in control, unconscious elements (the animus and shadow) have taken over, and women then behave as if possessed, because they are possessed. In the words of Esther Harding, the great writer and analyst, "Thus they fell once more under the dominance of the male. This time it was not without, that is under men, but under the rule of the male within."[2]

In presenting these ideas on how to make peace between the warring sexes, I do not think that my book merits a "peace protest," for such a response indicates the animus, collectively and individually. A dialogue is welcome, however.

As we have seen, animus opinions are not valid substitutes for thought. Thinking is characterized by reflection, sequential procedure, relevance, discrimination, reason, and logic. Honest thought is hard work, therefore.

By contrast animus opinion contains none of the above elements. A man, giving vent to an anima mood, is no nearer honest thought than the woman voicing the animus opinion. Here I should like to coin a new phrase, Antagonist Opinioning, recognizing that opinioning is not a dictionary word. The process of opinioning—in my coinage—implies an adversary or antagonist who in our *opinion* advocates the wrong or evil position. Therefore, we are not "reasoning together" in our discussion, but arguing to overcome, or vanquish our antagonist. There is no possiblity of our changing our mind, because our opinion is inflexible. Just when in our history thinking so deteriorated I cannot say, but it probably began when popularity overcame truth.

Unfortunately for our personal awareness and eventual growth, most of our individual "evil" remains unconscious, so that we do not see it in ourselves and cannot transform it to good, as the alchemist makes gold from lead. Without an awareness of our own faults, we project them, therefore, into the outer world, where evil appears everywhere in the form of persons who need "straightening out" by a strong hand wielded by ourselves. Ego regards itself as all good, and will not entertain anything to the contrary; hence, the shadow must retreat to the unconscious depths where it waits for a catalyst situation that will enable it to war on the goody-goody ego. One must ask, "How can wars be eliminated on the international level when most of us are incapable of owning up on an individual level to our own private shortcomings, whether or not they are of sufficient magnitude to be labeled "evil"? As Jung has said. "There is no cure and no means of improving the world that does not begin with the individual himself." The resolution of the war between the sexes depends upon how the warring masculine/feminine elements are handled in the individual psyche. Only when there is collective wholeness on an individual scale will there be mass wholeness in the world without.

Basically this perception is itself at war with another attitude which does not accept the fact that world change begins with individual transformation. This latter point of view is a kind of buck-passing that enables the individual to disavow responsibility by blaming "the system," which is seen as a kind of conspiracy beginning with the President, moving from there to the Pentagon, the military in general, and descending through state and local government to the utilities (gas, electric, and phone companies) to one's boss, finally encompassing all those in the immediate environment who do subscribe to one's point of view. "If you're not with us, you're against us," is the banner unfurled in their neighbor's face, and the epithet hurled is "fascist!" This is the worst kind of Antagonist Opinioning, because once branded, you can have no reply.

But the conflict between the individual and society is all too apparently rooted in the conflict between conscious and unconscious, and the warring masculine and feminine elements within the individual psyche. Needless to say, such a "the-buck-stops-here-with-me" philosophy is extremely unpopular.

The thrust of this book is to delineate the causes of the put down of women, and by so doing to defuse the war between the sexes, and to point the way to more abundant lives for both women and men, through the personal harmony of the *hierosgamos*. Personal harmony equals world harmony. *But this puts each of us on the spot, because we can no longer use extravert means to irradicate a problem that lies within each of us*, the warring pairs of opposites that foment the outer, social problems. Taking personal responsibility involves maturity, objectivity, and discriminating thought. There is a certain danger here because the finger of blame may swing around to point at us. So scapegoating, whether Jews or witches, has always been easier.

Antagonist Opinioning seems to be the predominate way of looking at the rest of the world in Third World countries, with the United States seen as the scapegoat; therefore, it is imperative that we have a closer look at this phenomenon. What are the characteristics of Antagonist Opinioning?

Basically it removes the psychological spot-light from each of us and turns it onto society, or the world, always promulgating external, sociological solutions to any and all problems, including individual. It views psychiatry as anathema, *since psychiatry undermines the view that society is best changed by a Marxist restructuring rather than by changing people.* Further, it will countenance no value judgments on its own people; therefore, individual persons cannot be faulted, including the tens of thousands of psychopaths that make up our prison population. They are *victims*, or so the line goes, of an unjust system. Of course, it's okay to call someone else a fascist if they don't agree with you. Value judgments are in order if they are deserved, and so on.

Again, the hierosgamos is a restructuring of the *psyche*, not society, in that previously unconscious contents constellating around the archetypes of shadow, animus, and anima, are partially brought into consciousness, and into a new relation with the ego. This process, which Jung has named the individuation process, transforms the individual. However imperceptibly, a change in one individual causes a change in society.

Contrarily, the Antagonist Opinioning abnegates individual change and activly prevents it. We all have heard of the fate of dissenters in the Soviet Union, so even leftists at home cannot argue that in the area of toleration of free expression of ideas, ours is indeed the preferable society. How then does Antagonist Opinionating prevent change? *If one advocates individual change, then there is an implied admission that the source of the problem lies not in the external structure of society, but in the internal or psychic make-up of its individual citizens.* This puts Antagonist Opinionating in an undesirable catch-22 situation in which only external, social change is necessary to achieve the desired society.

In order to substantiate this point of view, people must be stereotyped as a homogenous mass of equal intelligence, abilities, and without sexual differences in the psychic sense. Stereotyping is the primary characteristic of Antagonist Opinioning. Jungian psychology, observing a contrasexual archetype in the unconscious, which is masculine for women and feminine for men, concludes that there are very real psychic differences between the sexes. This confronts the unisex theory popular in stereotypical circles. To be true proletarians we have to be all alike. *Tabula rasa*, or the "clean slate" at birth theory is the cornerstone of Third World thinking. In order to be called a fascist you have only to give them the merest hint that you countenance differences at birth other than those of race and gender.

A Jungian analyst, Adolf Guggenbuhl-Craig, has done extensive research in the area of psychopathology, the study of socially unadaptable persons. This is of interest to us here because it correlates with our theory that the stereotypical thinking to which we are daily exposed at the hands of the media is promoting a society of psychopaths. Again, given the view that one wants to tear down traditional society as we know it, and, therefore, is antagonistic to it; then there is no reason to socially adapt to that society, since one has taken the adversary position with regard to it. This subculture seems to be saying, "We're all misfits," which is okay from their point of view, since what is wrong with the world is its present structure. In their own eyes, they become heroes of the cause to change the world from without, *without personal responsibility*. In their use of drugs and in the rock and roll songs a common plaint can be heard. "I'm okay—the world ain't."

The main task in the psychic growth of men is Eros development, the ability to relate. This is possible only through the evolution of the personal anima. But as our author notes, Eros is conspicuously absent in psychopaths. He then goes on to define the term psychopath.

"Psychopath," "psychopathy," comes from the Greek *psyche*, soul, and pathos, suffering. A psychopath, then, is one whose suffering is of the soul, which suffering manifests as anti-social behavior, or one who is mentally ill. It is no longer used in this sense, implying immorality, instability, unreliabilty, and even criminality.[2]

Next, a discussion of stereotypical thinking by the author presents us with some excellent examples of how even the scientific medical community have become permeated by it even though they should be above it, or so we assume. In recent years the scientifically correct term "homosexual" has become pejorative in society's eyes, so that usuage of the term implies prejudice, whereas "gay" is okay. This reveals two of the characteristics of Antagonist Opinioning: Psychiatry as anathema, and reluctance to make value judgement except on its antagonists.

For some reason neutral diagnoses assume negative qualities and significance. This can be partially avoided by re-naming or redefining the entire phenomenon or syndrome so that . . . psychopathy becomes 'Socio-pathic Personality Disorder'. The negative connotations of psychopathy can be alleviated through the use of the prefix 'socio'. At the same time, the phenomenon under consideration becomes more harmless, since one is no longer dealing with the psyche, 'Psycho', but with a conflict between the indiviual and society.

It seems that psychopathy has affected completely unforeseeable areas. It has called attention to the theory of equality in philosophy and political science. The question of inheritance has further led to practical political considerations: some analysts have gone so far as to label the idea of inheritance in psychopathy fascist or at least fascistoid. Leftist-oriented psychotherapists maintain that inheritance has little or no importance for human beings: we are all born with the same potential. The dispute extends even to zoology where, it has been observed animals are born with basic patterns of behavior. Consequently, zoologists like Konrad Lorenz are labeled fascist. Even Jung has been called a fascist, not because of the misplaced charges of anti-semitism, but because he maintained that human beings are born with certain patterns of behavior called archetypes.

People use the term fascism very loosely these days. In point of fact, it designated particular political movements of a dictatorial and elitist nature found primarily in Italy, Spain, and Roumania. Fascism is often confused with National Socialism in Germany, a movement with fascist qualities, but having distinctive and different elements such as the idea of the master race.

Those of leftist persuasion tend, therefore, to espouse the *Tabula rasa* or clean slate theory. Naturally, our image of ourselves and the world around us influences our scientific perspective, as evident in the discussion of intelligence. Recently I read an article in a medical journal which stated that the level of intelligence depends upon the functioning of the brain and, further, that brain functions are dependent upon the social environment. In order, the article continued, to raise human intelligence to the same level, society must undergo a Marxist restructuring.[3]

This is, of course, the final absurdity in stereotypical thinking. If one is not responsible for one's own brain, then we have reached the apotheosis of irresponsibility. The truly maddening element in the stereotypical point of view is that while purporting to serve the downtrodden, disenfranchised, and misfits of society, a genuine disservice is being done to them in that no change or growth is possible for them as long as the banner leading the grand parade says, "You're okay, society's wrong." For personal change begins with *personal* dissatisfaction not social. No change, now growth; it is as simple as that.

What then is the outlook for the future of humanity? Very bleak. For human evolution goes hand-in-hand with the evolution of consciousness. If consciousness stays pat and waits for society to change, we may have to re-invent the wheel in some distant future.

Adolf Guggenbuhl-Craig cites a number of primary and secondary symptoms of psychopathy which are germane to our discussion for two reasons. First, they all indicate the no-growth phenomenon which is given validation and a dubious stamp of approval by the "blame it on society" theory. Further, in the spirit of not making value judgments on any of their own kind, individual growth is no longer a necessity. Secondly, all of the symptoms of psychopathy have an opposite number in what we might call the symptoms of the individuated personality, the goal of Jungian psychology. And since these latter "symptoms" are possible only through the *hierosgamos* of masculine and feminine components, we shall return to animus and anima immediately after observing these symptoms.

First is the *inability to love*, the lack of Eros in the widest sense of the word...

The second primary symptom of psychopathy is the *missing* or *deficient sense of morality*.

The third primary symptom is . . .*the absence of any psychic development*.

The fourth primary symptom of psychopathy is what we call *background depression*. . . . The feeling that everyone is against him.

The fifth primary symptom of psychopathy is *chronic background fear*. A psychopath does not trust the world.[4]

These primary symptoms, when viewed in opposite, characterize the individuated personality, of which the psychopath is his or her opposite. First, the Eros is highly developed, enabling one to enter into very meaningful relationships. Secondly, there is a sense of moral purpose. By definition an individuated person has developed psychically. The libido is free for creative activity, not flowing back into the unconscious, a characteristic of depressive behavior. And finally, there is a great sense of personal confidence, as if living in the *tao*, flowing with the universal energies.

So if the popular point-of-view promotes psychopathy, however subtly and insidiously, we may not be too far away from a world in which psychopaths predominate. The first characteristic of psychopathy under the old, stigmatized definition was asocial or *criminal* behavior. Since the number of women incarcerated increases dramatically every year, we may well wonder whether or not there are forces or philosophies afoot which are sabotaging woman's natural facility for Eros relation.

THE NEUTERING OF WOMEN

Now since the Third World knows about the circumcision of 74 million women, why has nothing been done about it? The practice is a holdover from patriarchy, of course, but not something that can be blamed on the Judeo-Christian tradition, since it is a Muslim phenomenon. As I have noted, the West is largely unaware of this barbaric "religious" practice. The Third World parades behind a banner of a better life for its people, with which no one can argue. Why then is the mutilation of women not eradicated?

I believe the answer lies with what I call the neutering of women — the *tabula rasa*, unisex, no psychic differences party-line characteristic of Antagonist Opinioning. One envisions in the not too distant future armies of Third World macho men and animus possessed women fighting side by side to overturn the world. I believe this stereotypical way of looking at the sexes has been accepted by the vast majority of Third World women, *else circumcision would not be the general practice in their countries today*. Further, it can be surmised, since its sphere of influence is greater in the Third World than the West's, that the Soviet Union knows of the phenomenon but has done little—if anything—to eradicate it. The United States, Britain, Germany, France, Holland, and Belgium, represent the old colonialism, and we are suspect, and rightly so.

Let us begin with the physical neutering of women, and then proceed to psychic neutering. The only way the West has learned of circumcision is because of an influx of students from foreign countries seeking health care from hospitals and campus clinics. Our source, thanks to Dr. Dean Edell, is Evelyn Shaw, RN, MS, University of Arizona College of Nursing, and consultant to the Foreign Wives Club at the University. She is writing in the June, 1985, issue of the *American Journal of Nursing*.

Female circumcision encompasses a variety of female genital operations, which have been medically classified according to the degree of severity. *Sunna Circumcision* is the removal of the prepuce and/or the excision of the tip of the clitoris. *Excision* or *clitoridectomy* may include the excision of the clitoris, the labia minora, and the labia majora.

In *infibulation*, part or all of the clitoris, labia minora, and the medial aspect of the labia majora are excised. The raw areas on both sides are pulled together over the vagina and held with sutures, thorns, or paste-like material so that the opposite sides heal together and form a wall that closes the upper part of the vestibule. A small opening is left for urine and menstrual flow by inserting a matchstick-sized reed that is kept in place until the area heals. The child's legs are tied together to immobilize the wound, usually for three weeks.

A village woman or lay midwife usually performs the surgery. She also opens (usually by cutting) the infibulation scar on the wedding night if the husband is unable to do so, and opens it again during the birth of a baby. In some countries, trained midwives, barbers, paramedics, physicians, and nurses supplement their income by performing the initial and later surgery.

Usually the surgery is performed when the child is seven years old, but it may be done in infancy, toddler years, or puberty. Often anesthesia is not used, unless the circumcision is done in a hospital.

During and immediately after the initial surgery, there is danger of shock, hemorrhage, sepsis, and extensive lacerations of the surrounding area. The vagina, urethra, and rectal area may be damaged. As the wound heals, there is the possibility of sepsis, tetanus, and retention of urine if the infibulation opening closes or is too small. Often fluids are withheld from the child for three days after surgery to reduce urination; dehydration can become a severe problem.

When married, women who have been infibulated must be forcibly penetrated. If the husband cannot penetrate with his penis, a knife, sharp instrument, or fingernail, especially grown for this purpose, is used. The outcome obviously is painful intercourse and possible perineal laceration, infections, and hemorrhage.

During childbirth, the scar tissue must be cut and the opening enlarged, or the mother and infant may die of complications relating to the obstruction of the delivery by the inelastic scarred area. Again, there is danger of sepsis, lacerations, and bleeding.

Other reported complications include keloid formation, rectovaginal and/or vesicovaginal fistula, dysmenorrhea, pelvic inflammatory disease, endometriosis, infertility, cystocele, rectocele, and incontinence. Many of the mental health complications have not been researched extensively. However, it is believed that severe anxiety, prolonged pain, coital problems, and frigidity are all fairly common.

Many ethnic groups throughout parts of Africa, the Mideast, Indonesia, and Malaysia practice a variety of female genital operations. According to one researcher, about 74 million girls and women in Africa have been circumcised to date. Due to an increase in population in these areas, more female children than ever before are being "cut" every day.[7]

The author, Evelyn Shaw, then goes on to explain the rationale for female circumcision. "Economically, female circumcision is especially important in societies that are patrilinear and agrarian. The continuation of the patriarchal system is assured where infibulation is practiced since the new bride's virginity is visibly guaranteed by 'the chastity belt of the flesh' and therefore, succession and inheritance of property cannot be questioned. . . . Since an uncircumcised woman would not be considered marriageable—the only viable future for most of those women—many parents see no choice but to have their daughters circumcised."[8]

Is there then no way out of this dilemma? Suppose all the women in just one small village said, "No more marriages unless the mutilation stops!" Perhaps that could be the seed that spreads to other villages, towns, and countries.

The rest of the so-called reasons for female circumcision manifest the old masculine hysteria in the presence of feminine sexuality, an hysteria which one may have believed to have died out three hundred years ago with the execution of the last witch. These reasons do nothing so much as to substantiate the earlier charges I made against patriarchy, with regard to the fear of the female being linked to a fear of sex and death (the omnipotent power of life and death which she inherits from the Great Mother). All of the following reasons for circumcision are cited in Evelyn Shaw's article.

First, sexual control. "Excision of the clitoris is also believed to remove the masculine element in the young girl and prevent the organ from growing and thus increasing her desire for sex—which may not be matched by her husband's. In many areas, too much sex is considered bad for the husband. Furthermore, since a man is often allowed more than one wife, reduced sexual desire in wives is considered necessary. Some groups also believe that the clitoris contains a poison-like substance that can harm the husband."[9]

In the previous paragraphs, keywords are "harm," "poison," "bad," all indicative of the male fear of inadequacy. We also see a ritual kind of castration in removing "the masculine element in the young girl." Man has perpetuated every kind of barbarism upon the person of the female, why not castration? Castration in order to reduce female sexuality definitely reveals the same fear of the female which drove the monks into monasteries in the Middle Ages.

Secondly, we have the projection of the negative anima, the death-dealing aspect of the goddess, in that one of the reasons given for circumcision is the belief in some cultures that if during childbirth the baby's head touches the clitoris the infant will die.

Thirdly, there is the projection of evil onto woman as a daughter of Eve. Here the reader should know that the Bible is accepted by Muslims; therefore, all of the negativity which we discussed in connection with the Judeo-Christian tradition, in regard to Eve and the serpent, is also accepted by Islam. Thus, a reason given for closing the vagina by infibulation is to prevent evil spirits from entering. We do not even have to ask what horrendous things they might do in there to the male's penis!

Further, it should be noted that in keeping with "God's" edict that because of her sex the Fall of Man occurred, she shall bear children in pain. Infibulation results in painful intercourse, so it appears that Islam is trying to aid "God" in assuring that woman derive no pleasure from the sexual act.

Lastly, in some of the countries there is the belief that in regard to the genitals a man should be lumpy and woman smooth. This seems to me to be a variation of the castration theme, a further neutering of women. It also suggests a projections of the lowest anima level, women as non-threatening sexual toys, because a child-woman is "smooth," her sexual organs undeveloped

Now let us hear a personal account of what it is like to undergo a clitoridectomy. The writer is Nawal el Saadaw, an Egyptian physician and author of *Women and Sex*. Her books are banned in Libya and in Saudi Arabia:

> I was six years old that night when I lay in my bed. ... I felt something move under the blankets, something like a huge hand, cold and rough, fumbling over my body, as though looking for something. Almost simultaneously another hand . . .was clapped over my mouth, to prevent me from screaming.
>
> They carried me to the bathroom. . . . I realized that my thighs had been pulled wide apart, and that each of my legs was being held as far away from the other as possible, as though gripped by steel fingers that never relinquished their pressure. Then suddenly the sharp metallic edge dropped between my thighs and cut off a piece of flesh from my body. I screamed with pain despite the tight hand held over my mouth. The pain was like a searing flare that went through my whole body. After a few moments, I saw a red pool around my hips.
>
> I did not know what they had cut off, and I did not try to find out. I just wept, and called out to my mother for help. But the worst shock of all was when I looked around and found her standing by my side. Yes, it was she. In flesh and blood, right in the midst of these strangers, she was talking to them, and smiling at them, as though they had not just participated in slaughtering her daughter.
>
> They carried me to my bed. Then I saw them catch my four-year-old sister in exactly the same way they had caught me. I cried out with all my might. No! No! I could see my sister's face held between the big rough hands. It had a deathly pallor. Her wide black eyes met mine for a split second, a glance of terror that I can never forget. A moment later, she was gone, behind the door of the bathroom where I had just been. The look we exchanged seemed to say: 'Now we know what it is. Now we know where our tragedy lies. We were born of a special sex, the female sex. We are destined in advance to taste of misery, and to have a part of our body torn away by cold, unfeeling hands.'[10]
>
> My family was not an uneducated family. . . . Nevertheless, this custom of clitoridectomy for girls was very prevalent then, and no girl could escape having her clitoris excised, regardless of her social class or whether her family lived in a rural or an urban area. When I recovered from the operation and returned to school, I asked my friends about what had happened to me, only to discover that all of

them, without exception, had been through the same experience. For years, the memory of my clitoridectomy continued to track me down like a nightmare. I had a feeling of insecurity, fear of the unknown, waiting for me at every step I took into the future. I did not know if there were other such surprises being stored up for me by my mother and father, or my grandmother, or the people around me. Since that day, society had made me feel that I was a girl, and I saw that the word 'Bint' [girl] when pronounced by anyone was almost always accompanied by a frown.

Even after I grew up and graduated as a doctor in 1955, I could not forget the painful incident that made me lose my childhood, that deprived me during my youth and for years of married life from enjoying the fullness of my sexuality and the completeness of life that can only come from psychological equilibrium. Nightmares followed me throughout the years, especially during the period when I was working as a medical doctor in rural areas where I often had to treat young girls who had come to the outpatients' clinic bleeding profusely after this mutilation. Many died as a result of the primitive way in which clitoridectomies were performed. Others were afflicted with acute or chronic infections from which they sometimes suffered for the rest of their lives. And most, if not all, became the victims of sexual or mental distortions later on as a result of this savage experience.[1]

Savage experience indeed. My comment to Dr. Edell was, "This is worse than anything patriarchy has done to woman before!" But then the realization dawns that this barbarism commenced long before the witch hysteria, and has been going on ever since. Personally it makes me feel like starting another crusade and setting out for the Holy Land at once. Looking at the problem realistically, however, one realizes that Western women are going to have to mobilize their efforts in the interests of helping their Third World sisters. To me this is a cause with a capital "C".

Thanks to the persistence of the Feminist Movement, we may see an Equal Rights Amendment. The squeaky wheel get the oil, and the debt owed to feminists is considerable. Many women have put their jobs and marriages on the line to take a stand for right, and they deserve our collective thanks. The concept of woman as man's helpmate is as archaic now as it was when patriarchy first proposed it.

We now come to the psychic neutering of women. In the 20th century women have made positive strides forward—in the West at least. Suffrage and the social freedom provided by the Pill are merely two examples. Re-evaluation of what roles were once considered womanly has led to the realization that a woman may "play" any role in society without compromising her feminine principle. I use the word "play" because we must recognize that whatever our roles in life, we are like actors in a drama, and that the qualities of the role cannot be attributed to the actor. Thus woman may act the role of astronaut, longshoreman, fireman, or ditch-digger without compromising herself if she be true to the feminine principle.

If, however, she rejects her essence, considering it mere social conditioning or as chauvinistic stereotype, then she has lost the long battle with patriarchy and become psychically neutered, her Eros unwinged, her caring lamed, her nurturing hobbled, and her spirit decaying. Then have the rough patriarchal pillagers of the villages of the Great Mother won a final victory, and then is Yahweh exultant on high, the Tree of Immortality, Goddess, and Serpent toppled from the sky, flung headlong forever into Eden's fatal prison; and the will of a thousand thousand witches unbroken by inquisitors crushed on a mechanistic rack; then did Gaia feel, within her oceans, forests, and air, the spirit dwindle like clouds forsaking earth's atmosphere for the barren reaches of lonely space.

FOOTNOTES

EDEN : Chapter 1

1. The Nag Hammadi Library: "On the Origin of the World" (N.Y.: Harper & Row, 1981), p.172.
2. Ibid., p.173.
3. Ibid., p.174.
4. Roger Cook, *The Tree of Life* (N.Y: Avon, 1974), p.105.
5. Richard Allen,*Star-Names: Their Lore and Meanings* (Dover, 1963), p.208.
6. Ibid., p.209.
7. Ibid., p.207.
8. Cook, op.cit., p.107.
9. Ibid., p.105.
10. Sir Thomas L. Heath, *Greek Astronomy* (London: E.P. Dutton), pp.113-114.
11. Ibid.
12. Joseph Campbell,*The Masks of God: Occidental Mythology* (N.Y: Viking Press, 1964), p.259.
13. Ibid., p.258.
14. Ibid., pp.9 and 17.
15. Ibid., p.14.
16. *Larousse Encyclopedia of Mythology*(N.Y.: Prometheus Press, 1960), p.164.
17. *Occidental Mythology*, pp.20-21.
18. Joseph Campbell,*The Masks of God: Creative Mythology* (N.Y: Viking Press, 1968), p.155.
19. Ibid., p.156.
20. *Occidental Mythology*, pp.12-13.
21. Marija Gimbutas, *The Gods and Goddesses of Old Europe, 7000 to 3500 B.C.*, pp.93, 94, 34.
22. *Occidental Mythology*, p.24.

PATRIARCHY : Chapter 2

1. Joseph Campbell, *The Way of the Animal Powers*, Vol. 1. (N.Y: Harper & Row, Alfred van der Marck Editions, 1983) p.71.
2. Joseph Campbell, *The Masks of God: Occidental Mythology* (N.Y.: Viking Press, 1964), p.20.
3. Ibid., p.146.
4. Ibid., p.237.
5. Ibid., p.17.
6. *The Nag Hammadi Library*: "The Second Treatise of the Great Seth" (N.Y: Harper & Row, 1977), p.332
7. *The Nag Hammadi Library*: "The Gospel of Philip", p.131.
8. Ibid., p.132.
9. Ibid., pp.134-135.
10. John Dart, *The Laughing Savior* (N.Y: Harper & Row, 1976), pp.109-110.
11. *The Nag Hammadi Library*: "The Gospel of Philip", p.151.
12. Dart, *op.cit.*, p.128.
13. *The Nag Hammadi Library*: "The Gospel of Philip", p.138.
14. Elaine Pagels, *The Gnostic Gospels* (N.Y: Vintage Books, 1981) pp.72-76.
15. Max Weber, *Ancient Judaism* (Glencoe, Illinois: The Free Press, 1952) p.x.,xviix,viii.
16. Ibid., p.227.
17. Ibid., p.xxvi.

MATRIARCHY : Chapter 3

1. Erich Neumann, *The Great Mother* (N.Y.: Bollingen Foundation Inc., 1955), p.72.
2. Ibid., pp.48-49.
3. Walter F. Otto, "The Meaning of the Eleusinian Mysteries", Papers From The Eranos Yearbooks; Vol 2. Edited by Joseph Campbell. *The Mysteries*, (N.Y.: Bollingen Foundation Inc., 1955), pp.14-15.
4. Ibid., p.16.
5. Neumann, *op.cit.*, p.94.
6. Ibid., p.95-96.
7. Otto, *op.cit.*, pp.20-21.
8. Ibid., p.29.
9. Ibid., pp.29-30.
10. Ibid., pp.30-31.
11. Paul Schmitt, "Ancient Mysteries and Their Transformation", *The Mysteries*, pp.99-100.
12. Ibid., pp.100-102.
13. Neumann, op.cit., pp.305-308.
14. Ibid., pp.308-310.
15. Ibid., pp.313-314.
16. Ibid., p.318.
17. Ibid., p.319.

18. *Zur Psychologie des Weiblichen* (Zurich: Rascher Verlag, 1953).
19. Guiraut de Borneilh (c.1138-1200).
20. Genesis 3:24.
21. Genesis 3:22.
22. Joseph Campbell,*The Masks of God: Primitive Mythology* (N.Y.: Viking Press, 1959), p.435.
23. Esther Harding, *Women's Mysteries* (N.Y.: Harper Colophon Books, 1971), p. 31.
24. Robert Graves, *The White Goddess* (N.Y.: Vintage Books, 1958), p.vi.

WITCHES : Chapter 4

1. Heinrich Kramer and James Sprenger, *The Malleus Maleficarum* : Translated with an Introduction, Bibliography, and Notes by the Reverend Montague Summers (N.Y.: Dover, 1971), p.IX.
2. Ibid., p.xl.
3. Colin Wilson, *The Occult* (N.Y.: Random House, 1971), pp.415-457.
4. Sylvia Brinton Perera, *Descent to The Goddess* (Toronto: Inner City Books, 1981), pp.79-80.
5. Robert Graves, *The White Goddess* (N.Y.: Vintage Books, 1958), p.12.
6. Ibid., p.14.
7. Ibid., p.viii.
9. Kramer, *op.cit.*, pp.43-48.
10. Ibid., pp.117-118.
11. Ibid., pp.119-121.
12. John Demos, *Entertaining Satan*.
13. Joseph Campbell, *The Hero With A Thousand Faces* (N.Y.: Bollingen Foundation Meridian Edition, 156), pp.121-122.
14. Kramer, *op.cit.*, p.228.
15. Ibid., p.229.
16. Wilson, *op.cit.*, p.425.

NATURE, BODY, AND SEX : Chapter 5

1. *Larousse Encyclopedia of Mythology*(London, Batchworth Press Ltd., 1959), pp.89 and 91-92.
2. J.E. Lovelock, *Gaia: A New Look at Life on Earth* (Oxford University Press, 1979), p.3.
3. Ibid., pp. 145-150.
4. Peter Tompkins & Christopher Bird, *The Secret Life of Plants*, (N.Y.: Harper & Row, 1973), p.282.
5. Ibid.
6. Ibid.
7. Ibid., p.278.
8. Ibid., p.282.
9. Esther M. Harding: *Women's Mysteries* (N.Y.: Harper & Row, 1971), pp.110-111.

10. Tompkins, *op.cit.*, p.197.
11. Ibid., pp.101-102.
12. Sheila Ostrander and Lynn Schroder,*Psychic Discoveries Behind The Iron Curtain* (N.Y.: Bantam Books, 1970), p.217.
13. Ibid., p.218.
14. Tompkins, *op.cit..*, p.208.
15. Ostrander, *op.cit..*, p.216.
16. Ibid., pp.226-230.
17. John Michell, *The View Over Atlantis* (N.Y.: Ballantine Books, 1972), p.194
18. Ibid., p.159.
19. Tompkins, *op.cit.*, p.206.
20. Ibid., p.212.
21. Ibid.
22. Ibid., p.32.
23. Richard Roberts, *On Being Accused of Treason and Other Poems*, 1967.

EROS : Chapter 6

1. Esther M. Harding, *Women's Mysteries* (N.Y.: Harper & Row, 1971), pp.29-30.
2. Irene Claremont de Castillejo, *Knowing Woman: A Feminine Psychology* (N.Y.: Harper & Row, 1974), p.82.
3. Ibid., p.173.
4. John Rawson, *Tantra* (N.Y.: Avon, 1973), pp.25-26.
5. Ibid., p.16.
6. Ibid., p.27.
7. Ibid., p.15.
8. Ibid., p.18.
9. Ibid.
10. Ann Belford Ulanov,*Receiving Woman* (Philadelphia: The Westminster Press, 1981), pp.15-17.
11. Ibid., p.131.
12. Cyra McFadden, *The Serial* (N.Y.: Alfred Knopf, 177), p.56.
13. Barbara Hannah, *Striving Towards Wholeness* (N.Y.: G.P. Putnam's Sons, 1971), p.278.
14. Frances G. Wickes, *The Inner World of Man* (N.Y.: Henry Holt, 1948), pp.103-107.
15. Hannah, *op.cit*, pp.279-280.
16. Ibid., p.283.
17. de Castillejo, *op.cit.*, p.81.
18. Harding, *op.cit.*, p.69.
19. de Castillejo, *op.cit.*, p.80.
20. Hannah, *op.cit.*, p.278.
21. C.J. Jung, *Two Essays on Analytical Psychology* (Princeton University Press, 2nd Edition, 1966), pp.206-208.
22. de Castillejo, *op.cit.*, p.79.
23. Harding, *op.cit.*, p.67-68.

24. C.J. Jung, *Contributions to Analytical Psychology* (N.Y.: Harcourt Brace & Co., 1928), p.199.
25. Frances G. Wickes, *The Inner World of Choice* (Englewood Cliffs, N.J.: Prentice-Hall, 1976), p.180.
26. M.L. von Franz, "The Process of Individuation", in *Man and his Symbols*, edited by C.G. Jung, (N.Y.: Doubleday, 1964), p.177.
27. Richard Roberts,*Tales for Jung Folk* (San Anselmo, CA: Vernal Equinox Press, 1983), pp.68-69.
28. von Franz, *op.cit*, pp.194-195.
29. *Newsweek*, September 8, 1980.
30. Carol Gilligan, "Why Should a Woman Be More Like a Man?", *Psychology Today*.

SOCIAL HARMONY : Chapter 7

1. Esther Harding, *Women's Mysteries* (N.Y.: Harper & Row, 171), p.69.
2. Adolf Guggenbuhl-Craig,*Eros on Crutches. Reflections on Amorality and Psychopathy* (Irving, Texas: Spring Publications, 180), p.29.
3. Ibid., pp. 73-4.
4. Ibid., pp. 75, 81, 88, 92, 94.
5. Evelyn Shaw, "Female Circumcision", *American Journal of Nursing*, June, 185, pp. 685-6.
6. Ibid.
7. Ibid.
8. Dr. Nawal el Saadaw, *Ms.*, March, 1980.